Adobe® Flash®
Professional CS6
Digital
Classroom

Adobe® Flash®
Professional CS6
Digital
Classroom

Fred Gerantabee and the AGI Creative Team

WILEY

John Wiley & Sons, Inc.

Adobe® Flash® Professional CS6 Digital Classroom

Published by
John Wiley & Sons, Inc.
10475 Crosspoint Blvd.
Indianapolis, IN 46256

Copyright © 2012 by John Wiley & Sons, Inc., Indianapolis, Indiana
Published simultaneously in Canada
ISBN: 978-1-118-12408-6
Manufactured in the United States of America
10 9 8 7 6 5 4 3 2 1

For general information on our other products and services or to obtain technical support, please
contact our Customer Care Department within the U.S. at (877) 762-2974, outside the U.S. at (317) 572-
3993 or fax (317) 572-4002.

Wiley publishes in a variety of print and electronic formats and by print-on-demand. Some
material included with standard print versions of this book may not be included in e-books
or in print-on-demand. If this book refers to media such as a CD or DVD that is not included
in the version you purchased, you may download this material after registering your book at
www.digitalclassroombooks.com/CS6/Flash. For more information about Wiley products, visit
www.wiley.com.

Please report any errors by sending a message to errata@agitraining.com

Library of Congress Control Number: 2012934966

About the Authors

Fred Gerantabee is an award winning interactive designer, web developer and author based in New York City. He is a subject matter expert in Flash and ActionScript, standards-based web development and various scripting languages and platforms. Fred has worked with the AGI team for several years as a contributor to the Digital Classroom series, training events and currently leads the technology initiatives at Grey Worldwide in NYC. Fred is the author of several books in the Digital Classroom series on Flash and Dreamweaver, and co-author with AGI instructors Jennifer Smith and Christopher Smith of the *Creative Suite 6 Design Premium for Dummies*, also published by Wiley.

Greg Heald has 20 years of design and production experience in both Web and print environments. He has served as a contributing author or editor on a number of books on Dreamweaver, Flash, InDesign, and Acrobat. Greg has contributed to the development of Adobe's certification exams, and as Training Manager for American Graphics Institute, he oversees the delivery of professional development training programs for individuals and organizations. Greg holds a degree in Advertising Design from the acclaimed College of Visual and Performing Arts at Syracuse University.

Jeremy Osborn is the Content Director at American Graphics Institute. He has more than 15 years of experience in web and graphic design, filmmaking, writing, and publication development for both print and digital media. He has contributed to several of the Digital Classroom book series. Jeremy holds a MS in Management from the Marlboro College Graduate Center and a BFA in Film/TV from the Tisch School of the Arts at NYU.

The **AGI Creative Team** is composed of Adobe Certified Experts and experienced instructors from American Graphics Institute (AGI). The AGI Creative Team has authored more than 25 Digital Classroom books, and previously created many of Adobe's official training guides. They work with many of the world's most prominent companies, helping them use creative software to communicate more effectively and creatively. They work with design, creative, and marketing teams around the world, delivering private customized training programs, and teach regularly scheduled classes at AGI's locations. The Digital Classroom authors are available for professional development sessions at companies, schools and universities. More information at *agitraining.com*.

Acknowledgments

Thanks to our many friends at Adobe Systems, Inc. who made this book possible and assisted with questions and feedback during the writing process. To the many clients of AGI who have helped us better understand how they use Flash and provided us with many of the tips and suggestions found in this book. A special thanks to the instructional team at AGI for their input and assistance in the review process and for making this book such a team effort.

Thanks to the following photographers for the use of their images: Lesson 12: Shayna Zaid & The Catch photo by Jamie Santamour; Leslie Graves photo by Calvin Williams; Christopher Heinz photo by Calvin Williams; Shayna Zaid photo by William Kates; Oscar Rodriguez/Nakatomi Plaza photo by Dave Sanders; Emek Rave photo by Holly Danger..

Credits

Additional Writing
Greg Heald, Jeremy Osborn

President, American Graphics Institute and Digital Classroom Series Publisher
Christopher Smith

Executive Editor
Jody Lefevere

Technical Editors
Sean McKnight, Haziel Olivera

Editor
Karla E. Melendez

Editorial Director
Robyn Siesky

Business Manager
Amy Knies

Senior Marketing Manager
Sandy Smith

Vice President and Executive Group Publisher
Richard Swadley

Vice President and Executive Publisher
Barry Pruett

Senior Project Coordinator
Katherine Crocker

Project Manager
Cheri White

Graphics and Production Specialist
Jason Miranda, Spoke & Wheel

Media Development Project Supervisor
Chris Leavey

Proofreading
Jay Donahue, Barn Owl Publishing

Indexing
Michael Ferreira

Register your Digital Classroom book for exclusive benefits

Registered owners receive access to:

 The most current lesson files

 Technical resources and customer support

 Notifications of updates

 On-line access to video tutorials

 Downloadable lesson files

 Samples from other Digital Classroom books

Register at *DigitalClassroomBooks.com/CS6/Flash*

Register your book today at
DigitalClassroomBooks.com/CS6/Flash

Contents

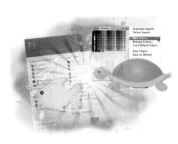

Lesson 2: Getting Started with the Drawing Tools

Lesson 3: Using Symbols and the Library

Lesson 4: Advanced Tools

Lesson 5: Creating Basic Animation

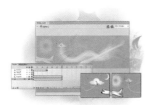

Lesson 6: Advanced Animation

Lesson 7: Customizing Your Workflow

Lesson 8: Working with Imported Files

Lesson 9: Introducing ActionScript

Lesson 10: Creating Navigation Controls

Lesson 11: Adding Sound to Your Movies

Lesson 12: Introducing Movie Clips

Lesson 13: Working with Video

Lesson 14: Delivering Your Final Movie

Lesson 15: What's New in Adobe Flash CS6?

Starting up

About the *Flash Professional CS6 Digital Classroom*

Adobe® Flash® Professional CS6 is used to create and deliver interactive content. Adobe Flash Professional CS6 is the authoring environment for creating rich, interactive content and advertisements for digital, web delivery.

The *Adobe Flash Professional CS6 Digital Classroom* helps you to understand these capabilities and to get the most out of your software so that you can get up-and-running right away. You can work through all the lessons in this book, or complete only specific lessons. Each lesson includes detailed, step-by-step instructions, along with lesson files, useful background information, and video tutorials.

Adobe Flash Professional CS6 Digital Classroom is like having your own expert instructor guiding you through each lesson while you work at your own pace. This book includes 15 self-paced lessons that let you discover essential skills, explore new ones, and understand capabilities that will save you time. You'll be productive right away with real-world exercises and simple explanations. Each lesson includes step-by-step instructions, lesson files, and video tutorials, all of which are available on the included DVD. The *Flash Professional CS6 Digital Classroom* lessons are developed by the same team of Adobe Certified Experts and Flash professionals who have created many of the official training titles for Adobe Systems.

Prerequisites

Before you start the *Adobe Flash Professional CS6 Digital Classroom* lessons, you should have a working knowledge of your computer and its operating system. You should know how to use the directory system of your computer so that you can navigate through folders. You also need to understand how to locate, save, and open files, and you should also know how to use your mouse to access menus and commands.

Before starting the lesson files in the *Adobe Flash Professional CS6 Digital Classroom*, make sure that you have installed Adobe Flash Professional CS6. The software is sold separately, and is not included with this book. You may use the free 30-day trial version of Adobe Flash Professional CS6 available at the *adobe.com* website, subject to the terms of its license agreement.

System requirements

Before starting the lessons in the *Adobe Flash Professional CS6 Digital Classroom*, make sure that your computer is equipped for running Adobe Flash Professional CS6, which you must purchase separately. The minimum system requirements for your computer to effectively use the software are listed on the following page and you can find the most current system requirements at *http://www.adobe.com/products/flash/tech-specs.html*.

Windows

- Intel® Pentium® 4 or AMD Athlon® 64 processor
- Microsoft® Windows® XP with Service Pack 3 or Windows 7
- 2 GB of RAM (3 GB recommended)
- 3.5 GB of available hard-disk space for installation; additional free space required during installation (cannot install on removable flash-based storage devices)
- 1024×768 display (1280×800 recommended)
- Java™ Runtime Environment 1.6 (included)
- DVD-ROM drive
- QuickTime 7.6.6 software required for multimedia features
- Some features in Adobe Bridge rely on a DirectX 9–capable graphics card with at least 64 MB of VRAM
- Broadband Internet connection required for online services

Mac OS

- Multicore Intel processor
- Mac OS X v10.6 or v10.7
- 2 GB of RAM (3 GB recommended)
- 4 GB of available hard-disk space for installation; additional free space required during installation (cannot install on a volume that uses a case-sensitive file system or on removable flash-based storage devices)
- 1024×768 display (1280×800 recommended)
- Java Runtime Environment 1.6
- DVD-ROM drive
- QuickTime 7.6.6 software required for multimedia features
- Broadband Internet connection required for online services

Starting Adobe Flash Professional CS6

As with most software, Adobe Flash Professional CS6 is launched by locating the application in your Programs folder (Windows) or Applications folder (Mac OS). If you are not familiar with starting the program, follow these steps to start the Adobe Flash Professional CS6 application:

Windows

1   Choose Start > All Programs > Adobe Flash Professional CS6.

2   Close the Welcome Screen when it appears. You are now ready to use Adobe Flash Professional CS6.

Mac OS

1   Open the Applications folder, and then open the Adobe Flash CS6 folder.

2   Double-click on the Adobe Flash CS6 application icon.

3   Close the Welcome Screen when it appears. You are now ready to use Adobe Flash Professional CS6.

Menus and commands are identified throughout the book by using the greater-than symbol (>). For example, the command to print a document appears as File > Print.

Access lesson files and videos any time

Register your book at *www.digitalclassroombooks.com/CS6/Flash* to gain access to your lesson files on any computer you own or watch the videos on your Internet-connected computer, tablet, or mobile device. You'll be able to continue your learning anywhere you have an Internet connection and a device that supports playing online video. This provides you access to lesson files and videos even if you misplaced your DVD.

Checking for updated lesson files

Make sure you have the most up-to-date lesson files and learn about any updates to your *Flash Professional CS6 Digital Classroom* book by registering your book at *www.digitalclassroombooks.com/CS6/Flash*.

Resetting the Flash workspace

To make certain that your panels and working environment are consistent, you should reset your workspace at the start of each lesson. To reset your workspace, choose Window > Workspace > Reset 'Essentials.'

Loading lesson files

The *Adobe Flash Professional CS6 Digital Classroom* DVD includes files that accompany the exercises for each of the lessons. You may copy the entire lessons folder from the supplied DVD to your hard drive, or copy only the lesson folders for the individual lessons you wish to complete.

For each lesson in the book, the files are referenced by the name of each file. The exact location of each file on your computer is not used, as you may have placed the files in a unique location on your hard drive. We suggest placing the lesson files in the My Documents folder (Windows) or at the top level of your hard drive (Mac OS), or on your desktop for easy access.

Copying the lesson files to your hard drive:

1   Insert the *Adobe Flash Professional CS6 Digital Classroom* DVD supplied with this book.

2   On your computer desktop, navigate to the DVD and locate the folder named fllessons.

3   You can install all the files, or just specific lesson files. Do one of the following:

   • Install all lesson files by dragging the fllessons folder to your hard drive.

   • Install only some of the files by creating a new folder on your hard drive named fllessons. Open the fllessons folder on the supplied DVD, select the lesson you wish to complete, and drag the folder(s) to the fllessons folder you created on your hard drive.

Unlocking Mac OS files

Mac users may need to unlock the files after they are copied from the accompanying disc. This applies only to Mac OS computers, and is because the Mac OS may view files that are copied from a DVD or CD as being locked for writing.

If you are a Mac OS user and have difficulty saving over the existing files in this book, you can use these instructions so that you can update the lesson files as you work on them, and also add new files to the lessons folder

Note that you only need to follow these instructions if you are unable to save over the existing lesson files, or if you are unable to save files into the lesson folder.

1   After copying the files to your computer, click once to select the fllessons folder, then choose File > Get Info from within the Finder (not Flash).

2   In the fllessons info window, click the triangle to the left of Sharing and Permissions to reveal the details of this section.

3   In the Sharing and Permissions section, click the lock icon, if necessary, in the lower-right corner so that you can make changes to the permissions.

4   Click to select a specific user or select everyone, then change the Privileges section to Read & Write.

5   Click the lock icon to prevent further changes, and then close the window.

Working with the video tutorials

Your *Adobe Flash Professional CS6 Digital Classroom* DVD comes with video tutorials developed by the authors to help you understand the concepts explored in each lesson. Each tutorial is approximately five minutes long and demonstrates and explains the concepts and features covered in the lesson.

The videos are designed to supplement your understanding of the material in the chapter. We have selected exercises and examples that we feel will be most useful to you. You may want to view the entire video for each lesson before you begin that lesson. Additionally, at certain points in a lesson, you will encounter the DVD icon. The icon, with appropriate lesson number, indicates that an overview of the exercise being described can be found in the accompanying video.

DVD video icon.

Setting up for viewing the video tutorials

The DVD included with this book includes video tutorials for each lesson. Although you can view the lessons on your computer directly from the DVD, we recommend copying the folder labeled videos from the *Adobe Flash Professional CS6 Digital Classroom* DVD to your hard drive.

Copying the video tutorials to your hard drive:

1   Insert the *Adobe Flash Professional CS6 Digital Classroom* DVD supplied with this book.

2   On your computer desktop, navigate to the DVD and locate the folder named videos.

3   Drag the videos folder to a location onto your hard drive.

Viewing the video tutorials with the Adobe Flash Player

The videos on the *Adobe Flash Professional CS6 Digital Classroom* DVD are saved in the Flash projector format. A Flash projector file wraps the Digital Classroom video player and the Adobe Flash Player in an executable file (.exe for Windows or .app for Mac OS). Note that the extension (on both platforms) may not always be visible. Projector files allow the Flash content to be deployed on your system without the need for a browser or prior stand-alone player installation.

Playing the video tutorials:

1 On your computer, navigate to the videos folder you copied to your hard drive from the DVD. Playing the videos directly from the DVD may result in poor quality playback.

2 Open the videos folder and double-click the Flash file named PLAY_FLCS6videos to view the video tutorials.

3 After the Flash player launches, press the Play button to view the videos.

The Flash Player has a simple user interface that allows you to control the viewing experience, including stopping, pausing, playing, and restarting the video. You can also rewind or fast-forward, and adjust the playback volume.

*A. Go to beginning. **B.** Play/Pause. **C.** Fast-forward/rewind. **D.** Stop. **E.** Volume Off/On. **F.** Volume control.*

Playback volume is also affected by the settings in your operating system. Be certain to adjust the sound volume for your computer, in addition to the sound controls in the Player window.

Hosting Your Flash content and websites

While you can work on everything in this book using only your computer, you will eventually want to post your Flash content to the Web and create sites to share with the world. To do this, you will need to place your website files on a web server, which is a computer that is persistently connected to the Internet and designed to handle multiple users at once.

If you don't want to get involved in hosting a website, there are a number of cost-efficient, web hosting services such as GoDaddy, FatCow, and Blue Host as well large, scalable cloud service providers such as Microsoft Azure and Amazon EC2. If you want to set up your own computer for hosting a web server on your own, and you are using a Windows computer, you can turn it into a web server at no cost by using the Web Platform Installer available at: *www.microsoft.com/web*. If you are a Mac OS user, you can get Mac OS X server from Apple to set up a Mac computer as a web server.

If you are just getting started, you may not need to worry about web hosting just yet. But you'll find this information useful once you start creating sites and content as you progress through this book.

Additional resources

The Digital Classroom series goes beyond the training books. You can continue your learning online, with training videos, at seminars and conferences, and in-person training events.

Training from the Authors

The authors are available for professional development training workshops for schools and companies. They also teach classes at American Graphics Institute including training classes and online workshops. Visit *agitraining.com* for more information about Digital Classroom author-led training classes or workshops.

Book series

Expand your knowledge of creative software applications with the Digital Classroom training series. Books are available for most creative software applications as well as web design and development tools and technologies. Learn more at *DigitalClassroom.com.*

Seminars and conferences

The authors of the Digital Classroom seminar series frequently conduct in-person seminars and speak at conferences, including the annual CRE8 Conference. Learn more at *agitraining.com* and *CRE8summit.com.*

Resources for educators

Visit *digitalclassroombooks.com* to request resources for educators, including instructors' guides for incorporating Digital Classroom books into your curriculum.

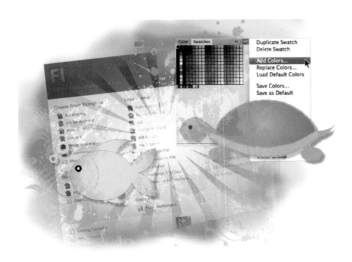

What you'll learn in this lesson:

- What is Flash and what can it do?

- Creating and saving new documents

- Getting familiar with the workspace and tools

- Try your first drawing and animation exercises!

Flash CS6 Jumpstart

This lesson takes you through the basics you'll need to get up-and-running with Flash Professional CS6.

Starting up

In this lesson, you will set up a new Flash document and work with several prepared files to explore Flash's tools and features. If you haven't done so already, install Flash Professional CS6 and the Adobe Media Encoder. Instructions for installation, system requirements, and information on how to use lesson files from the included DVD are in the Starting up section of this book.

Before starting, make sure that your tools and panels are consistent by resetting your workspace. See "Resetting the Flash workspace" in the Starting up section of this book.

Before you start, be sure to register your book at *www.digitalclassroombooks.com/CS6/Flash* to learn about updates to any of the lesson files and gain access to the accompanying video tutorials on any Internet connected computer, tablet, or smartphone.

You will work with several files from the fl01lessons folder in this lesson. Make sure that you have loaded the fllessons folder onto your hard drive from the supplied DVD. See "Loading lesson files" in the Starting up section of this book.

See Lesson 1 in action!

Use the accompanying video to gain a better understanding of how to use some of the features shown in this lesson. You can find the video tutorial for this lesson on the included DVD.

What is Flash?

You may have heard about Flash and seen it on eye-catching websites, online and social games, and banner advertisements. But did you know that you can use Flash for more than creating animated graphics? With Flash CS6 Professional, you can also manipulate video and sound, and even connect to databases to build web-based applications, such as shopping carts, or display news feeds of continuously updated information.

There are four key feature areas in Flash CS6 Professional:

Drawing environment. Flash features a complete set of drawing tools to handle intricate illustration and typography. Like its cousin, Adobe Illustrator CS6, Flash is a native vector-drawing application where you'll create rich, detailed, and scalable digital illustrations. Flash supports Illustrator and Photoshop files in their native file formats, .ai and .psd, making it easy to work with your favorite applications. All the content you create in Flash or these other programs can be brought to life through animation and interactivity.

Animation. Flash creates lightweight animation that incorporates images, sound, and video, and can be quickly downloaded through the Web. It has become a favorite—and essential—tool among web designers and developers who want to take their creativity to a whole new level. Flash animation is featured on websites and social networks, and is a primary tool for developing interactive, web-based advertisements. Flash's capabilities also extend beyond the Web, with tools and options for creating applications and content for smartphones and tablets, too.

Flash supports traditional frame-by-frame animation as well as its own method of animation, known as tweening. With tweening, you specify an object to animate, create starting and ending frames, and Flash automatically creates the frames in between (hence *tween*) to create slick motion, color, and transformation effects. You'll design your own Flash animations in Lesson 5, "Creating Basic Animation."

Flash's animation tweening easily generates animation between starting and ending frames.

Layout. The Flash stage gives you the flexibility to create extraordinary website layouts limited only by your creativity. You can position content anywhere on the Flash Stage with flexibility and precision, taking your layouts far beyond the "box" often associated with traditional web pages. Flash movies can also include any typefaces you choose, allowing you to use fancy typography and unusual fonts freely on your web pages, which is typically more involved and less consistent outside of Flash.

Programming. Hidden beneath the beauty of Flash Professional CS6 is the brain of ActionScript, a powerful, built-in scripting language that extends your capabilities beyond simple design and animation. With basic ActionScript, which you'll learn about in Lesson 9, "Introducing ActionScript," you can control movie playback or add functionality to buttons. If you venture deeper, ActionScript can turn Flash into a full-fledged, application-building environment to create shopping carts, music players, games, and mobile applications.

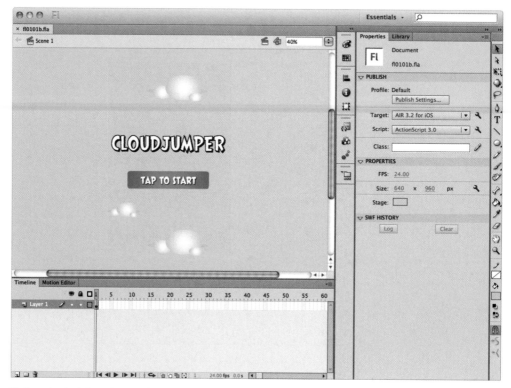

Flash can develop lightweight games for the Web and smartphones.

About Flash Player

The Flash Player is a stand-alone application found most often as a plug-in to such popular browsers as Internet Explorer, Safari, and Firefox. The Flash Player is required to play compressed Flash movies (.swf files), much like a movie projector is needed to play film reels.

The Flash Player is much more than just a playback machine, however. It is the platform that Flash content runs on and is the engine upon which ActionScript functions so you can incorporate rich interactivity within your movies.

As of this writing, the Flash Player is installed on more than 98 percent of Internet-enabled computers, so a majority of your online audience is already equipped to view your Flash creations. For users who do not have Flash Player installed, it is available as a free download from the Adobe website, *adobe.com*.

Flash Player 11 includes both a stand-alone application and browser plug-in, and is automatically installed with the Flash Professional CS6 application.

For environments where Flash player is not supported (such as on iPhones and iPads), you can publish Flash content as HTML and JavaScript, so it can run in nearly any device or browser.

Flash file types

You will encounter up to four types of files in Flash: .fla, .xfl, .swf and .html. Each one has a very specific purpose in the process of creating or delivering Flash movies.

Flash work files are generally created and saved in the .fla (Flash authoring) format. These are the working documents you'll use to design, edit, and store resources such as graphics, images, sound, and video. Additionally, each .fla document stores its own unique settings for final publishing. Because they are intended for designing and editing, .fla files can't be viewed with the Flash Player or in a browser—they're only used as the foundation to publish your final movie files in the .swf file format. You can also save source files in the .xfl file format, which allows for open exchange between Flash and other authoring applications. For nearly all examples in this book, however, it's assumed you are editing and saving to the .fla file format.

"Swiff", or .swf, files are completed, compressed movie files exported from your original .fla authoring files. These are played via the Flash Player in either a browser or your desktop. Although you can import .swf files into the Flash Professional CS6 application, you cannot edit them; you will need to reopen the original .fla files to make changes or additions. You can now also publish your movies to a variety of other formats, including HTML (for display in browsers and devices that don't support the Flash plug-in), AIR (for desktop applications), and popular mobile application formats for iOS and Android devices.

Now that you know what you're going to be working with, it's time to get your first Flash document started and begin exploring the Flash Professional CS6 workspace.

Creating a new document

Before you can draw or animate, you need to create a new document, or more specifically, an .fla file where all your work takes place. You can create and open documents from the Welcome Screen or from the File menu at the top of the screen.

The Welcome Screen is the launch pad for creating and opening files, including handy, built-in sample templates for common project types, such as Flash movies, advertising banners, and mobile phone application templates. The Welcome Screen appears when Flash is first launched or when no documents are open in the application.

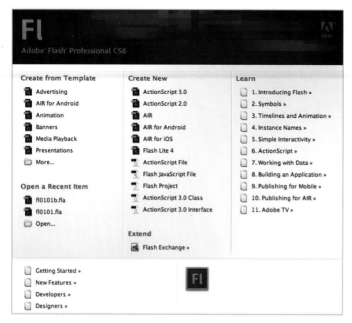

The Welcome Screen is the launch pad for new documents, including many templates for common projects.

1 To create a new .fla document using the Welcome Screen, open Flash CS6 Professional. If the application is already open, close any files that are currently open using File > Close All.

2 From the Create New column in the middle of the Welcome Screen, select ActionScript 3.0. Your workspace, including the Stage, Timeline, and Tools panel, appears.

3 Alternatively, you can create a new .fla document using the File menu. If you already created a new document using the Welcome Screen, this is not necessary.

To create a new document from the File menu, choose File > New. The New Document dialog box appears. Select ActionScript 3.0, and press OK to create the new document. Your workspace appears.

Setting up your new document

Now that you've created your new Flash file, take a moment to specify some important settings for it. These settings, or properties, will prepare your document before you get to work.

1   Choose Modify > Document or use the keyboard shortcut Ctrl+J (Windows) or Command+J (Mac OS) to open the Document dialog box.

2   Under the Dimensions section, locate the (width) and (height) fields and type **500** and **300**, respectively, to set the width and height of your movie in pixels. The size of the Stage is identical to the size of your final movie, so make sure the size accommodates the design you want to create.

3   Click on the Background Color swatch (▢) and the Swatches panel appears. This lets you choose the color of your Stage and, in turn, the background color for your final movie (.swf file) when it's published. If necessary, set the background color to white (#FFFFFF).

4   Note the Frame rate indicator field. Leave it set to the default (24 frames per second) for now. The frame rate determines the playback speed and performance of your movie, and you can adjust it later if you need to. You'll learn more about fine-tuning your frame rate in Lesson 6, "Advanced Animation."

The Match to Printer option sets your new document to match the paper size of your default system printer. This option is typically set to Default, requiring you to specify the width and height, or use the default Dimensions settings stored in Flash.

5 From the Ruler units drop-down menu, choose Pixels, if it is not already selected, to define the unit of measurement used throughout your Flash movie, including rulers, panels, and dialog boxes.

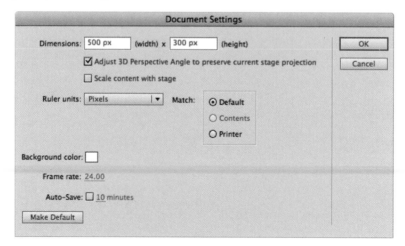

Use the Document Settings dialog box to specify settings.

If you are new to designing for the screen, the concept of pixels may feel a bit alien to you. It helps to remember that there are generally 72 pixels in one inch for size calculation. If you prefer, you can use the Document dialog box at any time to change the Ruler units for your file to a different unit of measurement.

6 Press OK to exit the Document Settings dialog box and apply these settings. Leave the new document open. You'll save it in the next part of this lesson.

Saving your Flash document

Your new document should be saved before starting any work or adding any content. By default, the application saves documents in Flash CS6 (.fla) format.

1 Choose File > Save.

2 In the Save dialog box that appears, type **fl0101_work.fla** into the Save As text field. Navigate to the fl01lessons folder, and press Save. Choose File > Close to close the document.

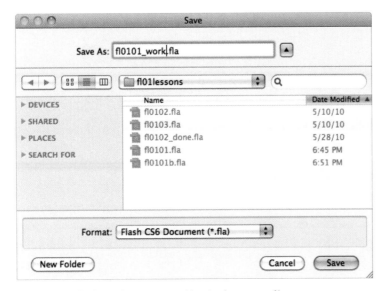

Use the Save dialog box to choose a name and location for your new file.

Always include the .fla extension at the end of your filename to make it easy to identify the file format.

To share your work with designers using Flash CS5, you can choose to save your document in Flash CS5 format. Flash Professional CS6 format files will not open in Flash CS5 or earlier. Flash CS6 Professional, however, can open files created in Flash CS5 or earlier.

Get started with sample templates

Flash includes a variety of sample templates to streamline the process of setting up common Flash projects. Creating files from these templates will pre-configure options such as document size and ActionScript version. Choose File > New and click on the Templates tab to view Flash's included templates.

In the Advertising section, templates include common banner sizes. Be aware that creating files from these templates sets the Flash player and ActionScript versions extremely conservatively for maximum compatibility. If you were planning on using the latest and greatest techniques and features in your project, this may be constricting.

New templates have been added for Animation, Banners, and Media Playback, and the Presentations templates have been enhanced for Flash Professional CS6. Sample Files, including animation examples, have been added as well. For more information on these new templates, see Lesson 15, "What's New in Adobe Flash CS6?".

Opening documents

Knowing how to open documents is as important as knowing how to save them. In addition to files created in Flash CS6 Professional, such as those included with this book, you can open documents created in previous versions of Flash. The steps are simple.

1   Choose File > Open. Use the Open dialog box to locate the fl0101_work.fla file you previously saved into the fl01lessons folder.

2   Select the fl0101_work.fla file, then press Open. Leave this file open. You will be using it in the next exercise.

Don't confuse the Open command with the Import options also found in the File menu. To access files created in other applications, such as Photoshop or Illustrator, you must use the Import menu. Importing files from other applications is explored in detail in Lesson 8, "Working with Imported Files."

If you want to reopen a document on which you have recently worked, there's a shortcut. To list the last ten documents you've opened, and to reopen one, choose File > Open Recent, then select the file you need.

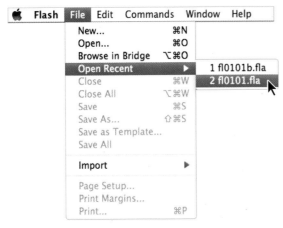

Choose File > Open Recent to access the last ten documents opened in Flash.

You can also open files using the Open button (📁) at the bottom of the Open Recent Items column on the Welcome Screen. Above this icon, you'll see the last several documents you worked on; this is a useful alternative to the Open Recent menu option.

The Flash workspace

Now that you know how to create, save, and open Flash documents, you're ready to get familiar with the workspace where you'll spend your time creating Flash content.

The Stage and work area

After you create a Flash document, the center of your workspace, called the *Stage*, is where the action happens. The Stage is the visible area of your movie, where you place graphics and build animations. By default, the Flash Stage appears white, but, as you saw earlier, you can change its background color from the Document dialog box using the Modify > Document command.

The gray area surrounding the Stage is the *pasteboard*; artwork you place or create here is not included in your final movie. Think of this area as the *backstage*; for instance, you can animate a character to enter from the pasteboard onto the Stage. The pasteboard is also a good place to store objects that are not ready to appear in your movie. The Stage reflects the actual size of the movie you create when it is published.

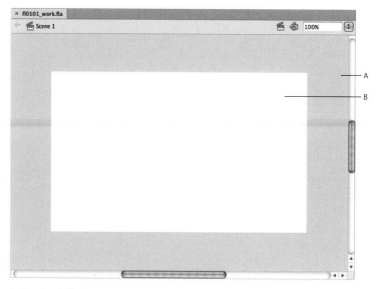

A. *Pasteboard.* *B.* *Stage.*

The Flash Tools panel

The Flash Tools panel includes everything you need to create, select, or edit graphics on the Stage. You can use the double arrows at the top of the Tools panel to collapse the panel to icon-only view, or to expand the panel and see all the tools.

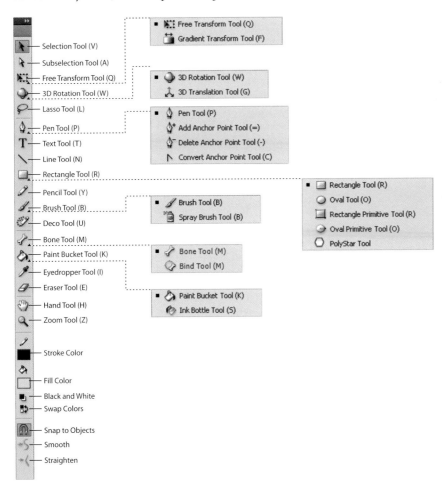

The Tools panel.

Selection tools

ICON	TOOL NAME	USE	WHERE IT'S COVERED
	Selection	Moves selections or layers	Lessons 1, 2
	Subselection	Selects and moves points on a path	Lesson 2
	Free Transform	Resizes, rotates, and skews objects	Lessons 2, 4, 5, 8
	Lasso	Makes selections	Lesson 3
	3D Rotation	Rotates objects in 3D space	Lesson 6

Drawing and Text tools

ICON	TOOL NAME	USE	WHERE IT'S COVERED
	Pen	Draws a vector path	Lesson 2
	Text	Creates a text box	Lesson 2
	Line	Draws straight lines	Lesson 2
	Shapes	Draws vector shapes	Lesson 2
	Pencil	Draws freehand paths	Lesson 2
	Brush	Draws freehand filled areas	Lesson 4
	Deco	Creates patterns using symbols	Lesson 4

Color tools

ICON	TOOL NAME	USE	WHERE IT'S COVERED
	Ink Bottle	Applies or modifies strokes	Lessons 1, 2, 3
	Paint Bucket	Applies or modifies fills	Lessons 1, 2
	Eyedropper	Samples colors and styles	Lessons 1, 2
	Eraser	Erases artwork	Not referenced in this book
	Bone	Creates Inverse Kinematic objects	Lessons 4, 6

Navigation tools

ICON	TOOL NAME	USE	WHERE IT'S COVERED
⟨ᵐ⟩	Hand	Navigates the page	Lesson 7
⚲	Zoom	Increases or decreases the relative size of the view	Lesson 6

Stroke and fill color selectors

ICON	TOOL NAME	USE	WHERE IT'S COVERED
✎ ■	Stroke Color	Selects stroke (outline) color	Lesson 3
◌ □	Fill Color	Selects fill (inside) color	Lesson 3
▣	Default Stroke/Fill	Sets stroke and fill to default colors: black and white	Lesson 3
▣	Swap Colors	Swaps stroke and fill colors	Lesson 3
▨	No Color	Sets selected color to none	Lesson 2

Tool options

ICON	TOOL NAME	USE	WHERE IT'S COVERED
⋒	Snap to Objects	Enables snapping between objects on the Stage.	Lesson 5

The Property Inspector

By default, the Property Inspector appears on the right side of your Flash workspace. Grouped with the Library panel, it displays properties and options for objects selected on the Stage, and also allows you to modify them. The Property Inspector is contextual, and so the information it displays is specific to the tool or object you select.

The Property Inspector is an essential part of the Flash workflow; it can display and set an object's properties, including width, height, position, and fill color. Let's take a look at the Property Inspector in action.

1 If the fl0101_work.fla file is not still open from the last exercise, choose File > Open to reopen it from inside the fl01lessons folder. Select the Rectangle tool (□) from the Tools panel.

2 At the bottom of the Tools panel, click the Fill Color swatch (⬚). When the Swatches panel appears, choose a yellow shade from the right side of the Swatches panel.

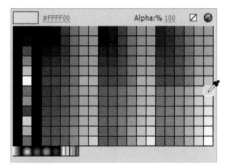

Choose fill and stroke colors using the swatches at the bottom of the Tools panel.

3 Move your cursor to the center of the Stage. Click and hold, then drag to draw a new rectangle. Release the mouse button after you have created a rectangle at the center of the Stage.

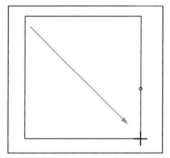

To draw shapes on the Stage, select a Shape tool, then click and drag.

4 Choose the Selection tool (▸) from the top of the Tools panel, and double-click the fill of the new shape to select it. If it's not already visible, click on the Property Inspector on the right side of the workspace to open it, and notice that it now displays the selected shape's width (W) and height (H) in pixels. Above the width and height, the object's X and Y positions on the Stage are also displayed.

5 Click the underlined number next to W: to highlight the current value, then type **250** to set the rectangle's width. Press Enter (Windows) or Return (Mac OS). Use this same method to set the height to **150**.

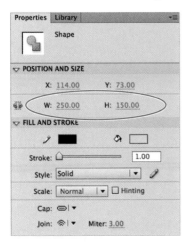

You can set properties for a selected shape using the Property Inspector.

6 Choose the Text tool (T) from the Tools panel. Click above the new rectangle you created and type the phrase **Flash CS6**. If it's not already visible, click to open the Property Inspector, and notice that it now displays text options such as font and size.

When text is selected, the Property Inspector displays relevant options such as font and size.

7 Click and drag inside the new text box to select all the text. In the Property Inspector, locate the Family drop-down menu and choose Arial (or, if that's unavailable, Verdana). Click on the Size and set the type size to **45**.

8 In the Property Inspector, click the Color swatch and choose a blue shade from the Swatches panel that appears to change the color of your type. In this exercise, the color #000099 was used.

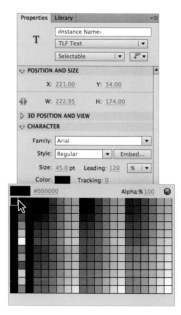

Select and format type directly from the Property Inspector.

9 Choose File > Save to save your work, then choose File > Close.

In addition to text and graphics, the Property Inspector also works with the Timeline, allowing you to set options and view information for specific frames. You will use this essential tool throughout the lessons to modify objects on the Stage, and frames in the Timeline.

The Property Inspector shows options for an active tool or information about a selected object, including the document itself.

Panels and panel groups

The Flash workspace is extremely flexible. It is organized into a series of panels, many of which you'll become quite familiar with, including the Library panel, Property Inspector, and Timeline. You're free to arrange any of these panels however you like. You can also open panels that are not available in the default workspace and arrange, group, and resize them to suit your needs.

Panels can be freely repositioned, resized, and grouped.

You'll explore the workspace in more detail in Lesson 7, "Customizing Your Workflow," but there are a couple things that you should be aware of in the interim.

Eventually you'll want to take control of your workspace and customize it to your preference, but for now, the flexibility of the workspace might be more confusing than advantageous. If you mistakenly drag panels around and start losing them, you can always reset your panels to their default positions by choosing Window > Workspace > Essentials. If you're migrating to Flash CS6 from an earlier version, you may also be interested in the Classic option found in this menu. For the sake of consistency, this book uses the default CS6 workspace.

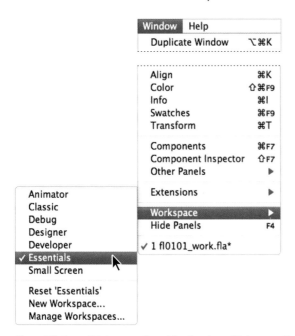

Choose Window > Workspace > Essentials, then choose Workspace > Reset 'Essentials'
to reset your workspace to the Flash CS6 defaults.

It's also important to note that each panel features a panel menu that can be accessed from the button in the top-right corner. This menu contains options that may or may not be available inside the panel. Sometimes this menu is superfluous; sometimes it's integral. Just remember to keep it in the back of your mind. This menu is usually the first place to look if you can't find an option that you're looking for.

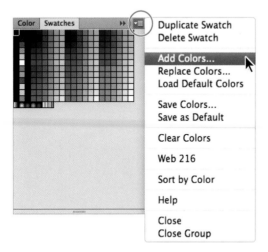

Panel menus are accessed using the button in the top-right corner.

The Timeline

The Flash Timeline is the heart of the action, where you create animations and sequence graphics with sound, video, and controls. The Timeline comprises frames, each one representing a point in time, just like a historical timeline. Graphics and animations are placed at specific points, or keyframes, along the Timeline to create sequences, slide shows, or movies. You can place ActionScript on individual keyframes to control playback and add interactivity, or place sounds along the Timeline to add sound effects, music, and dialogue.

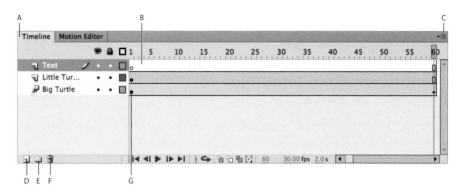

A. *Click and drag to undock the Timeline from the document window.* **B.** *Frames.* **C.** *Timeline panel menu.*
D. *Insert Layer.* **E.** *Insert Layer Folder.* **F.** *Delete Layer.* **G.** *Keyframe.*

The Timeline is composed of layers, which behave like transparent pieces of film stacked on top of one another. Each animation and piece of artwork can be placed on its own individual layer, which helps you organize and manage your work. If you've worked with other Adobe CS6 applications, such as Illustrator, Photoshop, or InDesign, you may already be familiar with the power and flexibility of layers.

Like all panels, the Timeline has a panel menu. Most of the options included in the Timeline's panel menu relate to customizing its display. Here you can adjust the size of layers and frames and turn on Preview mode to display the objects included on each layer as a thumbnail in the Timeline.

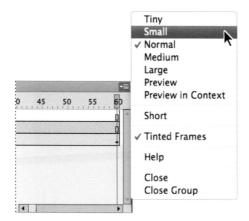

Change the Timeline settings according to how you'd like it to appear.

In this exercise, you'll explore a Timeline with multiple keyframes, animations, and layers to see how a typical Flash document looks.

1   Choose File > Open, and select the fl0103.fla document inside the fl01lessons folder. Press Open to open it for editing.

2   Examine the Timeline below the Stage. You'll see that it contains a layer, with a layer folder above it. Layer folders can contain layers and are used to organize the Timeline when layers start to add up. Click the arrow to the left of the Gears layer folder to expand it and reveal its contents. The three indented layers under the Gears name are the layers that are inside the folder.

 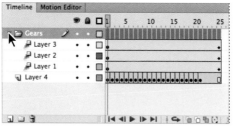

Click the arrow to the left of a layer folder to expand it.

3   Each of the three layers contains a separate animation that is marked at the beginning and end with a keyframe. Keyframes are special frames that are created along the Timeline where you want to introduce or remove a graphic, start or end an animation, or trigger something to happen with ActionScript. A blue background on frames indicates a Motion tween animation. Press Enter (Windows) or Return (Mac OS) to play the Timeline.

4   Look at Layer 4 in the Timeline, which contains several consecutive keyframes. Click once on each keyframe to jump to that frame and see what it displays at that specific point in time.

5   To shuttle through the Timeline, grab the playhead at the top (indicated by the red marker), and drag it in either direction.

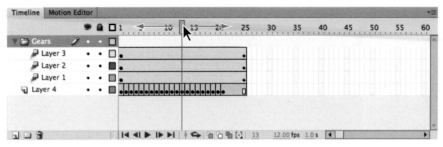

Scrub back and forth in the Timeline by dragging the playhead.

6   Choose File > Close to close the current document. If prompted to save any changes, press No (Windows) or Don't Save (Mac OS).

Tabbing between open documents

When you have more than one document open at a time, each document displays its own tab at the top of the document window. Click on a document's tab to switch to it and bring it forward for editing. To close the active document, you can choose File > Close, or use the small *x* that appears at the top of the document's tab. To close all open documents at once, choose File > Close All.

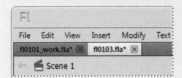

Tab easily between multiple documents at one time.

The Swatches panel

You'll see the swatch icon (▢) quite a few times in Flash—it opens the Swatches panel, which is used to set colors for backgrounds, fills, outlines, and type. You can choose from over 200 color presets and seven preset gradients, or create your own. You will learn how to add your own custom colors and gradients to the Swatches panel in Lesson 2, "Getting Started with the Drawing Tools."

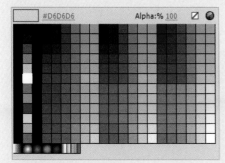

The Flash CS6 Swatches panel.

The six-character code at the top of the Swatches panel is hexadecimal code, the standard color-coding system for the Web. As you choose colors from the Swatches panel, you'll see the hexadecimal value for the selected color displayed at the top. The Color Picker in Adobe CS6 applications such as Illustrator and Photoshop also features hexadecimal values, so you can easily match colors between applications by copying and pasting the code shown.

Practicing with the Flash tools

Now that you've had a tour of the Flash tools and workspace, it's time to take them for a test drive. In the following exercises, you'll complete the illustration shown in fl0102_fish. fla while getting the feel for the selection, drawing, and transformation tools. You'll also use Flash tweening to create your first animation.

The drawing and selection tools in action

Your first steps will be to create and modify shapes and freehand artwork with the drawing tools, and then fine-tune your work with the selection tools. The selection tools work as a team with the drawing tools to position and modify shapes, illustrations, and type.

1   Choose File > Open and open the fl0102.fla file located in the fl01lessons folder.

2   Choose File > Save As; the Save As dialog box appears. In the Save As text field, type **fl0102_work.fla**, then navigate to the fl01lessons folder and press Save.

3   Choose the Selection tool (▸) in the Tools panel. This versatile tool can select, move, and manipulate objects directly on the Stage.

4   On the Stage, click once on the fin above the fish's body to select it. Click and drag it downward, making sure that the registration circle appears on the lower corner as shown in the image below, until it joins with the body. Release the mouse button.

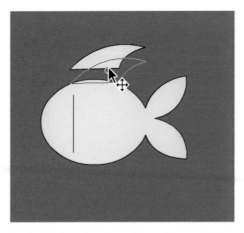

Use the Selection tool to select and move objects on the Stage.

5   You need to make a copy of this fin to use on the bottom of the fish. The easiest way is to clone it, or to drag a copy from the original. To do this, click the top fin once to select it, then, while holding the Alt (Windows) or Option (Mac OS) key, click and drag a copy away from the original fin.

Hold down Alt (Windows) or Option (Mac OS) and drag an object to clone it.

6 Because the new copy will serve as the bottom fin, you'll need to flip it around so it's pointed in the proper direction. Click once to select the new fin copy, and choose Modify > Transform > Flip Vertical. This Transform menu command flips the fin so it's pointed in the right direction.

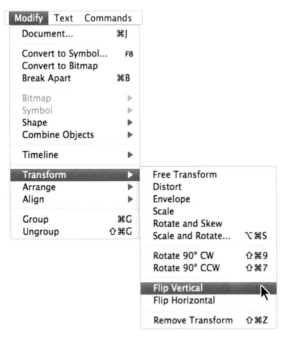

The Transform menu features commands that flip, skew, and rotate a selected object.

7 Still using the Selection tool, click and drag the new fin copy to the bottom of the fish's body, and leave it selected.

8 The new fin is almost there, but it's a bit big. There are several places within Flash where you can resize an object, including the Transform panel. Choose Window > Transform to open it.

9 With the new fin selected, type **60** in the horizontal and vertical Scale fields at the top of the panel and press Enter or Return to commit the change. The fin is reduced to 60 percent of its original size. If necessary, use the Selection tool to reposition the fin after reducing its size.

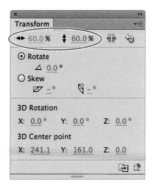

The Transform panel precisely resizes objects by a set percentage.

Notice the Constrain button (∞) next to the Transform panel's horizontal and vertical scale text fields. When you check this box, you can enter a size in only one field and Flash automatically resizes the selected object proportionally. A Reset button (◎) is also included to allow you to reset the selected object to its original proportions.

10 To add an eye to your fish, select the Oval tool (○) from the Tools panel. You may need to click and hold on the Rectangle tool (□) to access this tool. At the bottom of the Tools panel, click on the Fill color swatch and choose black as the fill color.

11 The Oval Tool Properties let you manipulate shapes even further; here, you'll add an inner radius to ovals to create ring-style shapes. In the Property Inspector, type **50** in the Inner radius text field and press Enter or Return.

12 Select Layer 1 in the Timeline by clicking on the name, and click and drag on the left side of the fish to draw a small oval, which will serve as the fish's eye. After you finish drawing the eye, make sure it is de-selected to avoid removing color from the fish below.

To create perfect circles, hold down the Shift key while drawing ovals.

Use the Oval tool with an inner radius to add an eye to your fish.

Congratulations! You've designed your first graphic object in Flash. However, this fish is rather basic.

Using gradient and color tools

Now you'll add some depth and more vibrant color to your fish, using the gradient colors and artistic stroke styles.

1 Choose the Selection tool (⬚) from the Tools panel, and click once inside the body of the fish. A dotted pattern indicates the fill area is selected.

2 To change the body's color, click on the Fill color swatch at the bottom of the Tools panel. In the resulting Swatches panel, choose the orange/yellow gradient located at the bottom of the panel to apply it to the selected area. Deselect the fish by choosing Edit > Deselect All or by clicking offstage in the gray work area.

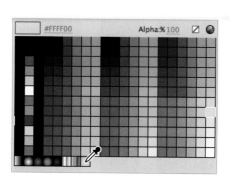 

Give your fish more depth by filling it with a gradient from your Swatches panel.

3 The Eyedropper tool (🖊) enables you to sample a color from one object and transfer it to another. You'll use it to apply the body color to the fish's fins. Using the Selection tool (⬚), hold down the Shift key and click once on each fin so that both are selected at the same time. Select the Eyedropper tool from the Tools panel. Click once on the body of the fish to sample the new color and apply it to the selected fins.

4 Choose Edit > Deselect All to deselect all items on the Stage. In the Tools panel, click and hold the Paint Bucket tool (⬚) and select the Ink Bottle tool (⬚) from the menu that appears. The Ink Bottle tool lets you change an object's stroke color. You'll use the Property Inspector to set a stroke color and style to apply.

5 In the Property Inspector, click the Stroke color swatch and type **#FF6600** (orange) into the hexadecimal field at the top-left corner of the Swatches panel that appears. Press Enter or Return to set this color.

6   Click on the Style menu that appears below the color swatches. Choose the ragged style from the drop-down menu. Click on the edge of the fish body to apply the new stroke color and style.

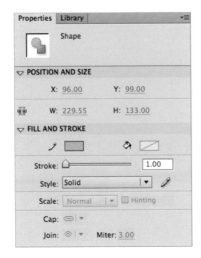

Choose a stroke color and style and apply them using the Ink Bottle tool.

7   Click on the edge of the remaining two fins and the gill line to apply the same color and stroke style to all three. Choose Edit > Deselect All to deselect any active items on the Stage.

8   Choose the Selection tool from the top of the Tools panel. Move the pointer slightly to the right of the gill line without touching it; a small curve appears below your pointer. Click and drag slightly to the right to bend the gill line into a curve.

The Selection tool can bend straight lines or distort shapes.

9 Click the Oval tool (○) in the Tools panel and select the Oval Primitive tool (⊝). Click the Fill color swatch at the bottom of the Tools panel, and choose a light blue color; #6699FF was used in this example. Click the Stroke color swatch and set your stroke color to No color (☑). Set the Inner Radius to **50** in the Property Inspector.

10 While holding down the Shift key, draw several ovals in front of the fish to create bubbles.

11 Choose File > Save to save your work.

Use the Oval Primitive tool to draw bubbles in front of your fish.

12 Choose File > Open, select the fl0102_done.fla file in the fl01lessons folder, and press Open to open it. Compare your work against the completed file fl0102_done.fla. Choose File > Close All to close all currently open documents.

You're off to a good start with the drawing tools. You will work with these tools in more depth in Lesson 2, "Getting Started with the Drawing Tools."

Animation in action

Flash is known for powerful, yet easy-to-use animation that you create directly in the Timeline. The Timeline displays content over periods of time, represented on the Timeline in frames. Each frame can be set as a keyframe, where items can be placed and animation can start or end.

Flash can generate animation with little more than a starting point and ending point; this method is known as tweening. You tell Flash where you want an object to start and stop its animation, and it figures out the frames in between.

1 Choose File > Open and, when prompted, select the fl0101.fla file in the fl01lessons folder. Press Open. Two tortoises appear on the Stage. In the next steps you'll animate the big turtle crossing the Stage.

2   Using the Selection tool (↖), click on the big turtle. Notice that the Big Turtle layer in the Timeline is highlighted in blue, along with the 60 frames included in the Big Turtle layer. Right-click (Windows) or Ctrl+click (Mac OS) on the big turtle and choose Create Motion Tween from the context menu.

Right-click/Ctrl+click on the Big Turtle and choose Create Motion Tween from the context menu.

Motion tweens allow you to easily create animations by simply adjusting an object's properties at different points on the Timeline. Flash takes care of all the heavy lifting.

3   Click and drag the playhead to frame 60.

Drag the playhead to frame 60.

4 Click and drag the big turtle to the left side of the Stage (just before the head reaches the edge). When you release the mouse, you will see a green motion path appear between his old location and his new one.

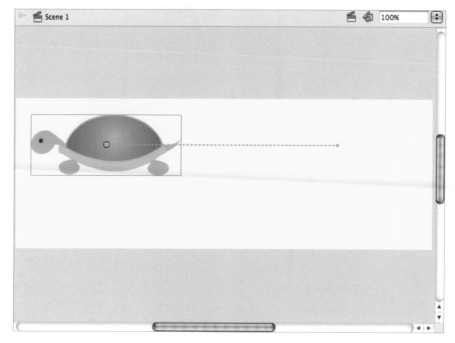

The big turtle repositioned.

5 Press Enter or Return to preview your first animation. It feels good, doesn't it?

Getting help

If at any point you can't find a specific command, want to know how a tool works, or want to learn how to complete a certain task, you can always consult the Flash Help menu. The Help menu launches the Help viewer (an all-in-one glossary, troubleshooter, and reference manual), and also provides links to key Adobe forums and support centers.

The Flash Help viewer is a good source for quick answers.

1 Choose Help > Flash Help.

2 When the panel appears, use the categorized list on the left, or type in a search term to get help on a specific topic or keyword.

Support forums

Adobe's Flash forums can be a rich source of answers, ideas, and tips from experts and other avid Flash users. You can search for answers to common questions or post your own topics and questions.

1   Choose Help > Flash Support Center. The Support forum launches in your system's default browser.

2   In the search text field in the upper-left corner, enter terms you want to explore, and then press the arrow to the right of the text field to select your desired application from the Adobe Community Help drop-down menu.

3   To post topics, questions, or replies, click the Account menu at the top of the page to log in with your Adobe ID.

You must register to post questions or replies to Adobe's Flash forums.

Moving forward

In the next chapter, you'll put pen to paper (or mouse to Stage, rather) to get your creativity flowing with the Flash drawing tools. Now that you've become familiar with the workspace, things should be just a bit easier. Don't hesitate to reference this chapter again to refresh your memory.

Going beyond Flash with HTML5

Many Flash designers are expanding their skills to also include HTML5, CSS3 and JavaScript for building highly interactive web pages and applications. This is especially necessary when targeting content for devices that don't support the Flash plug-in, such as the iPhone, iPad, and Windows Phone, and likely future releases of the Android OS.

Flash will continue to serve as a platform for gaming, video content delivery and web applications. Broadening your skills to include HTML5 and related technologies makes you more versitile as a designer or developer, and allows you to understand how to target your content for a wide range of browsers and devices. As a next step in your learning, after developing skills with Flash, you may want to look the *HTML5 Digital Classroom*, created by the same team that developed the *Flash CS6 Digitial Classroom*.

Self study

Create and save a new document in the fl01lessons folder. Use the Property Inspector to set dimensions, background color, and frame rate. Experiment with the drawing tools you've learned so far, to create artwork on the Stage, and use the Selection tool to move and adjust the artwork as needed.

To get a feel for the workspace, experiment with different panel setups and positions. The Workspace menu (Window > Workspace) features some presets that show how you can maximize the space in your work area.

Try animating the little turtle in fl0101.fla. Experiment with animating other properties using the Property Inspector.

Review

Questions

1   From what two locations can you open a document that was previously open?

2   What panel allows you to view information about a selected object, or set options for an active tool?

3   What method does Flash use to automatically create animation from a starting and ending point?

Answers

1   From File > Open Recent, or the Open a Recent Item column on the Welcome Screen.

2   The Property Inspector.

3   Tweening.

Lesson 2

What you'll learn in this lesson:

- Working with Shapes
- Organizing layers
- Transforming and combining graphics
- Working with Threaded and Multi-Column text
- Applying filters

Getting Started with the Drawing Tools

In addition to creating engaging animated content, Flash functions as a full-featured vector illustration program that enables you to create attractive graphics and digital illustrations for use in your movies. If you use industry-standard applications such as Photoshop or Illustrator, you'll find many similarities as well as some powerful tools that are unique to Flash.

Starting up

Before starting, make sure that your tools and panels are consistent by resetting your workspace. See "Resetting the Flash workspace" in the Starting up section of this book.

You will work with several files from the fl02lessons folder in this lesson. Make sure that you have loaded the fllessons folder onto your hard drive from the supplied DVD. See "Loading lesson files" in the Starting up section of this book.

See Lesson 2 in action!

Use the accompanying video to gain a better understanding of how to use some of the features shown in this lesson. You can find the video tutorial for this lesson on the included DVD.

Drawing in Flash

Adobe Flash Professional CS6 has many powerful tools to help you create shapes, paths, colors and patterns. Whatever you create with the drawing tools can then be animated using the Timeline. In this lesson, you will experiment with two different drawing models that you can use to create artwork in Flash: the Merge Drawing mode and the Object Drawing mode.

Using the Merge Drawing mode

The default mode is the Merge Drawing mode. At first, this mode may be difficult for new users to grasp, especially those already familiar with the drawing tools in Adobe Illustrator. In this lesson, however, you'll see how the Merge Drawing mode offers some unique benefits over traditional drawing tool behaviors. To view the finished project, choose File > Open within Flash CS6. In the Open dialog box, navigate to the fl02lessons folder and select the file, fl0202_done.fla, then press Open. Keep this file open for reference or choose File > Close to close the file.

The finished project.

Creating artwork in Merged Drawing mode

In Merge Drawing mode, shapes can be easily torn apart like clay—strokes can be separated from fills (and vice versa) and you can create partial selections to break up your shapes even further. Most importantly, two shapes drawn in this mode will automatically merge when they overlap, making it easy to create complex combined shapes. Mergeable artwork is easily distinguishable on the Stage by its stippled (dotted) appearance.

You'll first get familiar with how this unique mode behaves before diving into a more complex drawing lesson.

1   Launch Flash CS6 Professional, if it is not already open.

2   Choose File > Open and navigate to the fl02lessons folder that you copied onto your computer. Select and open the file named fl0201.fla. You'll start your artwork off with a basic shape drawn in Merge Drawing mode. First, you'll need to make sure you're in the right drawing mode.

3   Select the Oval tool (○) from the Flash Tools panel. This tool is grouped with the other shape tools, and you may need to click and hold down the mouse button on currently selected shape tool to select it.

Click your mouse button to reveal more shape tools under the Rectangle tool.

4   At the bottom of the Flash Tools panel, locate the Object Drawing button (○) and make sure it's *not* selected. This button controls whether or not you're drawing in Merge or Object Drawing mode. When selected, the button appears shaded.

5   Next, you'll choose your fill (inside) and stroke (outline) colors. At the bottom of the Flash Tools panel, locate the color swatch marked with a pencil icon (⌀) and click it. The Swatches panel appears—select black as your stroke color. Below it, click the color swatch marked with a paint bucket icon (⬧)—from the Swatches panel, select a light orange for your fill color. Click the Reset button at the bottom of the Property Inspector to make sure the Oval Options are all set at 0.

6   Click and drag in the middle of your Stage to draw an oval—once you're satisfied with the size and shape, release the mouse button. Switch to your Selection tool (⬈) at the top of the Tools panel; this tool allows you to select, move, and manipulate items on the Stage.

7 Click once on the fill (inside) area of your shape and the fill becomes selected without the stroke (outline). Double-click the fill, and both the stroke and fill become selected. You can now move or manipulate the shape as one whole object. Deselect the shape by clicking on the Stage.

8 Off to the upper-left corner, click and drag to create a marquee (selection area), and release it once it partially overlaps your new shape. You'll notice that the shape becomes partially selected; you can now use the Selection tool (k) to click and drag the selected portion away from the rest.

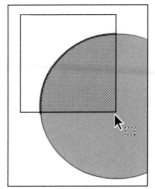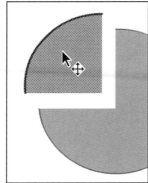

You can partially select mergeable shapes and pull them apart, which can create some interesting shape variations.

9 Next, you'll draw a new shape that overlaps the current one. Reselect the Oval tool (○) from the Tools panel on the right. You can leave your current color settings the same. Click and drag to draw a new shape that partially overlaps the first. Once again, switch to the Selection tool.

10 Double-click the fill of the new shape to select it, and pull it away from the existing one. You'll notice that the new shape has taken a piece out of the old one where the two overlapped!

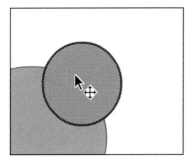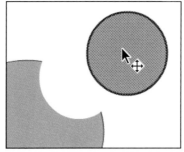

Overlapping shapes automatically merge, causing one to "knock" the other out when removed.

11 Choose File > Save As. In the Save As dialog box, navigate to the fl02lessons folder, then type **fl0201_work.fla** into the Save As text field. Press Save.

Keeping panels open

As a default, Flash collapses panels after it thinks you are done working with them.

You may find this to be inconvenient if you will be frequently using a panel. To have your panels remain open, choose Flash > Preferences (Mac) or Edit > Preferences (Windows) then uncheck the Auto-Collapse Icon Panels option.

Working with Drawing Objects

In contrast to artwork created in Merge Drawing mode (referred to simply as *shapes*), Object Drawing mode provides more rigid control over artwork created on the Stage. Much like drawing shapes in Illustrator CS6, shapes drawn in this mode group their stroke and fill together to avoid separation, and so partial selections are prevented. Drawing Objects give you the ability to stack and arrange shapes within a single layer, providing a deeper level of ordering amongst multiple pieces of artwork.

1 Select a green shade from the Fill color swatch on the Tools panel. Click and hold your mouse button on the Oval tool (○) to reveal the other shape tools, and select the Polystar tool (○).

2 Locate the Object Drawing button (○) at the bottom of the Tools panel, and click to select it. The button should be pressed in at this point, indicating that Object Drawing mode is enabled.

3 Click and drag to draw a new polygon on the Stage. You'll notice the shape appears inside a bounding box. Switch to the Selection tool (▶) and choose Edit > Deselect All.

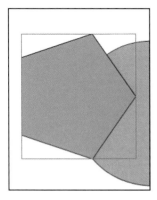

Drawing Objects appear inside of bounding boxes, and their strokes and fills can't be separated.

4 If you click once on the fill or stroke of the shape, the bounding box around the entire shape appears selected. Click and drag to draw a selection area (marquee) around part of the polygon, and you'll see that partial selections also result in the entire shape becoming selected.

5 Double-click the fill of the shape—you'll be brought inside the Drawing Object to edit its contents. Interestingly enough, the contents of the Drawing Object are simply the same, mergeable shapes you worked with in the last lesson. You can think of a Drawing Object as a container around a mergeable shape that keeps its parts grouped together.

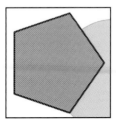 

Double-clicking a Drawing Object doesn't select it, but rather brings you inside to edit its contents.

6 Exit the Drawing Object by double-clicking on the Stage. Once again, return to the Tools panel and select the Polystar tool (○). Click and drag to draw another shape on the Stage that overlaps the polygon you drew in Step 3.

You can also exit a Drawing Object's Edit mode using the links shown above the Stage. Click on the Scene 1 link to return to the main Timeline, and you should no longer see the words Drawing Object appear to its right.

7 Choose the Selection tool and select the new shape. Pull it slightly away from the original shape—you'll notice the two shapes did not merge as they would with mergeable shapes. Leave the new shape selected and make sure that it still slightly overlaps the first polystar.

8 Next, you'll see how Drawing Objects can be meticulously stacked and arranged, even on the same Timeline layer. With the new shape selected, choose Modify > Arrange > Send to Back. The new shape is pushed behind the first. The Arrange menu allows you to restack Drawing Objects, groups, and symbols. Symbols are covered in more detail in Lesson 3, "Using Symbols and the Library."

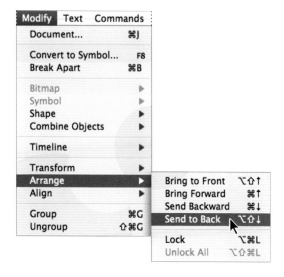
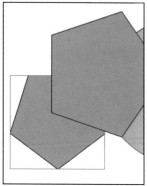

When a Drawing Object is selected, you have access to the Arrange menu (Window > Arrange), which allows you to change that shape's stacking order relative to other Drawing Objects on the Stage.

Mergeable shapes always fall below Drawing Objects, groups, or symbols on the Stage. To have a mergeable shape appear above other items, you need to place it on its own layer and move that layer to the top of the stack.

9 Choose File > Save, then choose File > Close.

Putting it all together

Now that you have a feel for how the two drawing modes work, you'll complete a piece of artwork using your new skills and become familiar with additional drawing tools.

1   Choose File > Open and navigate to the fl02lessons folder. Select and open the file named fl0202.fla.

2   Choose File > Save As. In the Save As dialog box, navigate to the fl02lessons folder, then type **fl0202_work.fla** into the Save As text field. Press Save.

3   On the Stage, you see a single oval—switch to the Selection tool (▶) and click once on the oval to select it. A bounding box appears, indicating that this is a Drawing Object. A look at the Property Inspector confirms this, as it should read Drawing Object at the top.

4   In order to dissect this shape further, you'll need to break it back down to a mergeable shape like the ones you created earlier. Make sure the shape is selected, and choose Modify > Break Apart. The shape now appears with a dotted pattern that indicates it is mergeable artwork.

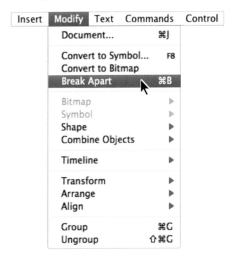

The Break Apart command allows you to break any artwork down to its next most basic form.

5 Deselect the oval shape by clicking on the pasteboard or a different area of the Stage. To create the mouth of your fish, click and drag with your Selection tool to create a partial selection that overlaps the left edge of the oval. Delete the selected portion by using the Backspace (Windows) or Delete (Mac OS) key. With mergeable shapes, you can delete partial selections to dissect shapes in unusual ways.

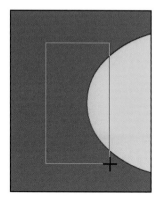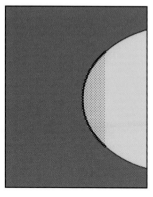

Create a partial selection around the oval where you'll form the mouth of your fish.

6 With the Selection tool active, move your cursor close to the open-ended stroke at the top of the oval. When an L-shaped angle icon (⬉) appears below your pointer, click and drag the anchor point down and to the left as shown below.

7 Continue using the Selection tool to click and drag the bottom anchor point up to meet the first anchor point as shown below.

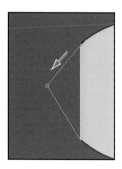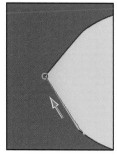

The Selection tool can pull open-ended paths to reshape an object.

8 Choose File > Save to save your file.

Paths on mergeable shapes automatically join when Snap to Objects is enabled. Snap to Objects can be enabled using View > Snapping > Snap to Objects, or by using the Snap to Objects button (⋒) at the bottom of the Tools panel.

Using the Line tool

Most illustration programs have a line tool, and while it's not the most creative tool in the box, you can use Flash's Selection tool to make it more useful. In the following steps, you'll form the tail of your fish using a few simple moves.

1   Select the Line tool (\) from the Tools panel. Make sure that Object Drawing mode is disabled (if necessary, deselect the Object Drawing button (◯) at the bottom of the Tools panel). Select Solid from the style menu on the Property Inspector to set a solid line.

2   Move your crosshair cursor close to the right edge of the oval, and click and drag to draw an upward diagonal line. Starting where your first line leaves off, click and drag to draw a second line that meets the oval again below where the first line began.

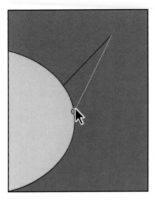

With Snap to Object enabled and Object Drawing disabled, diagonal lines automatically join if drawn close enough together.

3   Where the last line meets the oval, click and drag to draw a diagonal line moving downward. As you did in step 2, click and drag where the line leaves off to draw a second line that meets the oval again. These steps should have formed a spiky *tail* that you'll fine-tune in the next steps.

4   To change this from a spiky tail to a rounded, more appropriate one, you'll use the Selection tool. Choose the Selection tool (▶), and move your cursor toward the middle of the first diagonal line you created. Once you are close enough, a curved icon appears (▶) below your pointer. Click and drag upward to bend the line into a curve. As you can see, the Selection tool can also bend or reshape straight lines and curves.

5   Repeat step 4 for each of the three remaining lines until the tail is formed.

The Selection tool can be used to easily reshape lines and curves.

6   Next you'll need to fill the two sides of your new tail. By default, shapes drawn with path-centric tools such as the Line, Pen, and Pencil tools do not automatically fill. To fill these shapes, click and hold the Ink Bottle tool (◌), if necessary, to locate and choose the Paint Bucket tool (◌) from the Tools panel.

The Paint Bucket tool allows you to add fills where none exist, or to change the color of an existing fill.

7   Click on the Fill color swatch at the bottom of the Tools panel. Choose the light orange color marked #FFCC00. (You can also type this in the text field at the top of the Swatches panel to select the specified color.) Click inside of the tail fins to fill them with the selected color.

Add fills to empty paths using the Paint Bucket tool.

8   Switch back to the Line tool, and click and drag to draw two close, parallel, vertical lines in the middle of the oval. You will use these to form the gills for your fish.

9   Switch to the Selection tool (↖), and use the technique shown in steps 4 and 5 to bend each line into a slight curve in the same direction.

Use the same technique you used to create the tail to bend out some gills for your fish.

10   With the Selection tool active, click and select each of the two overlapping lines that separate the tail from the fish body. Press Backspace (Windows) or Delete (Mac OS) to clear the lines away.

11   Choose File > Save to save your file.

You can easily switch from any tool to the Selection tool by pressing the V key, without having to go over to the Tools panel.

What the hex is a hexadecimal code?

You may have noticed that each color you choose (including colors referenced in these lessons) is marked with a hexadecimal code, a 6-character code preceded by a pound (#) sign. A hexadecimal code is a binary representation of an RGB color, used to indicate colors within web-specific languages and applications (such as HTML, Dreamweaver, and Fireworks).

Each byte, or pair of two digits, represents the red, green, and blue values for that color, respectively, from 00 to FF (in decimal notation, the values 0 to 255). For example, white in standard RGB values is notated as 255,255,255—in hexadecimal notation, #FFFFFF.

While it's not at all necessary (and somewhat impossible) to memorize the hexadecimal values for every popular color, becoming comfortable with this notation will help you work your way through Flash's color panels as well as those of other applications.

A helpful hint: the Photoshop and Illustrator color pickers also display a hexadecimal code for any color selected, making it easy to match colors between applications.

Using the Pen tool

For precision illustration tasks, you will most likely want to use the Pen tool. The Pen tool allows for point-to-point drawing, and precise control over curves and lines in between. You can even add or remove points to fine-tune your work. If you've used the Pen tool in Illustrator CS6, you'll already be familiar with the Pen tool and its related tools.

You'll use the Pen tool to create fins for your new fish in the following steps.

1   Select the Pen tool (✒) from the Tools panel. In the Properties Panel or Tools panel, set your stroke color to black (#000000).

2   In the space above your oval, click and release the mouse pointer on the Stage to create a new point. Move your pointer to the left of the point you just created, and click and release again to create a second point. This point is joined to the first by a new path (line).

3   Position your cursor above and to the right of your last point. Click and hold down your mouse button, and then drag to the right. This forms a curve between your new point and the last one. Once you've gotten the curve just right, release the mouse button.

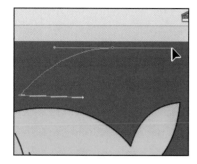

Creating precision lines and curves using the Pen tool.

You can create curves from any new point by holding down the mouse button and dragging in the direction you want to form the curve. (Be sure not to release the mouse button first!)

4   Next, you'll close up the shape. The next time you create a point, however, the Pen tool will attempt to draw a curve in the same direction as the last. To reset the last point drawn so that you can control the curve, click on the last point you created.

5   Move your pointer over the first point you created, and you should see a small loop appear below the pen cursor. Click and hold down your mouse button; drag to the right to form the final curve, and release the mouse to complete the shape.

6   As with other path-based tools, shapes created with the Pen tool do not automatically fill. To fill the new shape, choose the Paint Bucket tool (⬧) from the Tools panel. In the Tools panel, make sure the Fill color is still set to the orange color labeled #FFCC00.

7   Click once inside your new shape to fill it with the currently active fill color.

8   Now you'll move the fin into place and connect it with the rest of the body. Choose the Selection tool (↖), and double-click the fill of the fin to select the entire shape. Drag it into place at the top of the oval, slightly overlapping it. Click the Stage to deselect the shape; when you deselect the shape, the two become merged.

*Move your new fin into place
above the fish body.*

9   The fin should now be merged with the oval. Use the Selection tool and click once to select the portion of the stroke that overlaps onto the oval. Only that portion should become selected. Press Backspace (Windows) or Delete (Mac OS) to clear away the selected stroke.

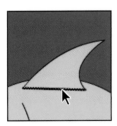

*Intersecting strokes in mergeable artwork become segmented
and can be individually selected and removed.*

By default, strokes that overlap between two merged shapes become segmented, and individual portions can be selected and removed.

10   Choose File > Save to save your file.

Using the Add and Delete Anchor Point tools

You can add or remove points along existing paths with the Add and Delete Anchor Point tools. These tools are found under the Pen tool and enable you to further fine-tune your illustrations. You'll add a bottom fin to your fish by manipulating the existing oval shape that forms its body.

1   Choose the Subselection tool (↖) from the Tools panel. Click on the edge of the oval; this reveals the points and paths that form this shape. From here, you can manipulate, add, or remove points along this path.

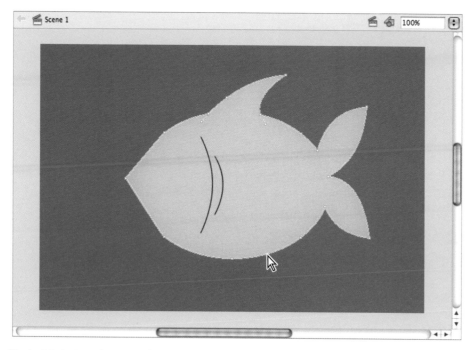

Use the Subselection tool to activate the points and paths that compose a shape.

2   Click and hold down your mouse pointer on the Pen tool (◊)—this reveals the Add, Delete, and Convert Anchor Point tools. Choose the Add Anchor Point tool (◊⁺). Note: You can also use the = and - keys to toggle between the Add and Delete anchor point tools.

3   At the bottom center of the oval, you'll notice a single anchor point. Using the Add Anchor Point tool, click once to the left and once to the right of that point to add two new anchor points.

If you add the anchor point(s) in the wrong place, or add too many, choose the Delete Anchor Point tool (◊) and click on any point to remove it.

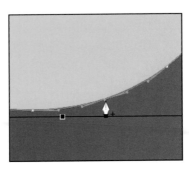

Use the Add Anchor Point tool to add two additional points surrounding the bottom point.

4   Choose the Subselection tool and, if necessary, click on the outline of your oval to reactivate the points and paths. Click the point at the very bottom of the oval to activate it—the point now appears solid instead of hollow.

5   Click and drag the point down and to the right, which extends that portion of the oval into a fin-like shape.

With more points in place, you can easily pull out and extend a fin from the existing shape.

6   Choose File > Save to save your file, and leave the file open.

Using the Combine Objects menu

If you need to create more complex combinations of shapes, you can use the Combine Objects menu, found at Modify > Combine Objects. This menu enables you to create punches, crops, or intersections between overlapping shapes, and even lets you convert mergeable artwork into Drawing Objects.

Before you can perform any Combine Objects menu commands on a piece of artwork, it first must be converted to a Drawing Object. To do this, you'll use the Union command to convert your fish from mergeable artwork to a Drawing Object.

1   Select the entire fish by choosing Edit > Select All. You can also use the Selection tool (⬆) to draw a selection area around the artwork if you prefer.

2   Choose Modify > Combine Objects > Union. This command converts the selected artwork to a Drawing Object, and a bounding box appears around your fish and its parts. Choose Edit > Deselect All.

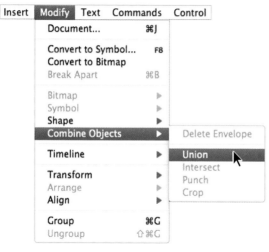

Convert mergeable artwork to Drawing Objects using Modify > Combine Objects > Union.

3   Select the Polystar tool (◯), and enable Object Drawing mode by selecting the button at the bottom of the Tools panel. From the Properties Panel, press the Options button. This opens the Tool Settings dialog box for the Polystar tool.

4   In the Tool Settings dialog box, type **3** for the number of sides. Leave the Star point size at its defaults and press OK to exit the dialog box. On the Stage, while holding your Shift key (to constrain the angle), click and drag to draw a right-pointing triangle.

If the new triangle appears unfilled, select any fill color from the Tools panel, and use the Paint Bucket tool to fill it.

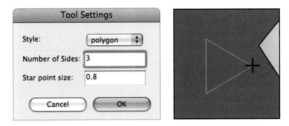

Use the Polystar tool to set and draw a triangle shape that you'll punch from the fish below.

5   With the shape still selected, choose the Free Transform tool (⊞) from the Tools panel. A bounding box with handles appears—grab the top middle handle and drag it downward to scale the shape down vertically.

Choose the Selection tool and move the shape so that it overlaps the fish on the left where a mouth should be.

6   Choose Edit > Select All so that the new shape and your fish both appear selected. Choose Modify > Combine Objects > Punch. The new shape is knocked out from your fish, leaving behind a mouth-like opening.

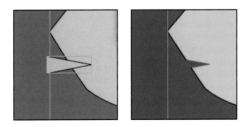

Use Modify > Combine Objects > Punch to subtract one shape from another.

7   Select the Oval tool from the Tools panel. Make sure you have a fill color selected (any color will do). With the Shift key held down, click and drag to draw a small, perfect circle. To match the figure shown in this example, use your Property Inspector to set the circle to a width and height of **50**. Switch to your Selection tool and position the circle on top of your fish above the mouth you created.

8 Choose Edit > Select All. With both the circle and fish selected, choose Modify > Combine Objects > Punch. This punches the circle into the body of the fish, making space for an eye.

Use the Punch command to create a space for your fish's eye.

9 Choose File > Save to save your file.

The Combine Objects menu

There are several commands available at Modify Combine Objects, not all of which you may use right away. Here's an overview of what each menu command does so that you can decide for yourself when and whether to use them.

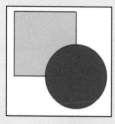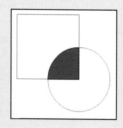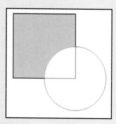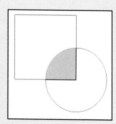

From left to right: Union, Intersect, Punch, Crop.

Union: Converts mergeable shapes into Drawing Objects. You can group several shapes into a single Drawing Object. In addition, shapes that are part of an Intersect, Punch, or Crop operation must all be Drawing Objects.

Intersect: Leaves behind only the overlapping area of two shapes.

Punch: Knocks out the top shape from the bottom shape.

Crop: Crops the bottom shape to conform to the top shape.

Using the Primitive tools (Smart Shapes)

The Rectangle and Oval Primitive tools provide you with an easy and time-saving way to create common variations on these basic shapes. From rounded or scalloped rectangles, to double-radius ovals, these smart shapes are especially powerful, because you can continue to modify them long after they've been created.

Using the Oval Primitive tool

Your new fish needs an eye, and the best tool for the job is the Oval Primitive tool, which allows you to create complex variations on ovals and circles.

1. Select the Oval Primitive tool (⊖) from the Tools panel. This tool can be found underneath the existing shape tools. From the Tools panel, choose black (#000000) for your fill color, and set the stroke to None (☑).

2. Choose View > Snapping, and select Snap to Objects to temporarily disable object snapping. While holding your Shift key (to constrain width and height), click and drag to draw a small circle on the Stage. Switch to your Selection tool (↖), and position the circle above the spot where the eye should appear on your fish (a hole should appear there from the last exercise).

    Use the W and H values on the Property Inspector to set the new circle's size to **45** by **45**.

3. In the Property Inspector, locate the three sliders at the bottom marked Start Angle, End Angle, and Inner Radius. Click and drag the Inner Radius slider toward the right, and you'll see that it forms a knockout in the center of the circle. Set the Inner Radius to suit your artwork (the figure and sample file use a value of around 49).

    You can also enter a precise value in the text field to the right of the slider.

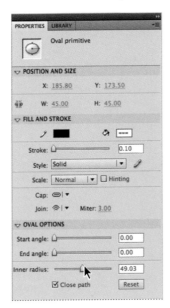 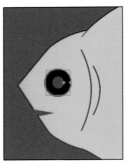

Use the Inner Radius slider to punch a center into an oval primitive.

4　Locate the Start Angle and End Angle sliders in the Property Inspector. Click and drag the Start Angle slider until its value reads somewhere between 40 and 45. You'll notice that as you increase the angle, the circle forms a *C* shape—this slider tells the circle to begin its circumference (shape) at a different angle, resulting in a partial shape!

5　You'll now perform the same action for the End Angle. Grab the End Angle slider and drag it to the right until the value reads about 330. The circle now ends at a different location as well. As you can see, this can be very powerful in any situation where you need to create wedges or partial circle shapes without the need for complex punch or knockout commands.

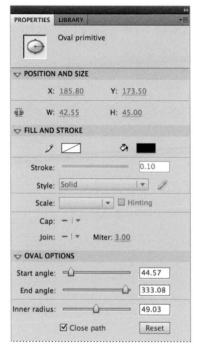
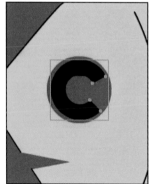

Use the sliders to affect your smart shape at any point. You can even deselect and return to the shape later on to edit its settings.

6 Choose View > Snapping > Snap to Objects to re-enable object snapping.

Oval Primitive shapes

For each oval primitive shape drawn, you'll see a discrete handle (it looks like an anchor point) on its right side. As an alternative to the Start and End Angle sliders, you can click and drag this handle in a clockwise or counter-clockwise motion to manually alter the start or end angle of the shape.

The Rectangle Primitive tool

The close cousin of the Oval Primitive tool is the Rectangle Primitive tool, which gives you control over corner radii on rectangles and squares. Like the Oval Primitive tool, you can easily set values for a new primitive shape, and return to edit it at any time.

It's time to give your fish a way to speak its mind, so you'll create a basic word balloon using the power of the primitive.

1 Choose the Rectangle Primitive tool (▢) from the shape tools group on the Tools panel. From the Tools panel or the Property Inspector, set a fill color of white (#FFFFFF) and a stroke color of black (#000000).

2 Click and drag to draw a rectangle to the upper left of your fish. It's okay if it goes off the Stage into the pasteboard. If you'd like to match the sample file, in the Property Inspector make sure the Lock width and height button (●) is disabled and set the rectangle's size to **200** pixels wide by **130** pixels high.

3 In the Property Inspector, locate the Rectangle Options section; you'll see four text fields and a slider. Here is where you set the corner radius for all or each of your rectangle's corners. By default, the four corners are locked together and use the same value.

Click and drag the slider to the right until the corner values read about 40—you see the corners of the rectangle begin to round out.

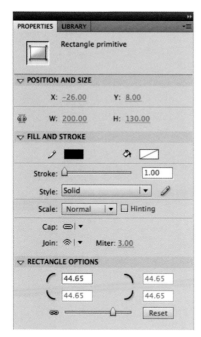 

Add a corner radius to the rectangle primitive using the slider in the Property Inspector.

To give each corner a unique value, click the chain link icon (∞) to the left of the slider to unlock the four corners. You can then type in a different value for each corner in its respective text field.

4 Next, you'll modify the corner radius using a slightly different technique. Instead of using the slider in the Property Inspector, you can grab the points adjacent to any corner and drag them to reshape the corner radius.

5 Switch to the Selection tool (↖), then click and drag the point in the upper-left corner of your rectangle to the left and right. As you can see, this modifies the corners of your rectangle—move slightly to the right to reduce the corner radius.

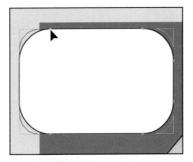

Using the Selection tool can be a more tactile way to modify corners.

6 Choose File > Save to save your work.

You'll now add the stem to make this a true word balloon—however, you may have noticed that primitive shapes behave unlike any other shape you've used so far. While they appear to look and function much like Drawing Objects, they actually can't be modified in the way that Drawing Objects can.

Neither the Selection nor Subselection tool will allow you to modify them in the way you've been able to do with Drawing Objects and mergeable artwork. To accomplish this, you need to break the shape down to artwork that you can manipulate freely. Keep in mind, however, that doing this is a one-way street: You can't convert a shape or Drawing Object back into a primitive shape once it's been broken apart.

7 If it's not already active, switch to the Selection tool (↖) and click once to select the rectangle primitive.

8 You'll now break this out of a primitive down to artwork you can manipulate further. Choose Modify > Break Apart, and the shape now appears with the dotted pattern that indicates it is now a mergeable shape. Keep in mind that you cannot go back.

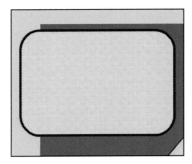

Use Modify > Break Apart to convert the primitive shape to a mergeable shape.

Choose the Subselection tool (⬚) from the Tools panel and click once on the edge of the shape to reveal its points and paths.

9   Switch to the Add Anchor Point tool (⬚). In the lower-right corner of the rectangle, click to create two new consecutive anchor points before the corner.

10   Switch to the Subselection tool, again, then click on the second point (the one closest to the corner) and drag it down and to the right to form the stem of your word balloon.

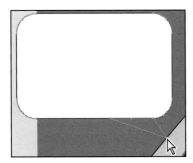

Form a stem by pulling out the second of the two new points you created.

11   With the shape still selected, choose Modify > Combine Objects > Union to convert the shape to a Drawing Object, which you can easily move and stack later on.

12   Choose File > Save to save your work.

Adding text to your artwork

Flash allows you to create and style text to include in your movies, which can also be incorporated into animations or rendered in 3D (see Lesson 4, "Advanced Tools," and Lesson 6, "Advanced Animation" for more on this). In addition, text is one of a few objects in Flash that can have filters applied to enhance its appearance.

Flash Text: TLF & Classic Text

Flash uses two different types of text—TLF and "Classic" text. The TLF Text engine superseded the Classic text engine in Flash CS5, and vastly adds upon the capabilities of the "classic" Flash Text tool. TLF Text boasts features such as multi-column text and threaded text frames, which most designers have become accustomed to working with in other Adobe applications such as InDesign and Illustrator. In addition, many subtle but advanced text options such as character rotation and vertical orientation are now available through an expanded character options panel in the Property Inspector.

You can continue to use Flash's Classic Text option in the Property Inspector, but for the purpose of the following exercises you'll be using the new TLF Text engine for all tasks.

In this lesson, you'll use the Text tool to add and style some cool text inside your fish's word balloon and alongside the edge of the Stage.

1   Select the Text tool (T) from the Tools panel. On the Property inspector, use the drop-down menu at the top to switch from Classic Text to TLF Text.

2   Click once and drag within your word balloon to create a new text box that's slightly smaller than the balloon itself. The box appears with a blinking cursor in the upper-left corner, indicating that you're ready to type.

3   Type the words **A Fish's Story:** within the text box. Click and drag across all the text within the box to select it.

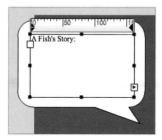

*Use the Text tool to add some text
to your word balloon.*

4   In the Property Inspector, locate the Character options, which include options to set Family (font), Color, and Size. Choose Arial (or equivalent) from the Family menu to change the typeface. Move your cursor above the Size value, and drag to set the type size to 24 points. Click the Color swatch and set the type color to black (#000000).

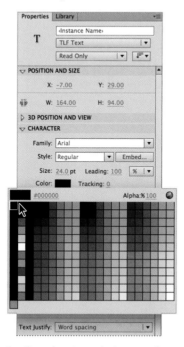

*Specify typeface, size, and color options for your new
text from the Property Inspector.*

5 Press the Escape key twice to exit the current text box and make the Text tool active again. You'll now add some text along the left side of the Stage for more visual impact.

6 At the top of the Property Inspector, locate the Change orientation of text drop-down menu. Click it and select the Vertical option. This will create vertically-oriented text next time you use the Text tool.

The Change orientation of text drop-down menu.

7 Click (but don't drag) near the left edge of the Stage to create a new text box, and type the words **Go Fish!** You'll see that the text now is created vertically alongside the left edge of the Stage.

You'll notice that you've created text on the Stage using two slightly different techniques: Clicking and dragging to create a pre-sized text box, or simply clicking on the Stage to begin a new type path. The former of the two will result in a text box that can take advantage of advanced type options and such as text-flow, multi-column text. The single click approach is a good way to create single lines of text for more basic and aesthetic purposes.

New: Text Ruler

When you create text boxes on the Stage, you'll notice a handy ruler appears above it. This shows you the width of your text field and allows you to set margins and other properties by dragging the available markers at the top.

A helpful ruler appears on top of text fields to set margins and size.

Working with Threaded and Multi-Column Text

Flash's TLF Text Engine brings a wealth of capabilities to type, many of which designers have become accustomed to in other Adobe applications, such as Illustrator and InDesign. This includes the ability to flow (thread) text across multiple text boxes, multi-column text and a variety of advanced character and paragraph options.

Next, you'll add more text to your fish's word balloon, and to catch the additional words you'll add a second text box on the Stage. You'll also take a look at splitting large blocks of type into columns for better presentation.

1 Choose Edit > Deselect All. If it's not already active, select the Text tool (T) from the Tools panel. Also, make sure that the orientation of your text is set back to Horizontal (select Horizontal from the Change orientation of text drop-down menu toward the top of the Property Inspector).

2 Click and drag in the lower-right corner of the Stage to create a second, empty text box (it should take up roughly the entire lower-right quarter of the Stage).

3 To resize the new text box, hover over any of the box handles on the sides or corners until you see a double-arrow. Click and drag to resize the text box until it's just right. The dimensions used in this lesson are 276px by 163px.

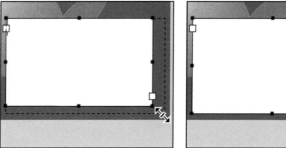

You can easily resize text boxes by dragging any of the four corners.

4 Now, you'll get some text to add to the first text box in the upper-left corner. Choose File > Open, and browse to this lesson's folder in the dialog box that appears. Select the story.txt file and click Open/Select to open it in Flash.

   You may need to make certain that All Files are set to display in the dialog box of the Open window in order to view and select a .txt file.

5 Select all the text within the text file you opened by triple-clicking within any point in the document, and choose Edit > Copy or Ctrl+C (Windows) or Command+C (Mac OS) to copy the selected contents.

6 Return to your Flash file by selecting its tab at the top of the workspace. Your text tool should still be active. Click within the first text box you created over the word balloon, and position your cursor following the words *A Fish's Story:*. Choose Edit > Paste or Ctrl+V (Windows) or Command+V (Mac OS) to paste the text into the frame.

7   You'll notice that the text is likely too long for the box, and gets cut off. You'll also note a small box with a red plus sign in the lower-right corner; this is the text frame's out port, and the red plus sign indicates an overrun, which means there's too much text for the box. You'll correct this by "flowing" the text from this box to the one you created on the bottom right corner of the Stage.

The newly added text overflows the text box, indicated by the red plus sign in the lower-right corner.

8   Click on the red plus sign, which is the out port of the text box; your icon should change to show a block of text attached. You are now carrying the overrun text, and can place it, or "flow" it to another text frame.

9   Locate the text box you created in the lower quarter of the Stage. Hover your cursor over the text box until you see a chain link icon (⊛), and click. The text from the word balloon should now continue in this text frame, and you'll see a line going from one to the other to indicate the frames are threaded together.

The final touch will be splitting that new text box with some attractive columns. Displaying text in multiple columns is a clean, easy way to read large blocks of text, and a technique commonly used in print publications and websites.

10   Using your Text tool, click within the new text box you created on the lower-right corner of the Stage. In the Property Inspector, locate the Columns value under the Container and Flow options (the default value should read 1).

11   Click and drag over the columns value until the value reads 2. This will split your text box into two columns.

12   If you'd like to adjust the gap between the two columns, locate the gap width value directly to the right of the Columns value (the default value should read 20px). Click and drag to the left or right to decrease or increase the gap, respectively.

13   Choose File > Save to save your document.

Now, if you add text to the frame within the word balloon, the text in the lower corner of the Stage will continue to adjust as needed, and format the overflowed text into two nice columns!

Adding filters

To enhance the appearance of text, you can add popular live filters such as drop shadows, blurs, glows, and more. Filters can also be applied to other objects in your movie, such as button and movie clip symbols (covered later in this book). For now, you'll add some basic filters to make your text stand out.

1 Switch to the Selection tool (↖), and click once on your text box in the lower-right corner to select it.

Pressing the V key while editing text simply types a v in the text box; it doesn't switch to the Selection tool as anticipated. To exit a text box, use the Esc (escape) key, and then press the V key to jump to the Selection tool.

2 At the bottom of the Property Inspector, locate and expand the Filters section. (Try collapsing the Container and Flow options to give your filter options more space.)

3 In the lower-left corner of the Filters section, press the Add Filter button (⊞) to add a new filter. A menu appears, showing you the various filters you can apply to your text. Select the Drop Shadow filter.

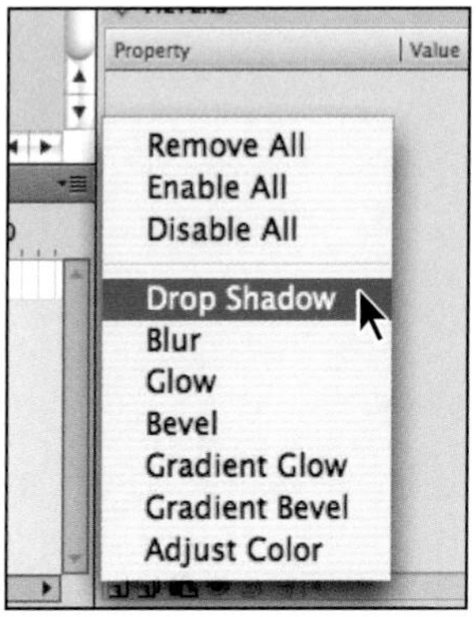

Apply filters to selected text from the Filters section of the Property Inspector.

4 Options appear for the new Drop Shadow filter, which you can fine-tune. To start, click and drag the Strength value to reduce the strength (opacity) to 30 percent.

5 Click and drag the Distance value to increase the distance to 10 pixels. Under the Quality setting, select High. Filter quality settings are discussed further in Lesson 12, "Introducing Movie Clips."

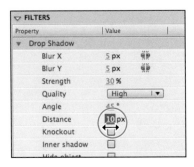

Set specific options for your filter, including color, strength, and distance.

6 Choose File > Save to save your file.

Working with colors

Flash offers a lot of options for creating, saving, and working with colors and gradients. In addition, the panels and workspace make it easy to choose and apply colors from virtually anywhere, or to save color sets that you can share between multiple Flash documents and projects.

Getting set up

1 First you'll want to make sure that the Color and Swatches panels are visible. Choose Window > Color. By default, the Color and Swatches panels are already grouped together.

The Swatches and Color panels are grouped together by default.

2 Drag the panel group by its title bar over the Property Inspector and Library panel on the right-hand side, releasing the mouse when you see a light blue line. The two panels should now appear docked in the panel group above the Property Inspector and Library panel.

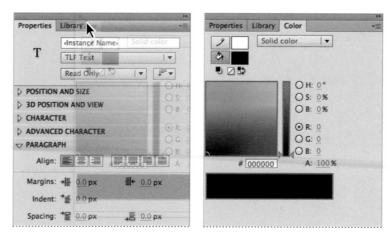

Move the Color and Swatches panel group to the Properties and Libraries panel group.

Creating gradients

A gradient is a gradual blend between two or more colors, and is often used for complex color transitions or to imply lighting effects. You can create and save gradients and apply them to fills or strokes within your artwork. Flash supports *linear* gradients and *radial* gradients. Both types can include any number of colors.

Linear gradients blend in a uniform manner and, as the name implies, in a straight line going in any direction or angle.

Radial gradients blend in a circular manner, either from the inside out or the outside in (depending on your perspective, of course).

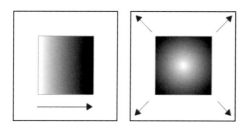

On the left, a linear gradient; on the right, a radial gradient.

Your fish is almost complete, so it's time to bring it to life with some dynamic and exciting colors.

1   Choose your Selection tool (⬧), and click once on your fish to select it. Choose Modify > Break Apart to separate the fish and its parts, and then choose Edit > Deselect All. Click once on the body of the fish.

2   Locate the Color type drop-down menu at the top-right corner of the Color panel. This allows you to choose a solid color or gradient for the currently active color. Choose Radial gradient to set a radial gradient to your fill. The fish displays the default black-to-white gradient.

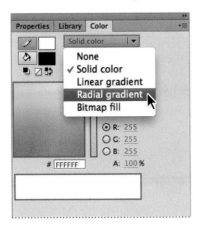

Choose Radial to switch your shape's fill to a radial gradient.

3   At the bottom of the Color panel, you see the color ramp, which now appears with two color stops (sliders), one for each color that forms your gradient. You'll need to assign a new color to each stop.

4   Double-click the right slider, and the Swatches panel appears. Choose the dark orange color marked #CC6600. Double-click the left slider, and from the Swatches panel, choose the light orange color marked #FF9900.

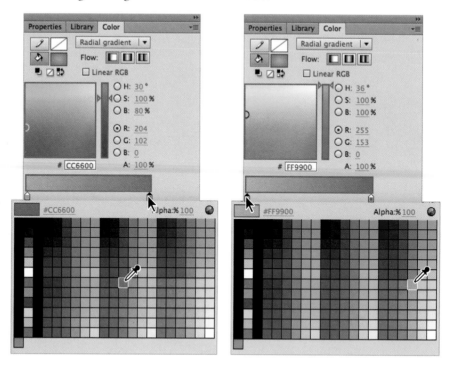

Set a unique value for each color stop on your gradient.

5   The position and distance between the two sliders determines the blend point. Moving one slider closer to the other changes the balance between the two colors.

Click and drag the left slider slightly toward the middle—this makes the lighter orange more prominent than the dark orange.

6   To add colors to your gradient, you'll add more color stops. Add a new color stop by clicking on the far left edge of the color ramp. A new stop should appear below the color ramp. Double-click the stop, and choose white (#FFFFFF) from the Swatches panel.

Now, you'll save this gradient for use later on.

7 Locate and open the Color panel menu (◦≡) in the upper-right corner of the panel. Choose Add Swatch to add your new gradient swatch to the existing swatch presets.

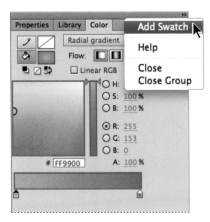

Save your new gradient as a preset that you can recall later on from the Swatches panel.

8 Choose File > Save to save your file.

Using opacity with gradient colors

A cool feature in Flash is the ability to set a unique opacity level for each individual color in a gradient. This can create some interesting effects, and add cool lighting-style effects to your illustrations. In this next exercise, you'll create and color some underwater bubbles using this interesting effect.

1 Choose the Oval tool (○) from the Tools panel. If it's not already enabled, activate Object Drawing mode by pressing the button at the bottom of the Tools panel.

2 From the bottom of the Tools panel, choose white (#FFFFFF) for your stroke color, and choose the black-to-white radial gradient preset for your fill color.

3 While holding the Shift key down (to constrain proportions), click and drag to draw a small circle to the left of your fish. Leave the circle selected.

4 If it's not already open, choose Window > Color to open the Color panel.

5 Double-click the black color stop to open the Swatches panel, and choose white (#FFFFFF).

6 With the stop still active, locate the Alpha slider; this sets the opacity of the selected color in the current gradient. Click and drag the slider downward until the value reads 0 percent. This produces an interesting light flare effect inside the bubble.

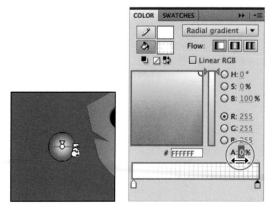

Draw a new oval, and use the Color panel to reduce the opacity of one of your oval's gradient colors.

7 Choose File > Save to save your file.

Creating custom colors

As you may have discovered, creating and saving a solid color swatch is nearly identical to creating and saving a gradient swatch. In this case, you'll set specific RGB values to create a color that you can apply to your artwork, as well as add to your existing swatches.

1 Choose the Selection tool (k) and double-click once on your fish to select it. In the Property Inspector, set the stroke color style to solid and the color to black (#000000).

2 Locate the R, G, and B text fields on the Color panel, click the stroke icon (✎ ■) to make certain the stroke (and not the fill) is selected, and type **250**, **100**, and **16**, respectively. This creates a dark orange color that is immediately applied to the stroke.

3 From the Color panel menu located in the upper-right corner, select Add Swatch to add your new color to the Swatches panel.

4 Choose File > Save to save your file.

Saving a custom color set

Once you've added new color swatches, you'll want to save that set for use with other projects and documents. If you've ever created and saved custom color swatches in applications like Photoshop or Illustrator, you'll find that saving color sets in Flash is very similar.

1 Press the Swatches panel tab located next to the Color panel tab to open the Swatches panel. Press the panel menu button (▾≡) in the upper-right corner of the Swatches panel.

2   From the panel menu, choose Save Colors.

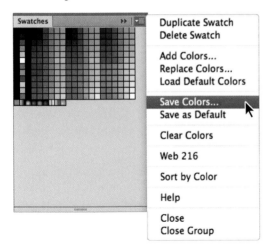

Save the current swatches as a new color set that you can recall at any time.

3   From the dialog box that appears, choose your Save location (for this lesson, you can choose the fl02lessons folder), and name the new file **fl02colors.clr**.

4   Press Save to save the color set into the selected folder. The color set appears in your destination folder as a single .clr (Flash Color Set) file.

You can also choose to save your swatches in .act (Adobe Color Table) format, which allows you to exchange it with Adobe applications such as Photoshop and Fireworks. You can even load .act color tables exported from Fireworks back into Flash if you'd like!

Organizing and layering graphics

As you build more complex graphics on the Stage, you'll want to position and layer them as needed to make your movie work for you. Flash gives you a lot of control over your Stage through a robust layer structure that you may already be accustomed to using in other Adobe design applications.

Working with layers

On a single layer, you have a great deal of flexibility to arrange Drawing Objects and grouped graphics—however, as your artwork becomes more complex, you'll want the power of layers to stack and arrange your artwork. In addition to controlling stacking order, layers let you hide specific graphics from view, and even lock those items from accidentally being edited or deleted.

You can think of layers as clear pieces of film that you can place graphics on and stack together; each layer sits above another, allowing you to reveal the items below, but also to control which items appear above or below another. Each layer and its contents can be isolated in view, toggled out of view, or locked to prevent editing.

In the next steps, you'll separate the graphics you've created so far onto individual layers for more control.

1 To start, you'll make sure that each set of graphics you want to assign to a layer is grouped or converted to a Drawing Object. This will make them easier to move and distribute.

Verify that your word balloon (leave the text separate) is a Drawing Object by selecting it and viewing its info in the Property Inspector. If not, use Modify > Combine Objects > Union to convert it to a Drawing Object.

2 Double-click to select your fish and the gills, then hold down the Shift key and select the eye. Convert them to a single Drawing Object by choosing Modify > Combine Objects > Union.

3 Shift+click to select the fish, the bubble, and the word balloon. Make sure to not select the text. Right-click (Windows) or Ctrl+click (Mac OS) on any of the selected items—a contextual menu appears.

Use Distribute to Layers to separate multiple objects at once to their own layers on the Timeline.

4 At the bottom of the menu, locate and select Distribute To Layers. All the items on your Stage are placed onto several new layers, which appear on the Timeline panel at the bottom.

The layers are named generically (Layer 2, Layer 3, and so on). To fix this, you'll identify which graphics belong to which layers and rename them appropriately.

5 Choose Edit > Deselect All. First, click on the fish on the Stage to select it, and look at the Timeline panel below. The layer that becomes selected is the one to which it belongs. Double-click directly on the layer's name to edit it, and type in the name **Fish**.

6 Repeat step 4 for the bubble and word balloon, naming them **Bubble** and **Word Balloon**, respectively. For Layer 1, rename this layer **Text** since all the text was left on this layer.

Double-click a layer's name to edit it. Rename your layers clearly so you know exactly what's on each one.

7 Choose File > Save to save your file.

Arranging, locking, and hiding layers

Once you've arranged your artwork on individual layers, you can easily control which layers are visible (or invisible) and editable, and easily rearrange the order and appearance of items in your movie.

1 Locate the layer titled Bubble, which contains the bubble you created earlier. Click to select it.

2 Click and drag upwards on the layer—you see a black beam follow your cursor within the layers. This indicates where the layer will be moved when you release the mouse.

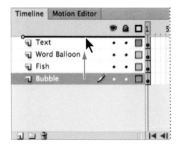

When dragging layers, follow the black beam to determine where your layer will be placed.

3 Drag the layer all the way up and release it at the top of the layer stack to move the bubble to the top.

4 Locate the two column headers above your layers—one appears with an visibility icon (👁) and one appears with a padlock icon (🔒), which means that it is locked. Under the padlock column, click on the Text, Word Balloon, and Bubble layers to lock those layers (a padlock icon should appear on the layer). Leave the Fish layer unlocked.

5 Click the Text layer below the visibility column—a red X appears and the text disappears. Toggle the layer's visibility back on again by clicking the red X.

Click under the padlock or visibility icon to lock, hide, and show specific layers.

To lock all layers except for the one you're targeting, hold down the Alt key (Windows) or Option key (Mac OS) and click on the target layer below the padlock column. All layers except for the one you clicked will lock. This also works for visibility!

Creating layer folders

As you accumulate more layers on the Timeline, it makes sense to try and group them logically so that you can easily view, lock, and hide related layers with a few clicks. You can create layer folders on the Timeline that can group several related layers together, making it easy to collapse, hide, and lock them as needed.

1 Click to select the Text layer, which should currently be the second layer on the Timeline.

2 Locate the New Folder button (📁) below the layer stack, and click it once to create a new folder above the current layer.

3 Double-click the Folder title, and type **Word Balloon and Text** as the new name.

4   Click and drag the Text layer up below the folder and to the right and release it—it should now appear indented below the folder, indicating it is now inside the new folder. (Follow the bar—it should appear indented below the layer folder before you release the mouse button.)

Move layers into your new layer folder.

5   Repeat step 4 with the Word Balloon layer to add it to the new layer folder. If necessary, rearrange the two layers within the folder so that the text appears above the Word Balloon.

6   Collapse the layer folder and hide its included layers by clicking the arrow that appears to the left of the folder name. The Word Balloon and Text layers temporarily disappear from view on the Timeline.

Collapse or expand a layer (and its contents) by using the arrow shown to the left of its title.

7   Choose File > Save to save your file.

You can now lock or hide all layers under that folder at once by clicking the layer folder under the Padlock and Visibility columns, respectively. To access individual layers again, simply expand the layer folder.

Layer folders can be created several levels deep, allowing you a lot of organizational control when you need it. To create a nested layer folder, select any layer inside of a layer folder and click the New Folder button below the Timeline.

Transforming graphics

Once you've created artwork on the Stage, Flash gives you a lot of options for scaling, rotating, skewing, and tweaking graphics and colors. Transforming existing graphics is as much a part of illustration as building them, so in the next steps you'll explore the various tools and panels at your disposal.

The Transform menu and Free Transform tool

The Modify menu at the top of your screen features a Transform menu, which provides shortcuts to many common transformation tasks as well as helpful dialog boxes. You'll use this menu in the next exercise to tweak the size and rotation of your fish.

1   Choose the Selection tool (➤), and click once on the fish to select it (make sure its layer is unlocked).

2   Choose Modify > Transform > Scale and Rotate. This opens the Scale and Rotate dialog box, where you can enter values for Scale (in percentage) and Rotation (in degrees).

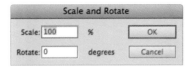

Choose Modify > Transform > Scale and Rotate
to open the Scale and Rotate dialog box.

3   Type **75** for the Scale value, and **25** for the rotation value; then press OK to exit the dialog box.

4   Your fish now appears smaller and rotated slightly upward. Use the Selection tool to move your fish to the center of the Stage, closer to the word bubble.

To fine-tune, you'll use the Free Transform tool, which offers a more tactile (but less precise) way of scaling and rotating your artwork.

Rotate the fish.

5   Leave the fish selected, and choose the Free Transform tool (⊕) from the Tools panel. The fish now appears inside a black bounding box with eight handles.

6   Move your mouse pointer over the top-right handle of the bounding box until you see a double-arrow icon appear. While holding down the Shift key, click and drag the corner handle down and to the left to resize your fish slightly smaller. If the text box makes it difficult to select the fish, you may move the text to another location on the Stage.

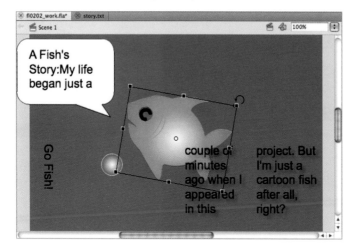

With the Free Transform tool, you can use corner handles to rotate or resize your artwork.

7   Move your cursor just above the same handle until you see the rotating arrow icon (↷). Once this icon appears, click and drag in a clockwise or counter-clockwise motion to adjust the rotation of your graphics to your liking.

8 Choose File > Save to save your file.

Getting the (transformation) point

What is that mysterious white dot that appears in the middle of your artwork when you use the Free Transform tool? That's your transformation point, which determines the point on a graphic from which scaling and rotation is set.

If you'd like to rotate a graphic around a different point than the center, for instance, you can move the transformation point to a different location within your graphic.

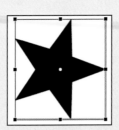  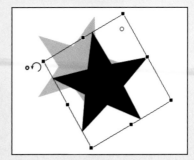

To do this, select your graphic with the Free Transform tool, locate the point, and click and drag it to a different part of your graphic.

The Transform panel

An alternative to the Free Transform tool and Transform menus is the Transform panel, which offers many of the same features plus some additional options for skewing and transforming graphics in the 3D plane.

1 Choose Edit > Deselect All. If necessary, unlock the Bubble layer for editing. Use the Selection tool (⬚) to select the bubble graphic.

2 Select Edit > Copy and then Edit > Paste in Center to make a copy of the bubble. Repeat this to make a third bubble. Use the arrow keys on your keyboard or the Selection tool to arrange the three bubbles vertically to the left of your fish's mouth.

3 Select the bottommost bubble. Choose Window > Transform to open the Transform panel. Locate the horizontal and vertical scale values at the top. Click the *Constrain* button (⬤) directly to the right, which will keep the horizontal and vertical values locked together.

4   Click and drag left over the horizontal value until the overall scale of the bubble is
reduced to around 50 percent.

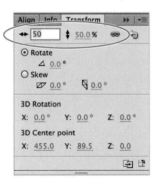

*Use the Transform panel to precisely scale
an object.*

5   Select the next bubble above the last, and repeat the same technique from step 4 to
reduce this bubble to 75 percent. This time, however, click and select the *Skew* radio
button. Click and drag the horizontal (left) skew value until it reads –20 degrees. This
adds a slight leftward tilt to the bubble.

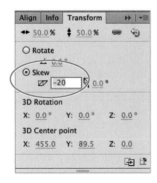

*Add skewing to an object by selecting
it and using the Skew values on the
Transform panel.*

6   Select the top bubble, and click to select the Skew radio button. Click and drag the
horizontal (left) skew value until it reads 15 degrees. Close the Transform panel.

*To remove all the transformation values from an object, select it and click the Remove Transform
button (⬛) at the bottom of the Transform panel.*

Transforming gradients

If you use gradients to fill or stroke graphics in your movie, you can precisely position, scale, and modify them using the Gradient Transform tool. Because your fish and bubbles both use gradient fills, you'll finalize your artwork with a little gradient tweaking.

1   From the Tools panel, click and hold down your pointer on the Free Transform tool (⬚) to select the Gradient Transform tool (⬚), then click on the body of your fish to select it.

2   A circular bounding box appears around your fish. Move your cursor over the center point of the bounding box until a four-way arrow appears. You can click and drag this point to shift the center point of the gradient. Click and drag the point up and to the left—this helps to imply a light source coming from the upper left.

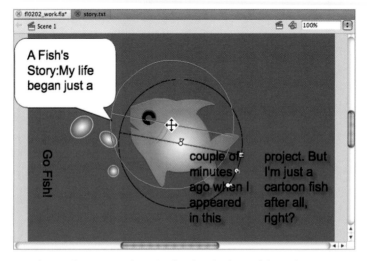

Move the point shown in a Gradient Transform bounding box to shift a gradient's center point.

3 Locate the scale handle in the lower-right corner of the bounding box. Click and drag it inward to scale the gradient down inside the fish. This increases the presence of the darkest color that makes up your fill.

Scale down a gradient using the handle shown. This also changes the perceived balance of colors.

4 Choose File > Save to save your file.

For linear gradients, the rotate handle allows you to change the direction of the gradient. This also works for radial gradients if the center point is offset from the middle.

Self study

Using the technique shown in the last exercise, shift the gradient points for your three bubbles to match the fish.

Review

Questions

1 Name two primary differences between Mergeable Shapes and Drawing Objects.

2 Which tool would you choose to manipulate individual points that make up a shape or path?

3 What three advantages does isolating artwork on a layer offer?

Answers

1 Drawing Objects can be arranged, whereas mergeable shapes cannot. Mergeable shapes can be partially selected, whereas Drawing Objects cannot.

2 The Subselection tool.

3 The ability to control stacking order, turn visibility on or off, and lock contents for editing.

Lesson 3

What you'll learn in this lesson:

- Working with the Library panel
- Adding symbols to the library
- Creating and managing artwork using symbols
- Editing and swapping symbols for easy updates
- Organizing the library

Using Symbols and the Library

Within each Flash Professional CS6 document, you'll find a powerful tool designed to help you effectively build and design your movies: the library. The library stores and manages symbols—reusable graphics, buttons, and animations—as well as imported photos, sounds, and video. In this lesson, you'll explore the advantages of using symbols and the library.

Starting up

Before starting, make sure that your tools and panels are consistent by resetting your workspace. See "Resetting the Flash workspace" in the Starting up section of this book.

You will work with several files from the fl03lessons folder in this lesson. Make sure that you have loaded the fllessons folder onto your hard drive from the supplied DVD. See "Loading lesson files" in the Starting up section of this book.

See Lesson 3 in action!

Use the accompanying video to gain a better understanding of how to use some of the features shown in this lesson. You can find the video tutorial for this lesson on the included DVD.

The project

You'll be learning how to create symbols from existing artwork and reuse those symbols throughout your movie to build a web banner for a department store's winter sale. After you build a layout for this season, you'll be able to easily modify it for other seasonal campaigns using the symbol's powerful swap and editing capabilities. Each exercise will introduce you to a new concept as you creatively evolve your ad campaign.

What are symbols?

As you create graphics on the Stage, you'll realize that you may want to reuse those graphics several times throughout your movie. Although you could copy and paste the artwork as many times as necessary, keeping track of each copy would be difficult because there's no way of letting Flash know they are related. Modifications, such as an overall color or shape change, would need to be applied to each copy individually, taking up creative time and opening the door to inconsistencies in your movie.

A better choice is to use symbols: reusable graphics, images, and animations stored in your document's library. You can create symbols from any graphics or imported images on the Stage, or from animations on the Timeline. A symbol is the original from which all copies are made; each copy of a symbol (called an *instance*) remains linked to the master symbol in the library. Changes made to the original symbol in your library affect all instances of that symbol throughout your movie.

As described in detail in the sidebar, "Symbol-ism: the symbol types," Flash uses three types of symbols:

- Graphic
- Button
- Movie clip

This lesson focuses on graphic symbols only: you'll be converting existing graphics to symbols as well as creating new symbols from the ground up. Lesson 10, "Creating Navigation Controls," explores buttons, while Lesson 12, "Introducing Movie Clips," covers the creation and use of movie clips—powerful symbols that can contain entire animations.

Symbol-ism: The symbol types

Each symbol type has different attributes and a unique purpose within your movie. Everything from basic graphics to full-blown animations can be stored as symbols in the library, making it easy to manage and build even the most complex movies. Each symbol is represented in the library and in the Property Inspector by a unique icon, so you can easily identify which symbol belongs to which category. Here's a closer look at what makes each symbol unique:

Graphic (🖼): Graphic symbols are the most basic of the three types and can contain graphics, type, imported artwork, or bitmaps. Use graphic symbols to store your artwork in the library or to get graphics ready for animation. Graphic symbols can contain other graphics, so you can make more elaborate symbols by converting groups of graphic symbols into a single, new graphic symbol.

Button (🖱): These symbols are designed for use as controls, and they contain multiple states that react to a user's mouse interaction, including clicks and rollovers. You'll learn how to create and work with buttons in Lesson 10, "Creating Navigation Controls."

Movie clip (🎬): Movie clips can best be described as super-symbols. They can contain anything from other symbols to full animations, even sounds and video. In addition, movie clip symbols have their own independent timelines, so they are capable of housing elaborate animations that can be treated as movies themselves. You'll learn to create and work with movie clips in Lesson 12, "Introducing Movie Clips."

A look at the Library panel

Each Flash document contains its own Library, where you can find images, sounds and video files that are being used in your movie. The library's contents are displayed and managed in the Library panel. This powerful organizational tool lets you view, sort, edit, and return information on symbols. Located on the right side of the screen behind the Property Inspector in the default workspace, the Library panel is the store-all management system for symbols and imported assets. For a detailed list of the panel's features, see the sidebar, "Library panel options."

Library panel options

As you've seen, the Library panel houses some additional features, and if you take a closer look at the Library panel, you'll see features that help you organize, sort, and view your symbols and assets.

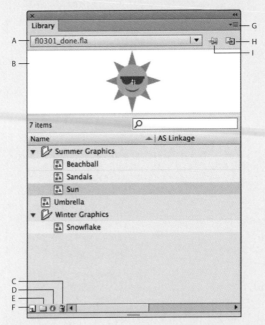

A. Library selector. *B.* Preview window. *C.* Delete. *D.* Properties. *E.* New Folder.
F. New Symbol. *G.* Panel menu. *H.* New Library panel. *I.* Pin current library.

Library selector: Allows you to navigate through the libraries of all currently open documents.

Preview window: Displays your symbol so you can see what it looks like. This is helpful if you have symbols with vague or similar names.

Delete: Deletes the currently selected symbol from the library. Choose Select Unused Items from the panel menu to highlight items that are not currently used by your movie or another symbol in the library.

Properties: Opens up the Symbol Properties dialog box for the currently highlighted symbol. From this dialog box, you can switch the symbol's type or assign it a new name.

New Folder: Creates a folder in the Library panel into which symbols can be sorted. Folders can go several levels deep, making fine-tuned organization possible.

New Symbol: Creates a new symbol in the library and is the same command as Insert > New Symbol or New Symbol from the Library panel's menu.

(continues)

Panel menu: This menu features additional options for working with symbols or modifying the display of the Library panel. This contains advanced options for linking symbols to ActionScript or setting up shared libraries.

New Library Panel: Opens a duplicate Library panel. Use this if you want to display libraries from multiple open documents at once, or to create several different views of the library you're working on.

Pin Current Library: Keeps the current library in view, even when switching between other open documents. The default behavior is for the Library panel to display the library for the currently active document only. This is useful if you'd like to copy symbols between movies and need to keep a previous library view available while you switch documents.

The Library panel opens up further possibilities by letting you export symbols for direct interaction with ActionScript, or share library items across multiple .fla documents. To open the Library panel, choose Window > Library or use the keyboard shortcut Ctrl+L (Windows) or Command+L (Mac OS).

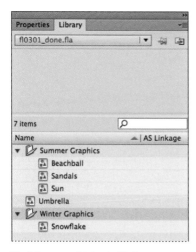

The Library panel is invaluable for managing symbols and imported assets.

Creating symbols

The first step toward taking advantage of symbols is to add some to the library. You can create symbols from existing artwork on the Stage, or you can create blank symbols with the option to add content afterwards.

Converting a graphic to a symbol

Open the fl0301.fla file located in the fl03lessons folder, and select File > Save As. The Save As dialog box appears. In the Save As text field, type **fl0301_work.fla** and press Save As.

On the Stage, you'll find all the artwork you need to construct an ad banner for the fictional department store Spacey's. This document was created using the 500 × 500 (Popup) sample template found in the New Document dialog box under Templates > Advertising, which you learned about in Lesson 1, "Flash CS6 Jumpstart."

The lesson file contains all the basic artwork you need to get your ad banner started.

In this exercise, you'll convert the six drawings on the Stage to symbols so you can store them in the library and reuse them several times throughout your movie.

1   Using the Selection tool (⮏), click and drag on the Stage and draw a selection area around the entire snowflake to select it.

2 Choose Modify > Convert to Symbol, or use the keyboard shortcut F8, to open the Convert to Symbol dialog box.

Choose Modify > Convert to Symbol to save any artwork on the Stage as a symbol in your library.

3 Assign the name **Snowflake** to the new symbol by typing it in the Name text field. You can name symbols just about anything you want, but try to keep names short and intuitive so you can easily figure out what's what when viewing the Library panel.

4 Choose Graphic from the Type drop-down menu.

5 Set the registration point for the new symbol by clicking the box in the center of the small grid shown on the right. Registration points serve as the *handles* by which you rotate and position symbols on the Stage. Registration point locations will vary, based on the shape of the artwork you're creating; here, a centered point works best.

6 By default, the Folder is listed as Library root. This means that your symbol will be in the main Library, not in any folders; you can leave this for now. Once you create folders, you'll be able to sort new symbols directly into a folder as you create them.

The Convert to Symbol dialog box.

6 Press OK. The new symbol appears in the Library panel, and the snowflake image remains exactly where you left it on the Stage. Click on the Properties tab to bring the Property Inspector forward. Click on the snowflake to select it. A special Graphic icon (▣) in the top-left corner of the Property Inspector will confirm that the artwork is now an instance of the newly created Snowflake symbol. After it is converted to a graphic symbol, the snowflake should have a registration point in its center and a blue bounding box surrounding it.

The basic snowflake artwork.   *The artwork as a symbol.*

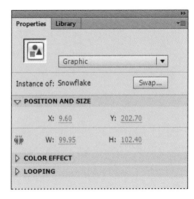

The Graphic icon and label verify that you have converted your symbol properly.

7 Repeat steps 1 to 6 for the Snowman, Beachball, Umbrella, and Sun designs on the Stage, using the corresponding names respectively. Leave the sandals design unconverted for now. When you're done, look at the Library panel and you'll see that the artwork pieces have been added to your library as graphic symbols.

8   Choose File > Save to save your work, and keep the document open.

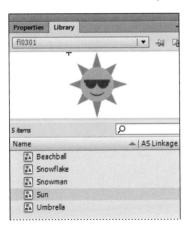

The new symbols in the library.

Don't confuse symbols with Drawing Objects. Although both appear inside bounding boxes, only symbols are stored in the library and have all the advantages discussed in this lesson. If you're unsure, select the artwork and use the Property Inspector to verify that what you're looking at is truly a symbol instance, and not a Drawing Object.

What's the point of registration points?

A symbol's registration point determines the measurement point by which the symbol is positioned on the Stage.

You specify a registration point when you first convert an object to a symbol, and you should choose a point subjectively based on the shape of the object. It is common to set a centered registration point for objects that are round or symmetrical (such as the beachball), or a top-left registration point for text or symbols that have no real point of symmetry (such as the snowman). When you edit your symbol, you can change the registration point by moving the artwork around relative to the crosshair that appears on the Stage in the symbol's Edit mode.

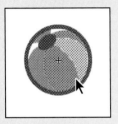 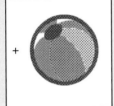

Change the registration point.

Creating blank symbols

You can create symbols of any type even when existing artwork isn't available. To do this, you can form an empty symbol, and add content later by drawing, pasting, or importing artwork into the new symbol. Here's how:

1 Select the entire drawing of the sandals on the Stage using the Selection tool (⭢).

You can also draw a selection area around the sandals using the Lasso tool (⌇) to make sure you get all the pieces.

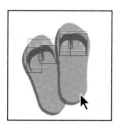

Use the Selection tool to select the sandals drawing.

2 Choose Edit > Cut to cut the artwork from the Stage and place it on the clipboard.

3 Choose Insert > New Symbol to open the Create New Symbol dialog box, which looks identical to the Convert to Symbol dialog box you used in the last exercise.

Type **Sandals** in the Name text field to name the new symbol.

4 Choose Graphic from the Type drop-down menu. Press OK to create the new symbol.

The Create New Symbol dialog box.

5 The new Sandals symbol appears in the Library panel, and you are presented with a blank Stage. You are now in Edit mode for the new symbol, where you can draw, paste, or import content for your symbol.

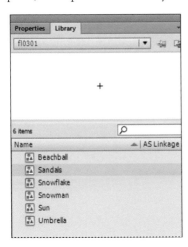

The Library now features your new Sandals symbol.

6 Select Edit > Paste in Center to paste the sandals artwork from the clipboard onto the symbol's Stage. This artwork is now included in your symbol, confirmed by the updated preview in the Library panel.

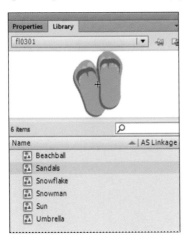

Paste the sandals onto the Stage in Edit mode.

7 Exit Edit mode by clicking the Scene 1 link above the Stage.

Select Scene 1 above the Stage to exit the symbol's Edit mode.

8 Choose File > Save to save your work.

You'll notice that the Create New Symbol dialog box didn't give you the option to specify a registration point. This is done when you paste, draw, or import artwork and position it relative to the crosshair in the symbol's Edit mode.

Whether you create blank symbols or convert existing artwork to symbols is completely up to you. Some designers prefer to have something tangible to work with before they create a symbol; others like to get symbols defined ahead of time.

Building artwork with symbol instances

With all the artwork added to the library as graphic symbols, you're ready to start building the layout for the banner advertisement. You'll find that working with symbols will be essential as the theme for your banner evolves. You'll soon discover how to easily place, swap, and update symbol instances to build and change the look and feel of your banner in a snap.

Positioning and snapping in symbol instances

To get the Spacey's ad banner started, you'll create a patterned background using some of your new symbols. The lesson is already sized and has visual guides to help you. To more accurately position symbols on the Stage, you'll use snapping. Snapping enables a magnet-like behavior, causing objects you move around the Stage to *snap* in place to guides, grids, or other objects when they are moved within a close-enough range of those objects.

1 Choose View > Snapping to open the Snapping submenu, and make sure the Snap to Grid and Snap to Guides options are checked.

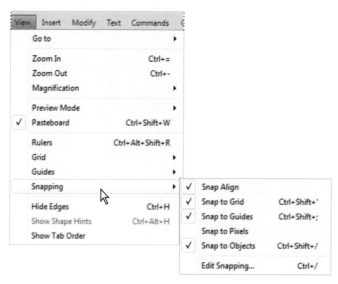

Set up your Snap options under View > Snapping.

2   Choose View > Grid > Show Grid to display the grid; in this document, it's set with the gridlines 50 pixels apart. You can store unique grid settings with each document.

3   Choose View > Guides > Show Guides. Vertical and horizontal guides appear, each one centered within the gridlines. These will help center and position symbols inside each box formed by the grid.

The visible grid and guides will help you align artwork on the Stage.

4   Choose Edit > Select All, and press Backspace (Windows) or Delete (Mac OS) to delete any existing symbols from the Stage. Now you have a clean start for the layout.

5   With the Library panel open, locate and drag an instance of the Snowflake symbol from the library onto the Stage.

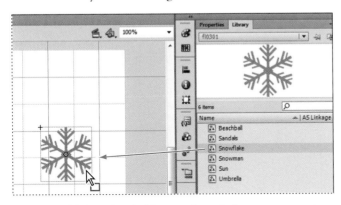

To place a symbol, drag it from the Library panel onto the Stage.

6   Using the snapping action behavior to help you, position the Snowflake symbol in the upper-left box.

7   To finish the background pattern, drag 12 more snowflake instances onto the Stage. Place one in every other box, checkerboard style, with the second row starting on the second box.

8 Choose File > Save to save your work.

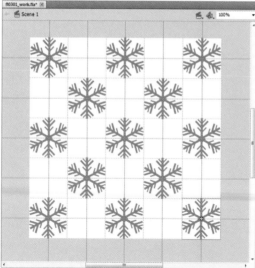

The completed background for your ad banner.

Editing and duplicating symbols

The beauty of working with symbols is that modifications to the master symbol automatically transfer to all instances throughout your movie. If you're not quite happy with the snowflake, for example, adjust it once and the entire background changes because all symbol instances are linked. You can update symbols in two places: from the master symbol in the Library panel or from any instance of that symbol on the Stage. In this exercise you'll explore both methods.

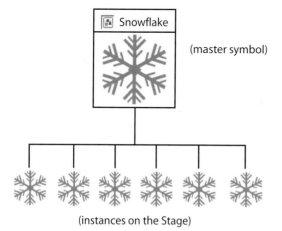

A master symbol controls all its instances throughout a movie.

To edit a symbol directly from the Library panel:

1   Double-click the Snowflake symbol in the Library panel to enter the symbol's Edit mode.

Double-click a symbol in the Library panel to edit it.

It now appears on the Stage in basic form, as it was before you added it to the library.

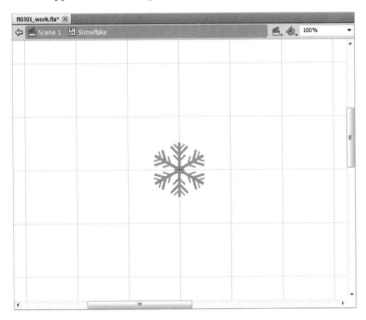

Inside the Snowflake symbol's Edit mode.

2 Select the snowflake with the Selection tool (▶), if it is not already selected. From the Fill color swatch in the Tools panel, select the light blue color labeled #CCCCFF.

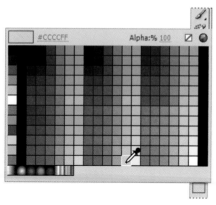

Select a new color for your symbol.

3 Exit the symbol's Edit mode by clicking the Scene 1 link above the Stage. Flash returns you to the main Stage. All 13 instances of the Snowflake symbol on the Stage now reflect the color change that you applied.

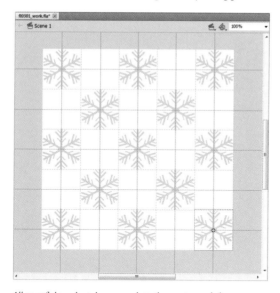

All snowflakes adopt changes made to the master symbol.

Editing symbols in place

The advantage to editing symbols directly from the Library panel is that you can focus on the symbol itself without the interference of other artwork on the Stage. Sometimes, however, you need to modify a symbol to better fit with the artwork surrounding it. In these cases, you can edit the symbol in-place on the Stage to see it in context as you make changes.

1   Double-click one of the snowflake instances on the Stage. The other instances *dim out* because they are no longer selectable. The snowflake you chose, however, is editable as basic artwork, just as it was in the previous exercise.

2   Click on the Properties tab to bring the Property Inspector forward. In the Property Inspector, type **80** in both the width (W) and height (H) text fields to set the width and height of the snowflake to 80 pixels. Notice that changes also affect the dimmed instances that are visible in the background and that changing the size of the symbol affects its alignment relative to your grid. To compensate for this, use the Property Inspector to set the X and Y positions of the graphic to **–40** each; this shifts the symbol instances enough to keep them each in their respective grid boxes.

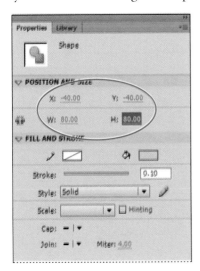

Reposition the Snowflake symbol to compensate for its size change.

3   Exit the symbol's Edit mode by clicking the Scene 1 link above the Stage. Back on the main Stage, you can see the changes you applied in context, exactly as you saw them when you were editing.

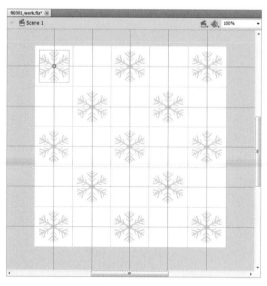

Edit in Place allows you to see a symbol in the context of other items onstage.

4   Choose File > Save to save your work.

Modifying individual symbol instances

What if you don't want a whole new look, but you just need to make a minor tweak to a single symbol instance? The link between the master symbol and its instances may seem constraining at times. The good news is that it doesn't have to be: Every instance of a symbol can be modified to take on its own color, dimensions, rotation, and transparency.

To resize or rotate a symbol instance, for example, select the instance on the Stage and use the Free Transform tool, Property Inspector, or Transform panel.

1   Using the Selection tool (⬀), select a single instance of your Snowflake symbol on the Stage, and choose Window > Transform to open the Transform panel, which allows you to enter exact values and resize and rotate a single instance of the Snowflake symbol.

2   In the Transform panel, make sure the *Constrain* option is active, and type **80%** in either the vertical or horizontal scaling boxes at the top of the pane. Press Enter (Windows) or Return (Mac OS).

Resize and rotate a single instance of the Snowflake symbol.

3   Type **45** in the Rotate text field to rotate your snowflake, and then press Enter (Windows) or Return (Mac OS) to apply the transformations. This, combined with the scaling in step 2, creates a nice variation from the other instances on the Stage.

Set the rotation in degrees for the Snowflake symbol.

Modifying instance color

To modify the color of a symbol instance, you will use the Color drop-down menu in the Property Inspector, which lets you create interesting variations by applying color tints, brightness, and transparency. Try it on one of the ad banner's Snowflake symbols:

1 Select the instance of the snowflake on the upper-left corner of the Stage. Make sure the Property Inspector is visible.

2 Open the Color Effect section of the Property Inspector by clicking on the triangle to the left of its label. From the Style drop-down menu, choose Tint. This produces several options, including a color swatch and tint amount (percentage).

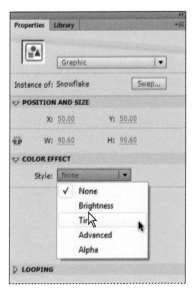

You can apply a unique color tint to any instance of a symbol using the Property Inspector.

3   From the color swatch, choose a blue (to match the example, use #0066CC). Set the tint amount to 100 percent by using the slider or typing **100** in the tint percentage text field. The symbol instance is now a darker blue, leaving the other instances and the master symbol unaffected. As you see, you can achieve some creative variations among your snowflake instances without modifying the original symbol in the library.

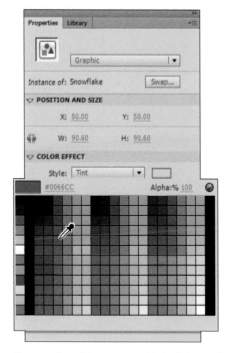

Choose a color and tint percentage with the Color menu's Tint option.

In the next exercise, you'll modify the background of your banner by changing the color and transparency of different symbol instances to create variety and texture.

Fine-tuning your background

You can take advantage of the unique characteristics that can be assigned to each symbol instance to add depth to your background. To make the snowflakes less obstructive to the type and additional artwork you'll add later, you can reduce the transparency (referred to as *alpha*) of all instances on the Stage. You can also use the Property Inspector to apply varying color tints to selected instances.

1 Choose Edit > Select All to select all instances of the Snowflake symbol on the Stage.

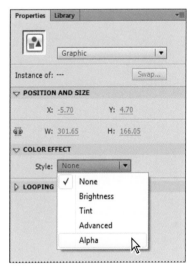

To select everything on the Stage, choose Edit > Select All.

2 In the Color Effect section of the Property Inspector, select Alpha from the Style drop-down menu. The Alpha percentage and slider should appear, enabling you to set the transparency (in percent) of your symbols.

The Alpha option is found in the Style drop-down menu in the Property Inspector.

3 Using the Alpha slider, change the transparency of the selected symbols to 40 percent. Or, if you prefer, type **40** in the text field next to the slider. Notice that the symbols immediately become more transparent on the Stage.

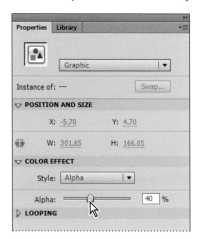 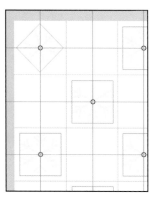

Set the Alpha amount to 40 percent to decrease the opacity of the symbol instances.

4 Choose Edit > Deselect All. Select only the snowflake instance in the lower-left corner. Adjust the Alpha setting in the Property Inspector to 90 percent to darken this instance of the snowflake, setting it apart from the others.

 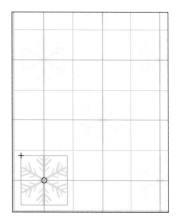

Set the opacity amount to 90 percent to darken the instance and make it stand out.

Duplicating symbols

Sometimes a variation on a theme is the best way to explore other possible design ideas. Perhaps you want to apply changes to a symbol beyond color or size (for instance, changing its actual shape). Rather than make edits that compromise the original symbol, consider making a duplicate of the symbol in the Library panel. Duplicating makes an exact copy of a symbol, and the new copy becomes its own symbol and is not associated with the original. Try creating a variation on the Snowflake symbol by duplicating it in the Library panel and making changes to the new copy.

1   Click on the Library tab to bring the Library panel forward. Select the Snowflake symbol in the Library panel.

2   Choose Duplicate from the Library panel menu. The Duplicate Symbol dialog box appears, prompting you to rename the symbol and, if desired, change the symbol type.

Duplicate the symbol through the Library panel menu.

3   Name the symbol **Snowflake 2**. Leave the Type as Graphic, and press OK. Flash adds the new symbol to the library. You can now use this symbol like any other, and it has no relationship to the original from which it was created.

Set the name for the snowflake copy in the Duplicate Symbol dialog box.

4   Double-click the new symbol in the Library panel to edit it. Add a different color, or use the Ink Bottle tool (🖋) to apply an interesting outline (stroke) to it. Click on Scene 1 to exit the Edit mode for this symbol and return to the main Stage. Notice that the modifications made to Snowflake 2 don't affect instances of the original Snowflake symbol on the Stage.

Make some changes to distinguish
Snowflake 2 from the original.

5   Choose File > Save to save your work.

A duplicated symbol has no relationship to the symbol from which it was created. Modifications made to the duplicate will have no effect on the original or any of its instances. They are regarded as completely different symbols.

Adding graphics and text to your banner

With your background complete, you're ready to add the headline text and feature graphics to advertise your sale. For your feature graphic, you'll use the snowman drawing you added to the library earlier in this lesson. For the type, you'll use the Text tool and skills you learned in Lesson 2, "Getting Started with the Drawing Tools."

1   If it is not already selected, choose the Selection tool (k) from the Tools panel.

2   Drag a copy of the Snowman symbol from the Library panel onto the right side of the Stage.

3   Toggle to the Property Inspector by pressing Ctrl+F3 (Windows) or Command+F3 (Mac OS). If it's not already selected, click the *Lock width and height values together* button (⇔) next to the W field to keep any adjustments to either the width or height proportional.

4   Type **350** in the H (height) field to resize the snowman. Type **350** for the X position, and **300** for Y position.

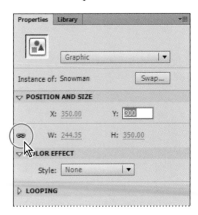

Use the Property Inspector to reposition and resize the snowman.

5   Select the Text tool (T) on the Tools panel. Text-related options such as Font and Font size (in points) appear in the Property Inspector. Choose Times New Roman (or equivalent) for the font, and type **40** in the Font size text field (or use the slider). For now, set your type color to black using the Text (fill) color swatch.

Use the Text tool and the Property Inspector to specify type options before creating the text on the Stage.

6 Click on the left side of the Stage, and type the words **SPACEY'S winter sale**, as shown below.

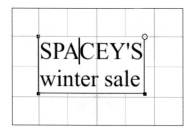

Type the words, SPACEY'S winter sale, on the Stage.

7 Use the Text tool to select only the words *winter sale* inside the text area.

8 In the Property Inspector, set the color of the selected text to blue. To match the example, use the color labeled #003399. Choose Italic from the Style drop-down menu to change the style of the selected text to italics.

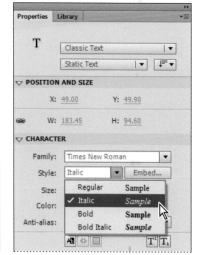

Use the Property Inspector to fine-tune the color and style of the selected text.

Your banner should be complete for the winter sale; choose View > Guides > Show Guides to toggle the guides off, and View > Grid > Show Grid to hide your grid. Creating and using symbols in this lesson allowed you to place and modify as many instances as you needed to complete your layout. In the next exercise, you'll discover how symbols can streamline your creative process even further.

Your completed banner, constructed using symbol instances.

Swapping symbols

Sometimes when you think you're finished, you're not—requirements change, new products are introduced, or those bright ideas you had in a late-night design session look dim the next morning. Symbols make such revisions easier; instead of starting from scratch, use the Property Inspector to swap any instance of a symbol with an instance of another symbol in the Library panel.

Consider your Spacey's winter sale banner, for example. If Spacey's wants a summer sale banner based on your successful winter design, you can easily reinvent your banner with a few quick symbol swaps.

1   Switch to your Selection tool, and click once on the instance of the Snowflake symbol in the upper-left corner to select it. Make sure the Property Inspector is visible.

2 Click the Swap button in the Property Inspector. The Swap Symbol dialog box appears, displaying all the symbols currently in the library. The Swap button lets you swap any symbol instance on the Stage with another symbol from the library.

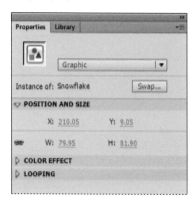

Swap any symbol instance on the Stage with another symbol from the library.

3 Select the Beachball symbol from the list and press OK, or double-click the Beachball symbol. A beachball replaces the snowflake in the upper-left corner. Swapped symbols inherit position as well as transformations.

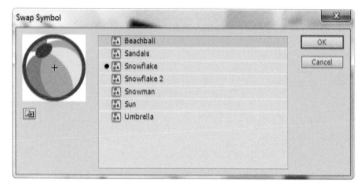

Select a different symbol from the library with which you can replace the current instance.

4 Repeat steps 1 to 3 for all remaining instances of the Snowflake symbol that appear in your background. If you'd like to change it up, try swapping some instances with the Sun or Umbrella symbols instead. Replacing each snowflake instance with other symbols in the library changes the whole theme. The best part is that positioning and other unique properties applied to the snowflake instances (such as Alpha) are maintained, even when a new symbol takes their place.

Swap out all the snowflake instances.

5 Select the Snowman symbol on the Stage. This is currently your feature graphic, which you need to replace with something that matches the new theme.

6 Click the Swap button to open the Swap Symbol dialog box, and double-click the Sandals symbol in the list that appears. An instance of the Sandals symbol replaces the snowman. There is no need to resize the sandals, because the new symbol instance inherits size properties from the previous one.

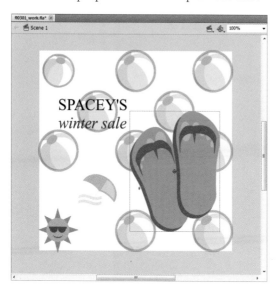

Away goes winter as you replace the Snowman symbol with the Sandals symbol using the Swap button.

7 Select the Text tool (T) from the Tools panel, and select the words *winter* inside the text frame to edit them.

8 Replace the word *winter* by typing **summer**, then select the words *summer sale*. Using the Property Inspector set the type color to orange (#FF9900).

9 Press the Escape key to commit the text changes. Choose File > Save to save your work.

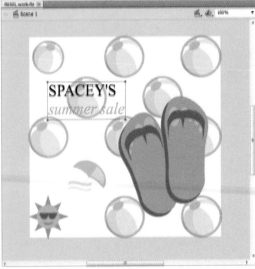

Your new summer sale banner.

Swapping symbols is not only great for use for a single instance, but also can be taken further to change the feel of an entire movie or layout.

Managing the Library

As you use symbols more and more, you may find the Library panel getting a bit crowded. Even with the panel's sorting abilities, you'll definitely need to get a handle on things with a bit of organization. The Library panel features several ways to clean house and make sense of your assets.

Organizing symbols with folders

Whether for papers in a file cabinet or files on your computer's hard drive, folders play an essential role in categorizing and organizing content. Flash's Library panel can use folders to organize symbols, sounds, and imported assets such as bitmap images and video.

You can create folders using the New Folder button (⬛) or by choosing New Folder from the Library panel's menu. For very flexible organizational possibilities, you can also nest folders inside other folders. Practice organizing your banner project's symbols.

1 Open the Library panel by selecting Window > Library, or pressing Ctrl+L (Windows) or Command+L (Mac OS).

2   Click the New Folder button in the lower-left corner to create a new folder in the Library panel. In the highlighted text field next to the new folder icon, type the phrase **Winter Graphics** to replace the default name, Untitled Folder 1. Press Enter (Windows) or Return (Mac OS).

Add a new folder for sorting symbols.

3   Click and drag the Snowflake symbol into the new Winter Graphics folder. Flash sorts it into the folder, and it appears indented under the new folder. Collapsed view hides the sorted symbols within their folders.

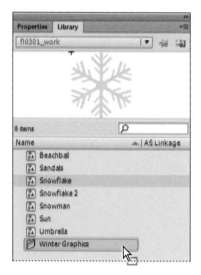 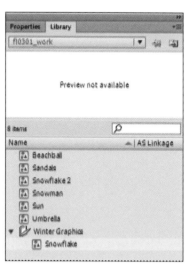

Drag symbols to sort them into folders. The Winter Graphics folder (shown expanded) now contains a symbol.

4   Repeat step 3 to add the Snowman symbol to the Winter Graphics folder.

The Move To command

A convenient alternative to these steps is the Move To command under the Library panel menu. Move To allows you to create new folders or move graphics to existing folders in one step. Sort the summer-themed graphics into a new folder to try it out.

1 Hold down the Ctrl key (Windows) or Command key (Mac OS), and select the Beachball, Sandals, and Sun symbols together.

2 Choose Move To from the Library panel's menu.

Move To creates, names, and sorts selected items in the Library panel into a new or existing folder.

3 In the Move To dialog box, select the New folder radio button. Type the name **Summer Graphics** in the text field, then press Select. The selected symbols now appear inside a new folder.

Name the new folder Summer Graphics.

4 Click the arrow to the left of the folder or use the Library panel menu's Expand Folder option to show or hide the sorted symbols in the new folder.

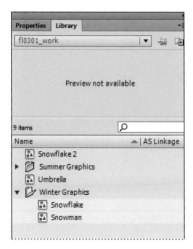

The Summer Graphics folder, shown collapsed.

5 Choose File > Save to save your work.

You can sort symbols into folders as you create them. The Folder option in the Create New Symbol and Convert to Symbol dialog boxes produces the Move to Folder dialog box, which you can use to sort the new symbol into an existing folder, and even create new folders on-the-fly.

Deleting items from the library

Over the life of a project, many symbols and assets may accumulate in the Library panel, some of which may not even be in use. If sorting your symbols is not enough to tackle this problem, you may want to select and trash unused items to eliminate clutter and reduce the size of your .fla file. Deleting unused symbols from the library is simple.

Keep in mind that a large amount of extraneous symbols and assets in your Library does not affect your final published movie size, only the size of your FLA file.

1 Open the Library panel, and choose Select Unused Items from its panel menu. Use this feature before you delete anything to avoid accidentally trashing items that are in use in your movie..

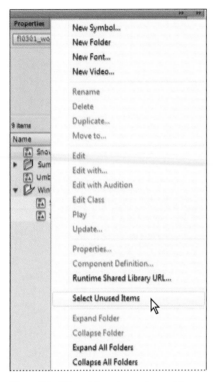

Choose Select Unused Items to reveal unused items in the library.

2 You should see the Snowflake, Snowflake 2, and Snowman symbols highlighted in the Library panel. Some of these symbols were never used; others, such as the Snowman, were retired when you changed the theme of your banner.

3 Delete the selected symbols by clicking the Delete button (🗑) at the bottom of the Library panel.

4 Choose File > Save to save your work.

Symbols that include other symbols create dependencies; one symbol can't be deleted without affecting the other. If a graphic symbol is composed of other graphic symbols, it requires those symbols to remain in one piece, like bricks that make up a wall. Always use the Delete Unused Items option to be sure; it accounts for symbols that are in use by other symbols.

Controlling library views

The Library panel's menu features some additional options you can use to adjust the appearance of contents in the library. If you combine this with the panel's sorting capabilities, managing and organizing the library will be easy, even with the most extensive Flash movies.

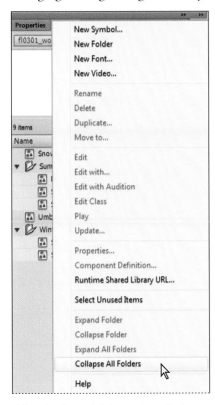

Collapsed and expanded views can be easily shown and hidden using the panel menu.

To expand all folders and view their contents, for example, choose Expand All Folders from the Library panel menu. To expand a single folder, select the folder and choose Expand Folder from the panel menu, or double-click the folder.

To collapse all folders and hide their contents, choose Collapse All Folders from the Library panel menu. To collapse a single folder, select the folder and choose Collapse Folder from the panel menu, or double-click the folder.

Choose File > Close to close the document.

Wrapping up

In this lesson, you've learned about the power of symbols, and how you can reuse, swap, and easily update artwork used throughout your design. As you'll see in later lessons, symbols also play an essential role in creating animation and adding interactivity in the form of buttons and movie clips.

Self study

Create new artwork in a fresh Flash file, and convert it to one or more graphic symbols. Use the new symbols to create a layout, and use the swap technique to substitute one symbol for another. Experiment with a variety of color and transformation modifications with each instance.

Review

Questions

1 What are the three symbol types that Flash supports?

2 True or False: You cannot modify the color or size of a symbol instance without changing all other instances of that same symbol.

3 What behavior allows objects on the Stage to magnetically move toward each other or toward visual aids in the work area?

Answers

1 Graphics, buttons, and movie clips.

2 False. Each instance of a symbol on the Stage can have unique transformation, scaling, or color effects applied.

3 Snapping. This behavior can be fine-tuned, enabled, or disabled by choosing View > Snapping.

What you'll learn in this lesson:

- Working with gradients
- Creating artwork with the new Deco and Spray Brush tools
- Masking artwork on the Stage
- Exploring the new IK tools

Advanced Tools

In Lesson 2, "Getting Started with the Drawing Tools," you explored the Flash drawing tools and combined shapes, paths, and colors to create rich graphics on the Stage. In this lesson, you'll learn some classic advanced techniques for drawing in Flash, and explore some of Flash CS6's advanced drawing tools.

Starting up

Before starting, make sure that your tools and panels are consistent by resetting your workspace. See "Resetting the Flash workspace" in the Starting up section of this book.

You will work with several files from the fl04lessons folder in this lesson. Make sure that you have loaded the fllessons folder onto your hard drive from the supplied DVD. See "Loading lesson files" in the Starting up section of this book.

See Lesson 4 in action!

Use the accompanying video to gain a better understanding of how to use some of the features shown in this lesson. You can find the video tutorial for this lesson on the included DVD.

The project

In this lesson, you'll be creating an ad for West Portland Homemade Textiles (WPHT). Their mascot, Stevie the Silkworm, showcases a multitude of WPHT's favorite patterns. Each segment in Stevie's body will feature a different pattern, which you will create using a combination of drawing tools. To see the finished file, navigate to the fl04lessons folder and open fl0401_done.fla. Keep this file open for reference or choose File > Close to close the file.

Stevie the Silkworm is a handsome beast!

Working with gradients

The first part of the silkworm that you will work on is his head. If you opened and viewed the finished file, you may have noticed the 3D appearance of this insect's visage. While this object is not truly 3D in the technical sense, a little fancy footwork with gradients can go a long way toward adding depth to your graphics.

1   Choose File > Open. Navigate to the fl04lessons folder and select fl0401.fla. Press Open.

2   On the Stage is the West Portland Homemade Textiles logo and not much else. Choose File > Save As. In the Save As dialog box, navigate to the fl04lessons folder and type **fl0401_work.fla** into the Save As text field. Press Save.

3 Add a new layer for your caterpillar to separate him from the logo layer by clicking the New Layer button (🖪) at the bottom of the layers section of the Timeline. Double-click the name of the new layer and type **Stevie** into the text field that appears. Press Enter (Windows) or Return (Mac OS) to commit the change.

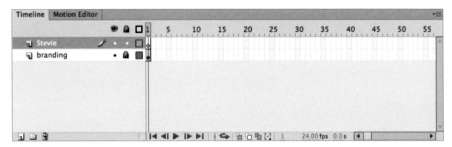

Create a new layer for Stevie.

4 Select the Oval tool (○) from the Tools panel. Make sure Object Drawing mode is enabled at the bottom of the Tools panel (the Object Drawing icon (◎) should be pressed in). Hold down the Rectangle tool (▢) to access the hidden Oval tool. At the bottom of the Tools panel, click on the Stroke color swatch to open the Swatches panel. Select None (◺) from the top-right corner of the Swatches panel.

5 Click on the Fill color swatch to open the Swatches panel and select the black and white radial gradient in the bottom-left corner. You'll adjust this gradient after you draw the oval.

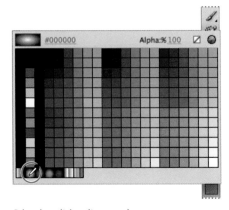

Select the radial gradient swatch.

6   While holding down the Shift key to constrain proportions, click and drag to draw a circle below the logo. If you need to move it, or draw it again, use the Selection tool (**k**) to select it and then click and drag to move it, or press Delete on your keyboard to remove it.

Draw a circle below the WPHT logo.

7   Choose the Selection tool from the Tools panel and select the circle. Choose Window > Color to open the Color panel. This panel can be used to choose colors, save them as swatches, and modify gradients. In this case, you'll be doing the latter.

8   Make certain that the fill is selected, then click on the gradient stop on the right side of the gradient slider. In the text field above the gradient slider, type **E3E33E** to set the black to yellow. Notice that the sliders above this field change to reflect its hue and brightness. You can use these sliders to create custom colors for your own gradients.

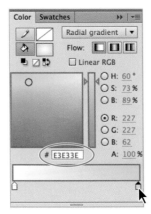

Set the black stopper to #E3E33E.

9   Close the Color panel and choose File > Save.

Adjusting gradients with the Gradient Transform tool

Gradients are pretty hip, but you'll probably want to customize more than just color. The Gradient Transform tool can help you exert some more control over the size, dimensions, and location of your gradient fills.

1   Hidden under the Free Transform tool (⬚) in the Tools panel is the Gradient Transform tool (▣). Choose the Gradient Transform tool, and click on the yellow circle on the Stage. Click and drag the center point down and to the right to offset the gradient.

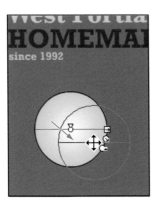

Drag the gradient off-center.

2 Click and drag the middle handle on the edge of the circle outwards to expand the size of the gradient.

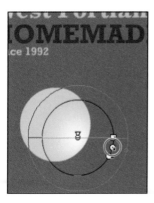

Use the handle in the middle to expand the size of the gradient.

Using the Gradient Transform tool to fine-tune gradients a bit can mean the difference between a convincing effect and a clumsy, amateurish effect. Keep it close at hand; it will serve you well.

3 For the finishing touches, drag out two instances of the eye graphic from the Library panel and use the Selection tool (➤) to position them on the circle.

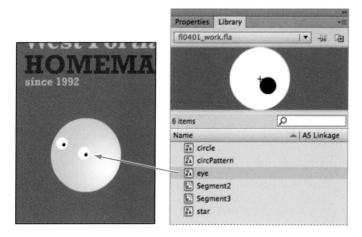

Stevie's got a new pair of eyes.

4 Now that the caterpillar has a respectable countenance, save it as a symbol. Use the Selection tool to click and drag a marquee around the circle and two eyes, and then choose Modify > Convert to Symbol. In the Convert to Symbol dialog box, choose Movie Clip from the Type drop-down menu, and set the registration point to the center. Type **head** in the Name text field and press OK.

5 Choose File > Save to save your work, and leave the file open for the next part of this lesson.

Flash CS6 tools for advanced drawing

Flash CS6 includes a number of tools that allow you to easily create effects that would otherwise be labor-intensive to create from scratch. In the next section, you'll use a few of these tools to create sections of the caterpillar's body. Perhaps more than any other features in Flash, these tools lend themselves especially well to experimentation. After you get a feel for the techniques in this section, you might find yourself staying up way past bedtime making strange compositions to astound your friends and family. It's highly recommended that you obey your impulses to do so.

Spraying symbols

For the first section of Stevie's body, you'll use the Spray Brush tool to create a field of stars, and then you'll mask out a circular section of this field.

1   Choose Insert > New Symbol. Much like the head, each segment of the body will be a Movie Clip symbol. In the Create New Symbol dialog box, choose Movie Clip from the Type drop-down menu and type **Segment1** in the Name text field. Press OK.

2   All the items on the Stage disappear as you enter symbol-editing mode. Select the Spray Brush tool (🖌), located beneath the Brush tool (✎) in the Tools panel. Click on the Properties tab to display the Property Inspector.

3   In the Property Inspector, press the Edit button in the Symbol section. In the resulting Select Symbol dialog box, choose the star graphic symbol and press OK.

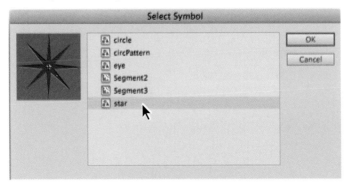

Select star from the Select Symbol dialog box.

4   In the Property Inspector, set the Scale width and Scale height to 50 percent. Make sure all three checkboxes at the bottom of the Symbol section are checked for Random scaling, Rotate symbol, and Random rotation. If you desire a more uniform effect, these checkboxes should be left unchecked, but in this case you're looking for maximum variety.

5   In the Brush section, type **200** in the Width and Height fields. Leave the Brush angle at its default setting.

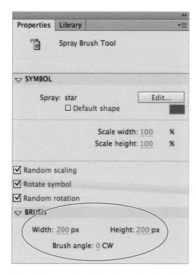

Adjust the properties of the Spray Brush tool.

6   Click and release in the center of the Stage. Each click sprays a number of symbols in a radius dictated by the brush width and height that you set in the last step. Clicking and dragging allows you to paint symbols onto the Stage.

7   Use the Spray Brush tool to create a field of stars. If you add too many stars, use the Selection tool to delete your work and try it again. In fact, try it a few times, even if you like the results of your first attempt. It's fun and easy, just like real spray paint, without the potential for legal trouble.

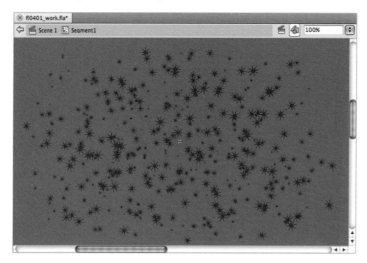

Spraying symbols.

Masking

Most graphics programs support some form of masking. In Flash CS6, the implementation is fairly simple, but it can be a powerful tool, especially combined with animation. Next you'll mask out the field of stars to finish the first segment of caterpillar Stevie's body.

1   Because you'll be working with more than one layer, and their arrangement will be crucial to success, you'll need to stay organized. Rename the default Layer 1, which now contains the field of stars you created in the last section, by double-clicking on the layer name and typing **stars** into the text field; then press Enter (Windows) or Return (Mac OS) to commit the change.

2   Press the New Layer button twice, then rename the two layers, **mask** and **background**, respectively. Drag the background layer below the stars layer in the Timeline.

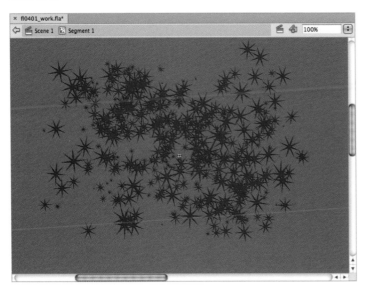

Add, rename, and rearrange layers.

3   Select the mask layer and choose the Oval tool (○) from the Tools panel. At the bottom of the Tools panel, choose none for the stroke, and set the fill to the blue labeled #6699CC.

4   Holding down the Shift key to constrain proportions, draw a circle over a section of the field of stars (use the crosshair as your guide as you paint). Any stars outside of this circle will soon be invisible, so if you've grown fond of them, adjust your circle accordingly.

5   Choose the Selection tool (▶) and click on the circle. Choose Edit > Copy. You will use this copy to populate the background layer in a couple steps.

6   Right-click (Windows) or Ctrl+click (Mac OS) on the mask layer in the Timeline and choose Mask from the context menu. Voila! Masking in Flash is just that easy.

Mask the stars you created with
the Spray Brush tool.

7   Select the background layer and choose Edit > Paste in Place. If the circle disappears, click on the Stage to deselect the newly pasted shape. This particular technique is often used in conjunction with masking to give an object a background color if the masked content contains transparent areas.

Paste the circle onto the background layer
to give Segment1 a background color.

8   Return to the main Stage by clicking on the Scene 1 link in the Navigation bar above the Stage. From the Library panel, drag an instance of the Segment1 symbol onto the Stage. Don't worry if it isn't the same size as Stevie's head; you'll adjust that in the next step.

9   Click and hold the Gradient Transform tool (⬚) in the Tools panel and select the Free Transform tool (⬚). Click on the Segment1 symbol on the Stage. Holding down Shift to constrain proportions, click and drag any of the corner points of the symbol's bounding box toward the center or away from the center to make Segment1 about the same size as the head. Click and drag Segment1 into place, attached to the head.

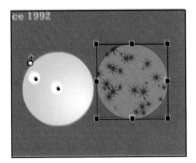

Use the Free Transform tool to get Segment1 sized-up and into place.

10   Choose File > Save and keep this file open for the next part of the lesson.

Introducing the Deco tool

The Spray Brush is a great way to throw symbols all over the Stage, but what if you want to distribute a number of symbols in a slightly more structured manner? Flash's Deco tool provides a number of customizable options for just this task.

1   Click and hold the Oval tool (○) in the Tools panel and select the Rectangle tool (□). Draw a large rectangle on the Stage. The dimensions are not too important, as you'll be using the mask technique from the last section to create this segment. This rectangle is just to contain the results of using the Deco tool.

Draw a rectangle on the Stage to contain the next pattern.

2 Choose the Deco tool (✎) from the Tools panel, then click the Properties tab to access the Property Inspector.

3 In the Drawing Effect section of the Property Inspector, choose Grid Fill. For Tile 1 press the Edit button and choose circPattern from the Select Symbol dialog box. Uncheck Tile 2, Tile 3 and Tile 4—you won't need these because we are using just one symbol for the pattern.

4 In the Horizontal and Vertical spacing text fields, type **2**. In the Pattern scale text field, type **60**.

5 Click inside the rectangle you created in step 1. A grid pattern is created inside this rectangle. The Grid Fill effect of the Deco tool is a handy way to whip up a grid of symbols; just be careful to fill only within a shape unless you really want to coat the entire Stage.

Fill the rectangle using the Deco tool. Note that fill results will vary from shape to shape.

6 Using the Selection tool (↖), click on the rectangle and press Delete to remove it. Click on the grid of circPattern symbols, and choose Edit > Cut. The rest of the segments have pre-created Movie Clips to streamline the process of finishing the project.

7 Double-click on the Segment2 Movie Clip icon in the Library panel to enter symbol-editing mode.

8 Select the content layer and choose Edit > Paste in Center.

9 Choose Window > Transform to open the Transform panel. This panel is the counterpart to the Free Transform tool (▦). It's a bit more precise, as you can plug in specific values, but the Free Transform tool is often more convenient for quick transformations.

10 Type **25** in the Rotate text field to rotate the field of circles. Close the Transform panel.

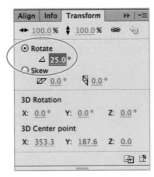 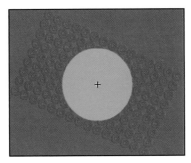

Use the Transform panel to rotate the grid.

11 Right-click (Windows) or Ctrl+click (Mac OS) on the mask layer and choose Mask from the context menu.

12 Click on the Scene 1 button in the Navigation bar to return to the Stage. Drag an instance of the Segment2 movie clip to the Stage, then reposition and transform your new segment with the Free Transform tool, if necessary.

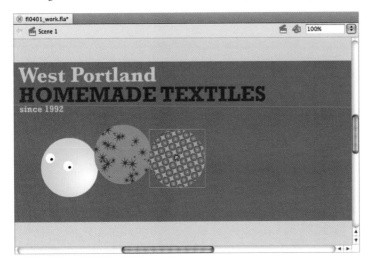

Move Segment2 into place as the caterpillar's body.

13 Choose File > Save. Leave this file open for the next part of this lesson.

Advanced Deco tool techniques

Now that you're starting to get the hang of the new Deco tool, you'll take it to the next level, making the caterpillar's third body segment. In this exercise, you'll see how to make complex geometric patterns by piggybacking Deco tool features.

1   Once again, you'll be using a Movie Clip with mask and background layers already created to streamline the process. Double-click the Segment3 movie clip in the Library to enter symbol-editing mode.

2   Select the content layer. The other layers are locked and invisible to keep them out of the way until you need them.

3   Select the Deco tool (⚘) and click on the Properties tab to access the Property Inspector. From the drop-down menu in the Drawing Effect section, choose Symmetry Brush.

4   Press the Edit button and select the circle graphic symbol from the Select Symbol dialog box. Press OK.

5   In the Property Inspector, make sure Rotate Around is chosen from the Advanced Options drop-down menu.

6   Click and drag outwards from the center of the Stage until eight circles appear as shown below. Be careful to not click at the intersection of the green lines. The Rotate Around option allows you to easily draw a circle of symbols.

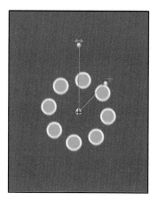

Drag to create a circular arrangement of eight circles.

7 Choose the Selection tool (↖) from the Tools panel. Click on the shape you created in the last step. You'll be using this shape to draw a more complex shape with the Deco tool, and so you'll need to convert it to a symbol. Choose Modify > Convert to Symbol. In the Convert to Symbol dialog box, choose Graphic from the Type drop-down menu, and type **halo** in the Name text field. Press OK.

When you draw with the Deco tool, you are creating groups. If you want to modify or swap parts of these groups, you can always choose Modify > Break Apart to break the group down to individual symbols.

8 Press Delete to remove the newly minted symbol from the Stage.

9 Select the Deco tool from the Tools panel. The Drawing Effect drop-down menu should still be set to Symmetry Brush. Click on the Edit button and select the halo symbol from the Select Symbol dialog box. Click OK.

10 In the Advanced Options section, choose Grid Translation from the drop-down menu. When the graph lines appear on the Stage, drag them by the intersection point to the center of the Stage.

11 Click and drag from this intersection point until four instances of the halo symbol appear. The Art Deco tool is very sensitive so place your cursor lightly on the green graph lines, small movements will create very different effects. We found putting the cursor on the horizontal axis of the green graph lines worked well.

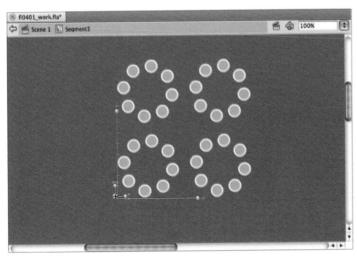

Drag four halos out onto the grid.

12 Change the Stage view to 50% by choosing 50% from the drop-down menu in the top-right corner of the work area.

13 Place your cursor on the circle on the far right of the horizontal graph line. Click and drag to the right to extend the graph line, as you do this, you create additional columns of the symbol, drag until there are four columns of circles. Now click and drag the circle at the top of the vertical graph line and drag upwards, this creates additional rows. Using these techniques you should make a 4-row by 4-column pattern. Now locate the small circle at the intersection of the graph, it has a small curved arrow. Drag this straight up to adjust the angle of the patterns.

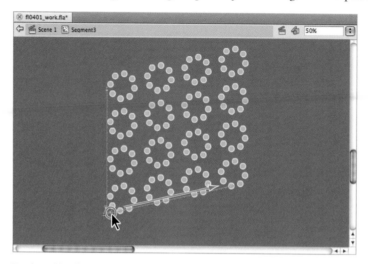

Use the grid handles to increase the size of the grid and skew the layout.

14 Choose the Free Transform tool (⊞) from the Tools panel. Drag to reposition the new grid in the center of the Stage, and then hold down Shift to constrain proportions and use the corners to resize the grid to about half of its original size.

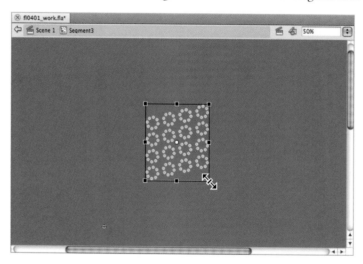

Use the Free Transform tool to reposition and resize the grid.

15 Make sure the halo graphic is centered on the Stage. If necessary, choose the Selection tool (↖) from the Tools panel and reposition it to the center of the Stage. Change the work area view back to 100%, then right-click (Windows) or Ctrl+click (Mac OS) on the mask layer and choose Mask from the context menu. Click on the red X's in the eyeball column of the mask and background layers to make them visible again and see the finished segment.

16 Return to the main Stage by clicking Scene 1, located above the Stage. Drag an instance of the Segment3 symbol out of the Library and move it into place to complete the caterpillar's body.

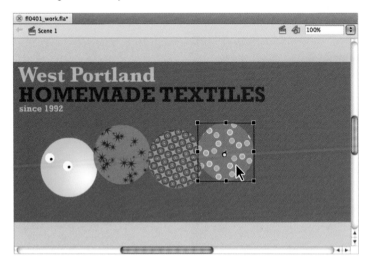

Stevie the Silkworm with three segments.

The Deco Tool's new options

The Deco Tool has a number of creative and fun modes that include anything from drawing flames and flowers to landscapes decorated with random buildings. They are way too much fun to explain, so check them out by selecting the Deco tool and selecting a mode from the Property Inspector.

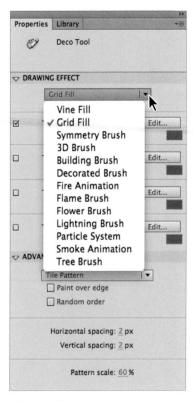

The Deco tool options.

Introduction to IK tools

Inverse Kinematics (IK) is used by 3D and character animators to help achieve more realistic motion, especially with jointed figures. Flash CS6 includes the Bone tool to add a skeletal structure to a group of symbols. In Lesson 6, "Advanced Animation," you'll explore animating with this feature; for now, you'll get your feet wet by making the caterpillar poseable.

1   Choose the Bone tool (⁄) from the Tools panel.

2 Click and drag from the center of Stevie's head to the center of Segment1. When you release the mouse, a bone is added, connecting Stevie's head to the first section of his body. As you may know from personal experience, bones can be a great way to keep your body from falling apart.

Use the Bone tool to connect Stevie's segments.

3 Still using the Bone tool, click and drag from the end of the last bone, to the center of Segment2. Do the same from Segment2 to Segment3.

4 Choose the Selection tool (⬉) from the Tools panel. Click and drag the segments of Stevie's body. They are now joined together to allow easy posing for character animation.

Stevie in all his glory.

5 Choose File > Save, then File > Close.

Congratulations! You have completed this lesson.

Self study

Create more segments for Stevie using the techniques from this lesson. Start by creating a small symbol to use with the Deco or Spray Brush tools, and then experiment by combining tools to create complex patterns. Mask the results within a new Movie Clip symbol to create a portable segment that can be added to Stevie's body.

Remember, you can use the Free Transform tool on Stevie to make room for more segments.

Review

Questions

1 What panel allows you to adjust the color of gradients?

2 What panel is the more precise counterpart to the Free Transform tool?

3 Can custom symbols be used with the Spray Brush and Deco tools?

Answers

1 The Color panel. Open it by choosing Window > Color. Adjust the stoppers in the gradient slider to customize your gradient.

2 The Transform panel. Open it by choosing Window > Transform. Because transformations made with the Free Transform tool can be adjusted from this panel, it's often a convenient way to refine transformation settings.

3 Yes. Simply create a symbol, choose the desired tool, and use the Edit button in the Property Inspector to select your custom symbol.

Lesson 5

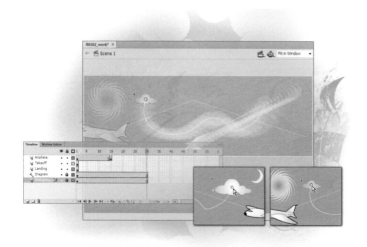

What you'll learn in this lesson:

- Using the Timeline
- Understanding the difference between frames and keyframes
- Setting up frame-by-frame animation
- Taking advantage of motion and shape tweens
- Using motion guides
- Testing your movie

Creating Basic Animation

Adobe Flash is widely regarded as one of the tools of choice for animation and motion graphics for the Web. With its ability to manipulate graphics in a variety of ways, the possibilities are endless when it comes to creating exciting, eye-catching animations for your projects. Now, with the ability to export HTML-based animation, there's no limit to where your creativity can be seen.

Starting up

Before starting, make sure that your tools and panels are consistent by resetting your workspace. See "Resetting the Flash workspace" in the Starting up section of the book.

You will work with several files from the fl05lessons folder in this lesson. Make sure that you have loaded the fl05lessons folder onto your hard drive from the supplied DVD. See "Loading lesson files" in the Starting up section of the book.

See Lesson 5 in action!

Use the accompanying video to gain a better understanding of how to use some of the features shown in this lesson. You can find the video tutorial for this lesson on the included DVD.

The project

To see a completed example of the animated web banner you'll be creating, launch Flash, open the fl0501_done.fla file, and choose Control > Test Movie > in Flash Professional to preview the final banner. Close the Flash Player and return to Flash Professional CS6 when you're done.

Introducing keyframes and the Timeline

One of the most important panels in the Flash workspace is the Timeline, which is where graphics, text, and media are sequenced and animation is created. The Timeline allows you to have items appear, disappear, or change appearance and position at different points in time.

The Timeline consists of three main components: layers, frames, and keyframes.

Layers

Layers enable you to stack and organize your graphics, media, and animations separately from one another, thereby giving you greater control over your project elements. If you've used other design applications such as Adobe Photoshop or Illustrator, it's likely that you've worked with layers before.

Flash also utilizes special types of layers for tasks such as tweening (animation), masking, and Inverse Kinematics, which you'll explore in this lesson and the next.

Frames and keyframes

On the Flash Timeline, time is represented by frames, which are displayed as small boxes across each layer of the Timeline. Time is subdivided into frames based on your frame rate. In a document set to the default frame rate of 24 fps (frames per second), every 24 frames on your Timeline represent one second of playback in your movie.

The playhead, shown as a vertical red beam, passes each frame when a movie plays back, much like movie film passing in front of a projector bulb.

When you decide you want to place a graphic, play a sound, or start an animation at a specific point along the Timeline, you must first create a keyframe. Keyframes are created to mark significant points along the Timeline where content can be placed. A keyframe can extend across the Timeline as long as you need it to keep its contents in view. By default, each new layer on the Timeline contains a single keyframe at frame 1.

The best way to understand the Timeline is to dive right in and work with it. In this next exercise, you'll sequence some items across the Timeline and work with layers to get started.

1   Choose File > Open, and locate and select the lesson file named fl0501.fla located in the fl05lessons folder. Choose Open to open the file.

    Examine the Stage, and you see an airplane graphic along with two pieces of text that read *Takeoff* and *Landing*. In addition to the background layer and diagram layer (which you'll use as a visual aid later on), each of these items sits on its own named layer.

    Note the frame ruler at the top of the Timeline, which marks frame numbers in 5-frame increments.

2   Choose File > Save As. In the Save As dialog box, navigate to the fl05lessons folder and type **fl0501_work.fla** in the Save As text field. Press Save.

3   Let's get a feel for sequencing items across the Timeline. Click directly on the Timeline on the Airplane layer at frame 15 to select that frame (it should appear highlighted in blue).

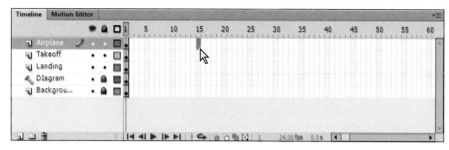

Select a frame directly on the layer to insert a keyframe at that position.

4   Right-click (Windows) or Ctrl+click (Mac OS) and choose Insert Keyframe to insert a new keyframe at this frame. The new keyframe appears with a border and bullet.

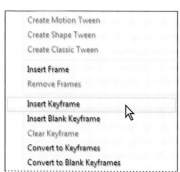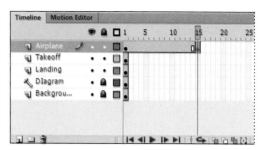

Insert a new keyframe.

Notice that the airplane on the previous keyframe (frame 1) has been duplicated on the new keyframe—you can now reposition this airplane on the Stage. However, you first need to extend the Background and Diagram layers so you can use them for reference.

5   Select frame 30 on the Background layer, then right-click (Windows) or Ctrl+click (Mac OS) and choose Insert Frame from the contextual menu that appears. This extends the Background layer up until frame 30.

Repeat step 5 for the Diagram layer so that it also extends up until frame 30.

Here, you added frames on the Diagram and Background layer to extend them up until frame 30.

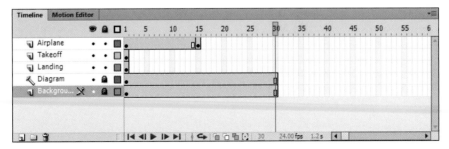

Add frames after a keyframe to extend it further along the Timeline.

6   Click on the Airplane layer and select keyframe 15. Using the Selection tool (⬧), grab the airplane that appears selected on the Stage, and drag it to the top-middle of the Stage. Use the Diagram layer as a reference.

7   Select frame 30 on the Airplane layer. Right-click (Windows) or Ctrl+click (Mac OS) on the selected frame, and select Insert Keyframe to add a keyframe at this position. Once again, the airplane from the previous keyframe is duplicated on this new keyframe.

8   Click on the Airplane layer and select keyframe 30. Using the Selection tool, grab the airplane that appears selected on the Stage, and drag it to the left edge of the Stage just above the ground. Again, use the dotted line and airplane images on the Diagram layer as a reference.

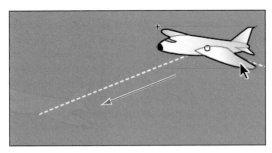

Move the airplane along the Stage.

9   Click on frame 1 of any Layer to bring your playhead back to the beginning of the movie. Press Enter (Windows) or Return (Mac OS) to play back your Timeline so far.

10 On the Landing layer, the text sits in the correct position but appears far too early in the movie. It shouldn't appear until frame 30, where the plane actually *lands*. Rather than create a new keyframe, you simply move the existing one by dragging it to a new location along the Timeline.

Click on the keyframe at frame 1 of the Landing layer to select it. Move your pointer over the frame again until a small white box appears below your cursor. Click, hold down your mouse button, drag the keyframe right, and release it at frame 30.

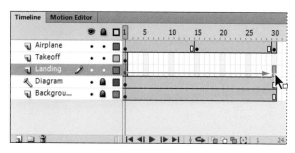

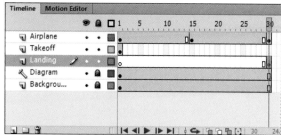

You can click and drag a selected keyframe to reposition on the Timeline.

11 The finishing touch is to ensure that the Takeoff text hangs out on the Timeline just a bit longer. You'll use the same technique you used to extend the Background and Diagram layers.

Click and select frame 15 on the Takeoff layer. Right-click (Windows) or Ctrl+click (Mac OS) on the selected frame, and choose Insert Frame to add a frame and extend the first keyframe up to frame 15.

12 Press Enter (Windows) or Return (Mac OS) to play your Timeline back. The airplane should appear in three different positions, and the text should appear and disappear at different points.

13 Choose File > Save to save your movie, then choose File > Close to close the file.

The final Timeline as it should appear in your file.

Keyframes can also be created using the F6 shortcut key or by choosing Insert > Timeline > Keyframe.

Building animation: Enter the tween

Flash's strength lies in its ability to create automatically generated animations, or *tweens*, making it easy and intuitive to get things moving on your Stage. You simply need to let Flash know where an object needs to start and where it needs to end, and Flash draws the frames in-between, saving you the painstaking work of creating dozens of frames by hand and moving or manipulating the artwork in small steps.

There are two types of tweens you can create on the Timeline: motion tweens and shape tweens. In the following steps, you'll focus on getting objects moving with motion tweens and tween layers.

Tween layers and automatic keyframing

The animation engine in Flash is designed to make creating animation easy and intuitive for new and existing Flash users. The heart of animation in Flash is the *tween span,* a single sequence of frames that can include any number of movements and tweens on a single object.

Within a single tween span, you only need to move or modify an object at a certain point in time, and Flash automatically creates keyframes to mark those movements where they occur on the Timeline. A layer that contains one or more tween spans is called a *tween layer.*

New Term: Motion Tween

A motion tween is an automatic animation performed on a symbol instance that can incorporate changes in position, scale, size, color effects, and filters. To create a motion tween, you right-click (Windows) or Ctrl+click (Mac OS) a keyframe that contains a single symbol instance and choose Create Motion Tween from the contextual menu that appears.

It's time to dive right in and get things moving on your Stage:

1   Choose File > Open and select the fl0502.fla file from this chapter's lesson folder.

You'll notice some familiar graphics from the last exercise—except this time you'll get things moving with some fluid animation.

2   Choose File > Save As. In the Save As dialog box, navigate to the fl05lessons folder and type **fl0502_work.fla** in the Save As text field. Press Save.

3   Let's begin with the Airplane layer—you'll want to move the airplane as you did in the previous exercise, but have it animate its movement from place to place. Right-click (Windows) or Ctrl+click (Mac OS) on the first frame of this layer and choose Create Motion Tween. A 24-frame tween span is created on this layer.

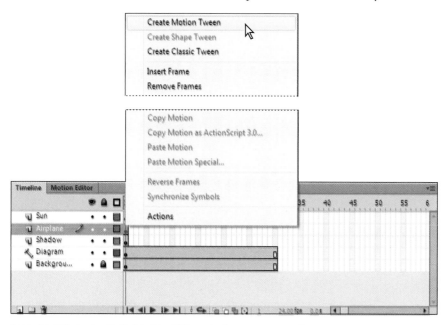

Right-click (Windows) or Ctrl+click (Mac OS) on a keyframe to create a motion tween.

4   To create animation, you simply need to move the playhead to a position on the Timeline and change the appearance or position of the graphic at that point in time. In this case, the goal is to get the airplane to the middle position at frame 15. To do this, click and drag the playhead to the frame 15 marker. Using the Selection tool (⟨), click and drag the airplane graphic to the middle position (using the diagram layer as a reference). Notice that a black dot marks an automatically created keyframe at this position.

5 You'll see a line appear on the Stage that outlines the motion of the airplane—this is referred to as a Motion Path. Click to select frame 1 on the Timeline ruler to return your playhead to the beginning of the movie, and press Enter (Windows) or Return (Mac OS) to play back your Timeline—you should see your airplane glide from one place to another!

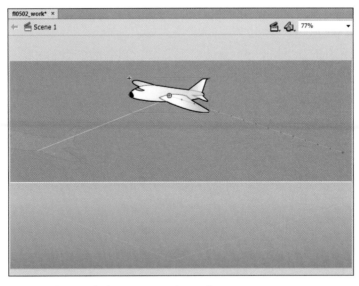

A motion path is created when you move an object within a tween span.

6 The next step is to get your airplane from the middle position to its final position on the left. To create an even number of frames for each movement, you're going to need to extend the tween span a bit. Move your mouse pointer over the last frame of the tween span (directly over the layer itself) until you see a double-arrow icon (↔). Click and drag to the right to stretch the span until it ends at frame 30.

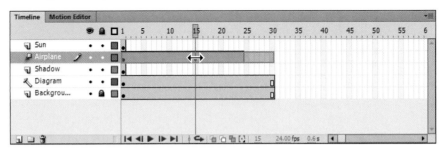

Extend or trim a tween span by clicking and dragging the last frame of the tween span.

You may notice that keyframe 15 moved slightly when you adjusted the length of the tween span. Keyframes shift as you readjust the length of a tween span; this is okay to leave as is.

7 On the frame ruler at the top, click on frame 30 to jump the playhead to this position. Select the airplane, being careful not to click on the small circle in the center and drag it to the left side of the Stage to the landing position (using the diagram layer as a reference). Another keyframe is created at this position in the tween span to mark the change.

8 Press Enter (Windows) or Return (Mac OS) to play back the Timeline, and you see your airplane glide from place to place.

9 Choose File > Save. Leave the file open.

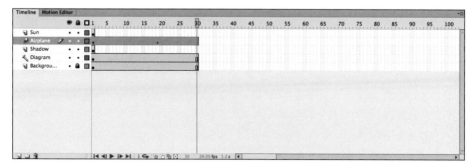

The finished Timeline.

The Tween rules

It most certainly does, but in this case, it refers to some rules that apply when creating motion tweens and tween spans on the Timeline.

- The length of any new tween span, by default, matches the frame rate of your movie. A movie at the default 24 fps frame rate will create 24-frame tween spans, and a movie at 30 fps will create 30-frame tween spans.

- To be included in a tween span, a graphic, text, or imported bitmap image must be converted to a symbol first. If you attempt to create a motion tween on a non-symbol, Flash will prompt you to convert the item to a symbol on the spot.

- Only one symbol or graphic can be tweened at a time. If you attempt to apply a motion tween to a layer with several objects, Flash will prompt you to convert the graphics to a single symbol.

- Tween spans can include changes to position, size/scale, color effects, and filters (for movie clips and buttons). To morph the shape of an object, you'll use shape tweens (discussed later in this lesson).

Tweening multiple objects

To tween multiple graphics simultaneously, you simply need to place each one on its own individual layer. Each animated item will always need to have a dedicated tween span and tween layer. In this exercise you'll add layers to animate the shadow and text elements to complete the scene.

1 Select the first keyframe of the Shadow layer. Right-click (Windows) or Ctrl+click (Mac OS) on this keyframe and choose Create Motion Tween from the menu that appears. A tween span is created on this layer, and the shadow graphic is ready to be tweened.

2 Click on the Timeline ruler and drag the playhead to frame 15. At this frame, use the Selection tool (✦) to select and move the shadow so it sits below your airplane (using the diagram as a guide).

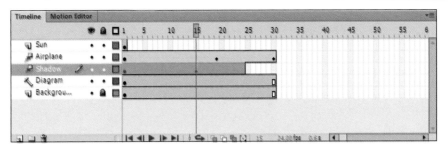

Create a tween span on the Shadow layer, and reposition the shadow on frame 15.

3 Move your mouse pointer over the last frame of the new tween span, and click and drag it to extend it to frame 30 (it should be as long as the airplane layer's tween span).

4 Click and drag the playhead to frame 30. On this frame, select the shadow once again and position it so it sits below the airplane in its landing position (using the diagram as a guide).

5   Press Enter (Windows) or Return (Mac OS) to play back your animation, and you should see the shadow move in tandem with your airplane!

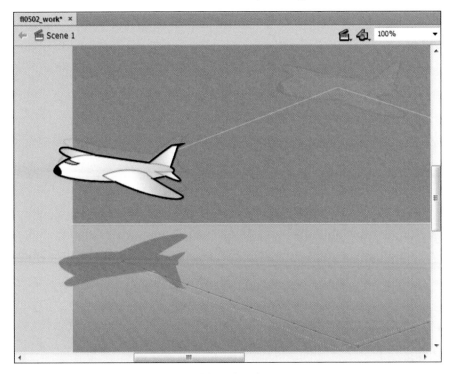

Reposition your shadow to match the movement of the airplane above.

6   Choose File > Save to save your work. Leave the file open.

A tween layer won't allow you to place or draw additional graphics on it once it's been created. You will get a warning dialog box if you attempt to add content to an existing tween layer.

Previewing animation with Test Movie

Pressing Enter (Windows) or Return (Mac OS) (referred to as Live Preview) is a quick way of seeing your animation as you build it, but the performance of your animation is based on many factors, including frame rate, the complexity of Stage graphics, and the number of simultaneous animations running on the Stage at once.

To get a more accurate picture of your animation as your end user will see it, use the Control menu's Test Movie command. This command temporarily publishes your movie and displays it as your user will see it in the Flash Player.

1   With the current file open, choose Control > Test Movie > in Flash Professional.

2   The Flash Player opens, and displays and plays your movie. At this point, you can only stop the movie by using the Control menu in the Flash Player window. Choose Control > Stop.

You may have noticed that your Diagram layer never shows in the final, published movie. The Diagram layer is a special type of layer called a Guide, whose contents are used strictly for visual reference and don't publish to your final movie. You can convert any standard layer to a Guide layer.

Generally, performance will be better in the Flash Player as you're viewing a flattened and optimized version of your movie.

3   Close the Flash Player window and return to your file.

You can use Ctrl+Enter (Windows) or Command+Return (Mac OS) as a shortcut instead of Control > Test Movie. This shortcut key combination will be used several times throughout the lesson.

Moving and transforming tween paths

Once a tween has been created, you may decide that the entire animation needs to be repositioned or shifted. Thanks to the motion paths that appear on the Stage, this task is easier than ever.

1   Click the Shadow layer in the Timeline and locate the motion path that your shadow graphic follows along the bottom of the Stage.

2   Using the Selection tool (⬑), click once on the motion path to select it in its entirety.

3 Click anywhere on the motion path and then drag it straight down—this moves the path and the entire animation along with it. Move it down until the bottom of the motion path touches the bottom of the Stage. Note that you can disregard the positioning shown on the Diagram layer at this point.

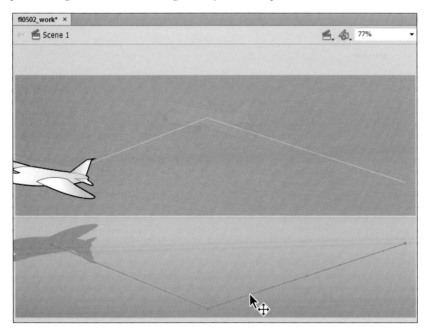

Click and drag a motion path to move it and the animated objects that follow it.

4 Leave the path selected, and choose the Free Transform tool (⬚) from the Tools panel. Handles appear on either end, and in the middle of, the motion path. You can transform the motion path just as you would a graphic to change its position or rotation.

5 Position your cursor to the bottom-right of the right handle and pull it upwards slightly to change the rotation of the path. You may notice that while the rotation of the path changes, the actual shadow does not!

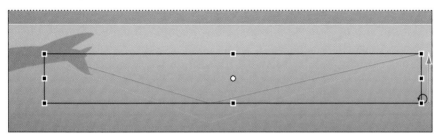

You can transform a motion path just as you would a piece of artwork. This has no effect on the animated object that follows it, however.

6 Press Enter (Windows) or Return (Mac OS) to play back your modified animation.

7 Choose File > Save to save your file.

Incorporating color effects and scaling

The cool thing about motion tweens is that you can have several properties of your graphic all animate at once, even within the same tween span. In addition to position, you can tween opacity (transparency), color tints, scaling, and rotation of an object to create more complex animation behavior.

For your airplane shadow, you'll want to manipulate the size and opacity of the shadow as the plane flies at different heights from the ground.

1   Select frame 19 of the Shadow layer. This brings you to the part of the tween span where the shadow appears in the middle of the Stage. Because the plane is at a higher altitude, the shadow should appear lighter and smaller.

2   Choose the Selection tool (⬉), then select the shadow directly on the Stage at frame 19, and locate the Color Effect options under the Property Inspector panel on the right. If necessary, click on the arrow to the left of Color Effect to display the Style menu below it.

3   From the Style menu, choose Alpha, which controls the transparency of your symbol instance. Use the slider to set the Alpha back to 50 percent. Leave the shadow selected.

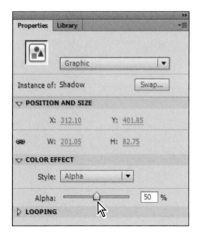
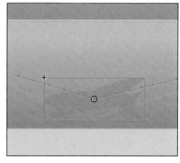

Select the shadow and use the Color Effects options to set its Alpha (transparency) to 50 percent.

4   Next, you'll reduce the size of your shadow slightly, as the airplane is higher off the ground. Choose Modify > Transform > Scale and Rotate. This opens the Scale and Rotate dialog box. Set the scale value to **60** percent, make sure the Rotate value is set to 0 degrees, and press OK.

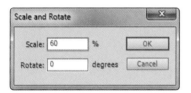

Scale the shadow graphic down to 60 percent at frame 19.

5   Drag the playhead to the beginning of the Timeline, and press Enter (Windows) or Return (Mac OS) to play back your animation—notice that the Alpha and scaling effects have been added to your tween!

However, also notice that the size and Alpha of the shadow don't return to their original values when the animation reaches frame 30. You'll fine-tune this in the next lesson.

6   Choose File > Save to save your movie.

Introducing the Motion Editor

Docked behind the Timeline panel is the Motion Editor, a powerful panel that enables you to fine-tune and modify animation with precision. The Motion Editor displays all properties of a selected tween span in a graph-like format where you can adjust individual properties (such as position and Alpha) in a tactile, precise way.

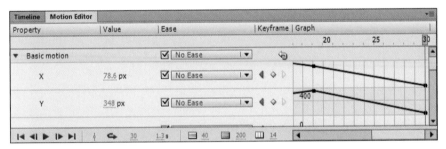

The Motion Editor is a powerful feature that allows you to see and adjust every aspect of your animation in a graph-like format.

Previous Flash users will find this to be a welcome addition, but if this is your first time animating in Flash, you'll also enjoy the flexibility that comes with the Motion Editor.

Let's take a look at the Motion Editor, and see how it works:

1   Click the Motion Editor tab to bring it forward. The Motion Editor appears docked behind the Timeline panel at the bottom of your workspace.

2   Before you can use or view properties in the Motion Editor, you'll first need to select a tweened object on the Stage. Click on the Shadow graphic on the Stage to select it and view its animation properties in the Motion Editor.

3   Each row across represents a different property that is either being tweened or can be tweened if desired. Use the vertical scroll bar on the right side of the Motion Editor to scroll down and see more properties.

You should see that every property you've tweened for your Shadow graphic, such as x position, y position, and Alpha, all have lines running across. These lines represent the value of each property at different points along the Timeline. As the line goes higher, so does the value.

4   Within the Basic Motion category click on the X property to expand it. This expands the row to full height. Click on the X property again to collapse it to its original height. You can also make more room for the Motion Editor by dragging the divider in between the bottom of the Stage and the top of the Motion Editor/Timeline panels.

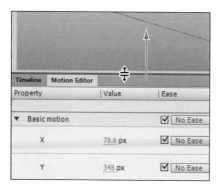

Click and drag between the Motion Editor and the Stage to expand its height.

5   Scroll down and take a look at the Skew X and Skew Y properties. These rows display dashed lines, which indicate that there is no value for these properties. You haven't applied any skewing to your graphic.

6   Leave the Motion Editor open for the next exercise.

Modifying the animation using the Motion Editor

Let's go ahead and put the Motion Editor to use by modifying the animation you created earlier.

You'll remember that the Alpha and scale values of your shadow didn't switch back even as the airplane returned to the ground in frame 30. You'll need to adjust these values to change later in the animation, and the Motion Editor will help you do that.

1   If the Motion Editor is not already visible, click its tab above the Timeline to bring it forward. Note: If you accidentally collapsed the panel, you can reopen it by choosing Window > Motion Editor.

2   Using the Selection tool (⬈), click to select the Shadow graphic on the Stage to reveal its properties in the Motion Editor. Scroll down if necessary and locate the Alpha/ Alpha amount row nested inside the Color Effect category.

3   If necessary, expand the Alpha amount row by clicking on it. Use the horizontal scroll bar to scroll across, and watch as the line starts at 100 percent (top), dips down at frame 19 to 50 percent, and remains there. A dashed line appears from that point on. You'll need to add a keyframe along this line to change its value at a different point in time.

4   Scroll right until you reach the end of the Alpha amount line (frame 30). Right-click (Windows) or Ctrl+click (Mac OS) on the very end of the line, and select Add Keyframe from the small contextual menu that appears.

This creates a draggable point on the line at frame 30. From here, you can either drag the point up or down to change the Alpha value, or specify an exact value on the left.

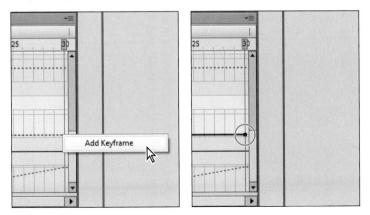

Right-click (Windows) or Ctrl+click (Mac OS) at any point along a value line to add keyframes that you can use to adjust values.

5   Leave the point selected, and on the left side of the row, locate the Alpha amount value. Click and drag on the value until it reads 100 percent. You should see the point (keyframe) you created move to the top position on the right and the shadow on the Stage become opaque.

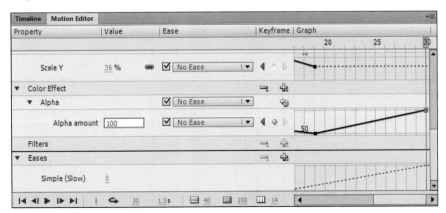

Adjust values of a selected keyframe using the slider/type-in box on the left side of a row.

To expand the height of the current row for a larger view, click on the row anywhere within the gray area on the left side of the Motion Editor.

6   Directly above the Alpha row, locate the Scale X and Scale Y rows, which affect horizontal and vertical scaling (respectively). You animated these properties when you scaled down the shadow earlier. Once again, scroll to the end of the row so that the end of the value line is visible.

7   At the end of the Scale X line, right-click (Windows) or Ctrl+click (Mac OS) directly on the line and choose Add Keyframe from the contextual menu that appears.

Note to make sure the Link X and Y property values button is not active so that you can set independent values for each axis.

Another way that you can create additional points along the value line is by holding down Ctrl (Windows) or Command (Mac OS) and clicking directly on the line. Add the Shift key to this combo to remove an existing point.

8   Click and drag the new point (keyframe) straight up until the value on the left reads 60 percent. The value is shown on the left side of the Motion Editor directly to the right of where it reads Scale X. As you change this value, you will also see the plane shadow scale.

9   The Scale Y value should have automatically scaled back up to 60%. This is because Scale X and Scale Y values are linked together to maintain proportion. If you had disabled the Link X and Y Property Values button, repeat steps 7 and 8 for the Scale Y value, also returning its value to 60 percent at the end of the line (frame 30).

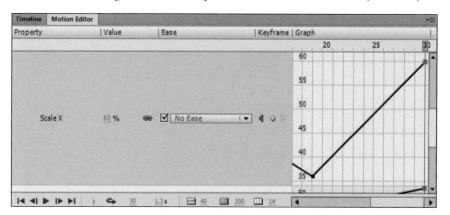

Add keyframes to the end of the Scale X and Scale Y value lines and change their final value to 60 percent.

10 Press Ctrl+Enter (Windows) or Command+Return (Mac OS) to preview the animation with the new adjustments you've made. You should see the shadow animate back to full opacity and its original size as the animation reaches its completion. Close the Flash Player once you've viewed your movie.

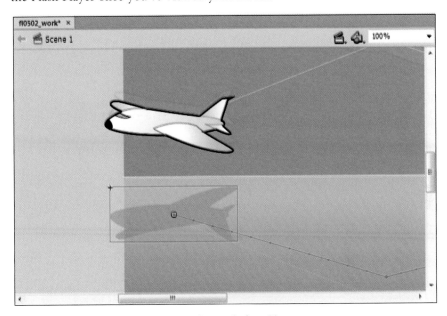

The airplane's shadow now returns to full size and opacity by frame 30.

11 Choose File > Save, and leave this file open.

The Motion Editor displays a frame ruler and playhead at the top just like the Timeline, so you can easily preview your changes as you go, without the need to switch back to the Timeline panel.

Making moves: Navigating the Timeline

Now that you are working across several frames and tween spans across the Timeline, you'll want to be able to navigate the Timeline and view animation sequences in a number of ways.

Here are a few short tips for navigating the Timeline that you'll find useful:

Preview an animation by pressing Enter (Windows) or Return (Mac OS) to start playback of the Timeline and view an entire animation sequence.

Move frame-by-frame through the Timeline by using the , (comma) and . (period) keys.

Move in any direction at any speed by clicking and dragging the playhead back and forth across the frame ruler. This is referred to as *scrubbing*.

Rewind and jump to the beginning of the Timeline by choosing Control > Rewind or pressing Shift+, (comma).

Tweening rotation

If you need to incorporate one or more full rotations in a tween, you'll find that rotation has its own special option in the Property Inspector. Rotations may need to occur more than once (for instance, three full revolutions)—behavior that Flash can't figure out from a graphic's position alone.

In the following steps, you'll add a tween to the Sun graphic on your Stage, and rotate it using the Property Inspector's rotation menu.

1 Bring the Timeline panel forward by clicking its tab below the Stage, or by choosing Window > Timeline. Select keyframe 1 of the Sun layer on the Timeline.

2 Right-click (Windows) or Ctrl+click (Mac OS) on the keyframe and choose Create Motion Tween from the contextual menu that appears. The layer is converted to a tween layer and a new tween span is created.

3 Just as you did with the other tween layers earlier, move your pointer over the last frame of the tween span, and then click and drag it to the right until it ends at frame 30.

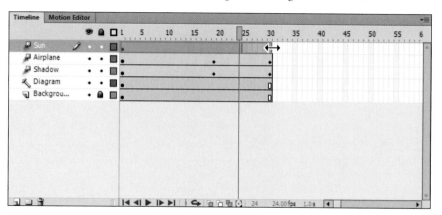

Add a motion tween to the Sun layer, and expand the tween span to frame 30.

4 Leave the frame selected, and locate (and if necessary, expand) the Rotation options in the Property Inspector on the right of your workspace.

5 Place your cursor over the 0 in the Rotate property and then click and drag to set the rotate count to 3 times. This sets the number of revolutions the sun will complete during the course of the tween span.

6   Under the Rotate value, click on the Direction drop-down menu. This allows you to choose the direction (clockwise or counter-clockwise) of the revolutions. Select CW for clockwise if it's not already selected.

Set the rotations to 3 on the Property Inspector.
If necessary, set the direction to CW (clockwise).

7   To put the finishing touches on your animation scene, select the Sun layer, and then click and drag it directly below the Airplane layer.

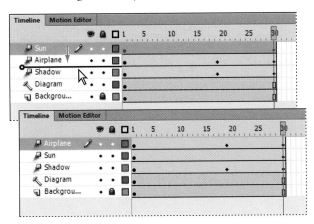

Drag the Sun layer below the Airplane layer to complete the scene.

Press Enter (Windows) or Return (Mac OS) to play back your movie, and you'll see the sun rotate three times clockwise! Experiment with different numbers of revolutions to increase the perceived speed of the rotation.

Remember, increasing revolutions without increasing the length of the tween span will result in faster rotation.

8 Choose File > Save to save your file.

New Feature: Rotation

The Rotation options feature the ability to add a specific number of degrees to the number of full rotations you've chosen. For instance, you can set three rotations and 45 degrees if you'd like! Previous versions of Flash only accepted whole number rotation values.

Controlling animation paths

You may have noticed how all the tweens you've created so far move in a straight line. While this may work in certain situations, there will certainly be a time when you want an animated object to follow a curved or unusual path.

To accomplish this, you can manipulate the motion path that your animated object follows. This motion path behaves much like any other path, and can be curved or manipulated using the Selection tool.

1 Select the Airplane layer in the Timeline. Choose the Selection tool (↖), and move your pointer over the right half of the airplane's motion path (animation path). You should see a curved line appear below your cursor (↖) when you get close enough to the line.

2 Click and drag up to bend the line into an upward curve, as shown in the figure below.

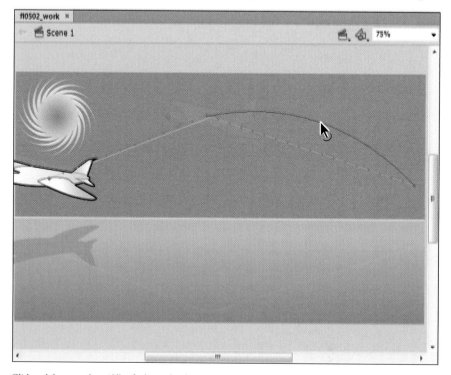

Click and drag over the middle of a line to bend it into a curve.

3   Move your pointer over the second half of the motion path (where the plane begins to fly down again) until the same curved icon appears below your cursor. Click and drag down to bend the line into a downward curve.

4   Press Enter (Windows) or Return (Mac OS) to play back your animation, and you'll see your airplane follow the new curve of the motion path.

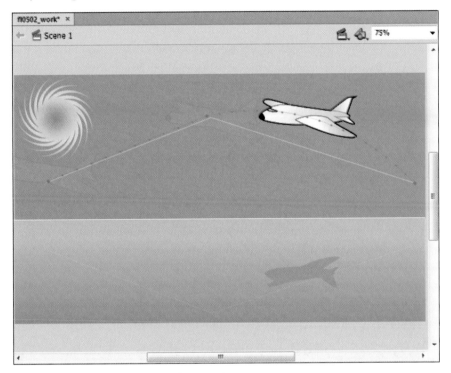

The airplane now follows the newly adjusted motion path.

5   Choose File > Save to save your file.

Where did Motion Guide layers go?

Users of previous versions of Flash who are revisiting the application may notice the absence of the Add Motion Guide icon below the Timeline. Changes in the animation engine, as well as the addition of motion paths in Flash, have essentially removed the need for Motion Guide layers.

More complex path manipulation is covered in Lesson 6, "Advanced Animation," where you will learn to create and manipulate complex animation paths to accomplish the same effect you may have previously achieved with Motion Guide layers.

What happens to my existing Flash files that use Motion Guide layers?

The good news is that Flash CS6 continues to support Motion Guide layers from previously created documents. You will be able to modify motion guides paths, and any tweens using them are treated as *classic* tweens (discussed later in this lesson).

How do I create a motion guide if I still want to?

Interestingly enough, despite the removal of the Add Motion Guide button, it is still possible to create a Motion Guide layer, but in a very non-obvious way. The Flash CS6 team thought enough to include a discreet way to create motion guides using standard guide layers.

Because traditional motion guides only work with classic (old-school) tweens, they are discussed in detail later in this lesson under "Legacy techniques: Creating classic tweens."

Morphing graphics and colors with shape tweens

So far, the tweens you've created have involved moving, scaling, or rotating symbol instances across the Stage. However, you may want to create some cool animations by having an object change its shape or color.

For these tasks, you'll explore shape tweens, which allow you to animate changes in shape and color between two graphics. You can also create cool *morphing* effects by having one object gradually transform into another.

Shape tween basics

The good news for experienced Flash users is that the process of creating a shape tween has not changed. For new users, shape tweens differ in some important ways from the motion tweens you learned about earlier in the chapter.

Some major differences are:

- Unlike motion tweens, shape tweens don't work with symbol instances. You can only use mergeable artwork or drawing objects. Primitive shapes can be used, but they must be broken down first.

- Shape tweens require the creation of two keyframes to contain the starting and ending shapes of the tween.

- Shape tweens do not have motion paths, so their motion, if any, is always linear (they move in a straight line).

- The Motion Editor can't be used to adjust shape tweens.

In this section, you'll create a shape tween to transform a moon into a bird in your animation scene.

1   Make sure the Timeline panel is visible by clicking its tab below the Stage, or by choosing Window > Timeline.

2 Select the Airplane layer and click the New Layer icon (⊒) below the Timeline to create a new layer; rename it **Shape Morph**. At this time, lock your other layers so you don't accidentally disturb their contents.

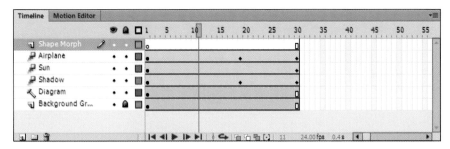

Add a new layer and name it Shape Morph.

To lock all layers except for the one you want to work on, hold down the Alt (Windows)/Option (Mac OS) key and click the dot below the padlock icon on the layer you'd like to use. All other layers except for the selected one automatically lock.

3 Click and drag the playhead to the beginning of the timeline at frame 1. Bring the Library panel forward by clicking its tab—you'll find it docked behind the Property Inspector on the right. In the Library panel, locate the Moon graphic symbol, and drag an instance of it to the upper-right corner of the Stage. It is automatically placed on the new layer you just created.

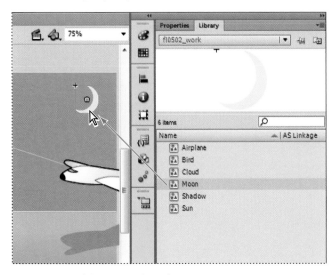

Drag an instance of the Moon graphic to the Stage.

You won't be able to drag a symbol to a locked layer, so if you're having difficulty, make sure that you have that Shape Morph layer selected on the Timeline, and that it is unlocked.

4   Because shape tweens can't work with symbol instances, you'll need to break this symbol back down to basic artwork again to use it in your shape tween. Use the Selection tool to select the new symbol instance, and choose Modify > Break Apart to break it down to non-symbol artwork.

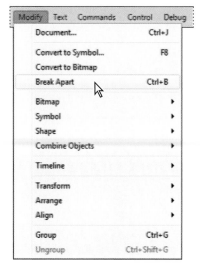
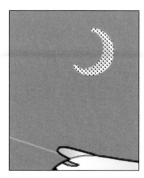

Choose Modify > Break Apart to break a symbol instance apart and prepare it for shape tweening.

5   Next, you'll need to add a second keyframe that will contain a new shape that your moon will transform into. Click and select frame 30 on the Shape Morph layer. Right-click (Windows) or Ctrl+click (Mac OS) on the selected frame and choose Insert Blank Keyframe to add a new empty keyframe at this position.

The only difference between inserting a keyframe or a blank keyframe is whether or not Flash copies the contents of the previous keyframe to the new one. For a shape tween, you generally aren't reusing the shape from the starting keyframe, so adding a blank keyframe is a better choice.

6   Click to select the new keyframe (30). Locate the Bird graphic symbol in your Library panel, and drag an instance of it to the middle of the Stage, slightly above the ground.

7   Once again, choose Modify > Break Apart to break the symbol instance down to basic artwork. Now that you have two unique shapes on keyframes 1 and 30, you're ready to create a shape tween to have one transform into another.

Place and break apart the Bird graphic to prepare it for shape tweening.

8   Click to select keyframe 1. Right-click (Windows) or Ctrl+Click (Mac OS) on the keyframe and choose Create Shape Tween from the contextual menu that appears. A green shaded area and an arrow appear between the two keyframes, letting you know that the shape tween has been successfully created.

9   Press Enter (Windows) or Return (Mac OS) to play back your animation, and watch as the first shape gradually morphs into the second!

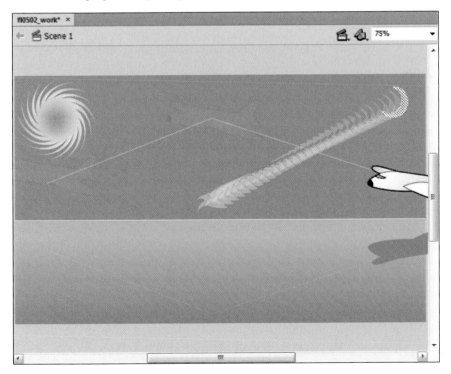

Your completed shape tween. (Shown here in Onion Skin view)

10 Choose File > Save to save your file.

If your tween displays a dashed line instead of an arrow, be sure to check that both pieces of artwork have been broken out of their symbol form. If either piece of artwork still exists as a graphic symbol, the shape tween can't be properly created.

Getting in shape: Making the most of shape tweens

Shape tweening is part technique, part luck of the draw. Every pair of shapes will yield a unique result, but in some cases the transition between two shapes may not be what you expect. In some cases, the transition may not be pretty at all. To get the best results from your shape tweens, here are some general pointers to consider:

1 Try using solid, whole shapes. For instance, if you have a face and two eyes, avoid trying to morph all three in a single shape tween. Consider breaking each element out onto its own layer for best results.

2 Try and keep the number of starting and ending shapes the same. Two shapes to two shapes, as opposed to two shapes to three shapes, will yield cleaner results.

3 If your starting shape includes a stroke, try to include one on the ending shape as well.

4 Use Shape Hints to fine-tune the quality of your shape tweens and anchor common points between starting and ending shapes (Shape hints are discussed in detail in Chapter 6).

Legacy techniques: Creating classic tweens

In previous versions of Flash, the process of creating motion tweens was very different. In fact, it was much more like creating shape tweens, whereby a set of keyframes had to be manually created to mark the beginning and end of a motion tween.

While it's highly recommended that you use the new tween model, there may be cases where you need to create or modify a *classic* motion tween within an older Flash file. The next lesson illustrates this technique for just those times.

1 Press the Insert Layer button (⊡) below the Timeline to add a new layer. Name this new layer Classic Tween.

2 From the Library panel on the right, locate and drag an instance of the Cloud graphic symbol to the first keyframe of the new layer. Use the Selection tool (▸) to position it in the upper-right corner of the Stage.

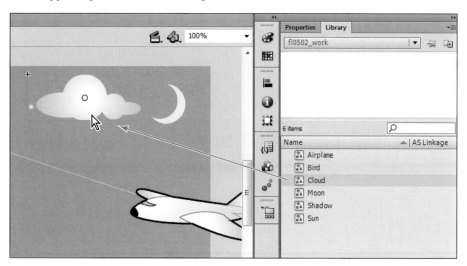

Drag instance of the Cloud graphic from your Library to the Stage.

3 Classic motion tweens require a starting and ending keyframe, so you'll need to create the ending keyframe further down on this layer. Select frame 30 of this layer, and press the F6 shortcut key (Windows) or choose Insert > Timeline > Keyframe (Mac OS) to create a new keyframe at this position.

4 The cloud from keyframe 1 has been duplicated onto this new keyframe—you'll change the position of this copy to mark where the cloud should go during the course of the animation. Click and drag the cloud instance on keyframe 30 straight to the left so it sits beside the sun.

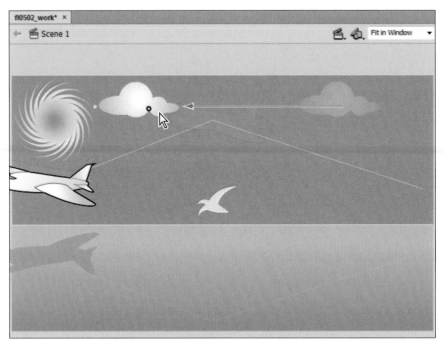

Move the cloud to the left to indicate where it will travel to (shown here in Onion Skin view).

5 Now it's time to finalize the tween. Click and select keyframe 1. Right-click (Windows) or Ctrl+click (Mac OS) on the keyframe and choose Create Classic Tween from the contextual menu that appears. A purple, shaded area and arrow should appear in between the two keyframes, indicating the tween has been successfully created.

6 Choose Control > Test Movie > in Flash Professional to preview your animation. The cloud moves to the left across the Stage!

7 Close the Flash Player, and choose File > Save to save your work.

Classic tween rules

As with tween layers and tween spans, classic motion tweens have some rules that need to be followed to ensure that they are created properly.

- Classic tweens require a starting and ending keyframe.

- Classic tweens can only use symbol instances.

- Both keyframes require an instance of the same symbol; you can't tween between two different symbol instances.

- Only one object can be tweened at a time on a single layer.

Adding color effects and scaling to a classic tween

When using classic tweens, you can animate several properties at once, just as you did with the airplane's shadow earlier in the lesson. By making changes to the starting or ending instance of the cloud, you can incorporate transparency, scaling, and other properties in the tween along with the existing motion.

1 If it's not visible, bring the Property Inspector forward by clicking its tab on the right side, or by choosing Window > Properties.

2 Click keyframe 30 directly on the Classic Tween layer to select it. The cloud on this keyframe should also appear selected on the Stage. Click once more on the cloud so it's active in the Property Inspector on the right.

3 Under the Property Inspector's Color Effect options, locate and click on the Style menu and select Alpha. When the Alpha slider appears, click and drag it to the left to set the Alpha value to 50 percent.

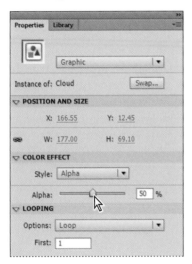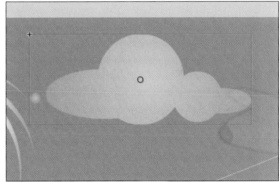

Select the cloud on frame 30 and use the Color Effect options on the Property Inspector to set its Alpha to 50 percent.

4 Leave the cloud selected, and choose Modify > Transform > Scale and Rotate. In the Scale and Rotate dialog box that appears, type **50%** for the Scale value, and press OK to apply the new value.

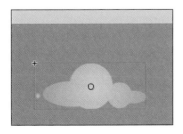

The cloud shown after color effects and scaling have been applied.

5 Press Enter (Windows) or Return (Mac OS) to play back your Timeline, and watch as the cloud fades and shrinks as it moves across the sky.

6 Choose File > Save to save your file.

There is a big difference between selecting a keyframe and selecting the contents of a keyframe. If an object on the Stage appears selected, but you don't see its options in the Property Inspector, click once more on the object to make it active. This is sometimes referred to as focusing an object.

Unlike tween spans, classic tweens will not prevent you from adding other objects to the same layer. While this will not generate a warning, adding graphics or text to a layer that contains a classic tween will likely break the tween.

(Re)creating motion guides for classic tweens

Experienced Flash designers may have already noticed the apparent removal of the Add Motion Guide button below the Timeline, and, in turn, the ability to create Motion Guide layers. A technique still exists for creating *classic* motion guides when and if necessary. In the following steps, you'll change the path of animation for your classic tween using good, old-fashioned motion guides.

1 Click and select your Classic Tween layer on the Timeline.

2 Click the Add Layer button (⌐) below the Timeline to create a new layer above the Classic Tween layer, and rename it **Motion Guide**. You'll use standard drawing tools, such as the Pencil tool, to create a random path that your cloud can follow.

3 Select the Pencil tool (✐) from the Tools panel, and make sure that you have a stroke color selected. In addition, make sure that Object Drawing is *not* enabled. The button at the bottom of the Tools panel, (◯), should be popped out.

4   On the new layer, use the Pencil tool to draw a single interesting path that starts about where the cloud begins, and ends about where the cloud ends on the left side of the Stage. This path is what your classic tween will follow in just a few moments.

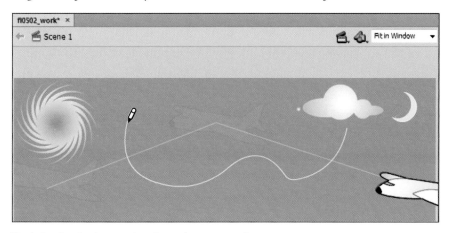

Use the Pencil tool to draw a path on the new layer you created.

5   The trick to making sure the classic tween will follow this path is to first convert this layer to a Guide layer. Right-click (Windows) or Ctrl+click (Mac OS) on the title area of the Motion Guide layer, and choose Guide from the contextual menu that appears. The layer icon is replaced by a T-square icon (✎), indicating that this is now a Guide layer.

6   Next, select the Classic Tween layer, and carefully drag it up and to the right below the Motion Guide layer until it appears indented underneath it. This lets the Classic Tween layer know to follow whatever path it finds on the Motion Guide layer above it.

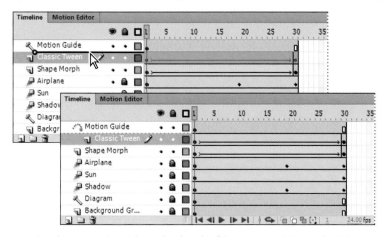

Move the Classic Tween layer below and to the right of the Motion Guide layer to bind the two together.

7   To get your cloud following the path, you'll need to snap the cloud instances at the beginning and end keyframes of the classic tween layer to the beginning and end of the path, respectively. Choose the Selection tool (↖), click on keyframe 1 of the classic tween layer, and drag the center of the cloud on this keyframe over the beginning of the path you created until the center snaps in place.

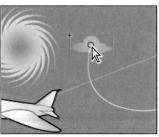

Snap the cloud instances on keyframes 1 and 30 to the beginning and end of the path, respectively.

Select keyframe 30 of the classic tween layer, and click and drag the cloud on this keyframe to the end of the path until it again snaps in place.

For symbol instances to properly snap in place to a path acting as a motion guide, make sure Snap To Objects is enabled. Choose View > Snapping > Snap To Objects to make sure it is checked.

8   Press Enter (Windows) or Return (Mac OS) to preview your animation—your cloud should now follow the path you created on the Motion Guide layer.

9   Choose File > Save to save your file.

Troubleshooting Motion Guides

Motion guides can be a bit tricky the first few times around. If your animation is not following the motion guide you created, use the following points to troubleshoot your animation:

• Make sure that both the starting and ending instance are snapped directly onto the path you created. If either instance is not seated properly on the motion guide, it will not work. Think of it as putting a train on the tracks.

• Make sure your motion path is NOT a drawing object, group, or symbol. Animations can only follow paths drawn in Merged Drawing mode. A telltale sign that you may not be using the right type of artwork is if your path appears inside a bounding box.

• Avoid using unusual stroke styles, such as dashes, dots, or ragged strokes. These occasionally cause unpredictable behavior if used on a motion path.

Adjusting animation with onion skinning

One of Flash's most useful visual aids is the Onion Skin, which allows you to view all frames of an animation at once on the Stage. This helps you make crucial decisions, such as how far to move or scale an object during the course of an animation. It also helps you see how your animation works alongside other items on the Stage as the Timeline plays back.

Onion skinning can be enabled for a single layer or multiple layers at once; simply unlock a layer if you want to view it as onion skins, or lock it if you don't.

In the following steps, you'll see how you can adjust your existing tweens in Onion Skin view.

1   On the Timeline, lock all layers except for your Shadow, Shape Morph, and Classic Tween layers. If necessary, click and drag the playhead to the end of your Timeline to frame 30.

2   At the bottom of the Timeline, locate the cluster of five small buttons, and click the second button from the left, (▣), to enable Onion Skin view. Two brackets appear on the frame ruler at the top of the Timeline. These brackets allow you to select the range of frames that you'd like to view in Onion Skin mode.

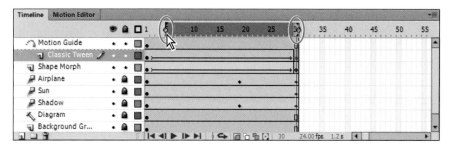

Adjust the brackets on the frame ruler to choose how much of the Timeline you want to reveal in Onion Skin mode.

3 Click and drag the left bracket to position it at the very beginning of the Timeline (frame 1). With the playhead at frame 30, the right bracket is at the end of the Timeline. You should now see all frames of animation on the unlocked layers.

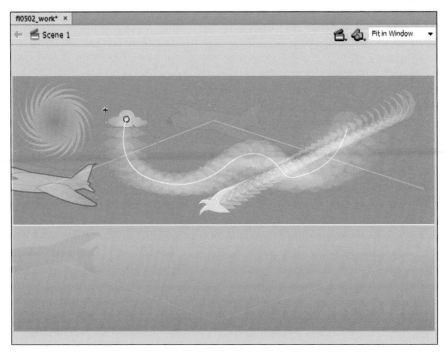

With Onion Skin enabled, you can view all frames of animation on all unlocked layers.

4 Click on the Timeline ruler at Frame 1 to return the playhead to the beginning of the Timeline. On the Shape Morph layer, select the moon shape and drag it slightly downward, click anywhere in the background and you will see the frames in between adjust automatically. Adjust the angle of the frames in between until you get the shape morph moving in a straight line from right to left.

5 On the Shadow layer, grab the starting shadow symbol instance on the right side of the Stage and drag it down slightly. You see the trajectory of the tween change, and the motion path readjusts as well.

6 Use the same technique to adjust the starting and ending position of your Cloud graphic on the Classic Tween layer. Try relocating the cloud to the opposite side of the Stage by moving the starting and ending instances individually, and watch how the frames redraw in between.

If the full-color frames in Onion Skin are difficult to look at, try Onion Skin Outlines. Click the button directly to the right of Onion Skin (third from the left in the button cluster below the Timeline). This displays all frames in an outline view that's easier to see in certain situations.

7 Choose File > Save to save your file, and choose File > Close to close the file.

Looking ahead

Now that you have a feel for creating basic animation and working with multiple layers of animation at once, you will move on to more advanced techniques in Lesson 6, "Advanced Animation."

You'll work more with the Motion Editor, learn to simulate gravity and inertia effects with Easing, and create more advanced motion paths. You'll also learn to incorporate 3D properties into your tweens, edit and align several frames of content at once, and create cool frame-by-frame animation using Flash CS6's IK (Inverse Kinematics) behavior.

Self study

Add a new layer to your lesson file, and drag an additional airplane from the Library panel to the new layer. Create a tween that incorporates changes to position, color and size. Add a second layer, and draw a shape that you'd like to morph. Create a second shape on a new keyframe at the end of that layer, and create a shape tween between the two shapes.

Review

Questions

1 What three types of tweens can be created in Flash?

2 What are two reasons why you would create a keyframe on a layer along the Timeline?

3 How many objects can be tweened at the same time on a single layer?

Answers

1 Motion tweens, shape tweens, and classic tweens.

2 To have an object appear at that point in time, or to start or end an animation sequence (tween).

3 One.

What you'll learn in this lesson:

- Creating and fine-tuning shape tweens

- Masking animation layers

- Using the Copy and Paste Motion features

- Editing multiple frames at once

Advanced Animation

You'll take it to the next level by creating more elaborate animation sequences and effects. You'll learn to save time by duplicating motion across several objects, to create unique effects with filters, and to harness the power of Flash CS6's 3D and Inverse Kinematics tools.

Starting up

Before starting, make sure that your tools and panels are consistent by resetting your workspace. See "Resetting the Flash workspace" in the Starting up section of this book.

You will work with several files from the fl06lessons folder in this lesson. Make sure that you have loaded the fllessons folder onto your hard drive from the supplied DVD. See "Loading lesson files" in the Starting up section of this book.

See Lesson 6 in action!

Use the accompanying video to gain a better understanding of how to use some of the features shown in this lesson. You can find the video tutorial for this lesson on the included DVD.

The project

You'll explore more complex animation techniques and new features by completing a complex ad banner for the skyPod portable music device.

Copying, pasting, and saving animation

As you develop more complex movies, you'll likely want to animate several objects in the same way throughout a single movie. Once you've created a tween span (or several), Flash gives you many options for copying and pasting animation between objects. Another more reusable option is motion presets. Motion presets allow you to capture, save and apply an animation behavior later onto any number of objects across objects or even different movies. Motion presets are discussed later in this chapter.

Using Copy and Paste Motion

The Copy and Paste Motion menu options enable you to copy animation behavior from one object and paste it to another. This means you can apply the same tween behavior to several symbols at once, or have two objects move in tandem with each other without having to manually recreate the same tween twice.

Copy Motion captures all aspects of a selected tween, including position, scaling, color effects, easing, and filters. You can paste motion as-is between two symbols, or use Paste Motion Special to pick and choose exactly which aspects you want to apply.

You'll use Copy and Paste Motion to create and apply the same tweening behavior to several text taglines in your skyPod banner.

1   Choose File > Open and open the fl0601_start.fla file in the fl06lessons folder. Choose File > Save and name the file **fl0601_work.fla**.

2   On the Timeline, locate and expand the Tag Phrases folder by clicking on the arrow to the left. This reveals five layers: Jam, Dance, Skip, Bounce, and 65 Trillion, each of which contains a tag line that you'll animate.

3 On the Jam layer, right-click (Windows) or Control+click (Mac OS) on frame 1 and choose Create Motion Tween from the contextual menu that appears. This creates a new, 24-frame tween span. Move your cursor over the last frame of the new tween span, click and drag to the right, and expand the tween span to frame 40.

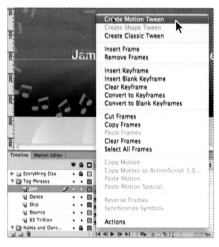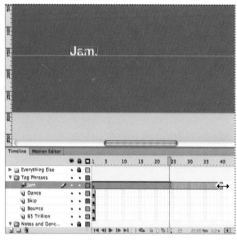

Create a new motion tween and expand it to frame 40.

4 Drag the playhead to frame 1, and select the word *Jam* on the Stage, which is a movie clip symbol from your Library. On the Property Inspector, locate Filters. Click the Add Filter button at the bottom of the panel and select Blur from the filter menu that appears. Type **15** for the Blur X value to set a 15-pixel blur and press Enter (Windows) or Return (Mac OS). Choose High from the Quality drop-down menu.

5 Above the Filters options, locate the Color Effect options, and choose Alpha from the style menu. Use the Alpha slider that appears to set the alpha to 0 percent (full transparency)—the word *Jam* disappears (for now).

Next, you'll gradually fade the text back in, using a motion tween.

6 Position the playhead at frame 15, and reselect the word *Jam* at this frame.

If you are having difficulty finding fully transparent items, you can click the colored box to the right of the layer name to temporarily enable Outline view.

Set a layer to Outline view for the layer to temporarily reveal transparent items.

7 With the word selected, return to the Property Inspector and use the Alpha slider (under Color Effect) to return the alpha to 100 percent. Notice that a keyframe has been automatically created at frame 15 to mark the change.

8 Position the playhead at frame 40, where the tween span ends. Again, select the word Jam. Locate the settings you created earlier for the Blur filter (under Filters). Change the Blur X and Blur Y values to 0 pixels, then press Enter (Windows) or Return (Mac OS) to remove the blur.

9 Press Enter (Windows) or Return (Mac OS) to play back your animation so far. Notice that the word Jam fades in, and then gains focus as it reaches the end of the tween. Your next step will be to copy all the animation behavior you've just created, and paste it to the next word in the sequence: Dance.

10 On the Jam layer, click anywhere in the tween span to select it—all frames within the span should appear selected. Right-click (Windows) or Control+click (Mac OS) on the tween span and choose Copy Motion from the contextual menu that appears. The Animation behavior contained with the span, including motion, filters, and color effects, has been captured to memory.

Right-click on a selected motion tween and choose Copy Motion from the contextual menu to copy its animation behavior.

11 Select frame 1 on the Dance layer. Right-click (Windows) or Control+click (Mac OS) on the selected frame and choose Paste Motion from the contextual menu that appears. A tween span is created on the current layer of the same length, which includes all the same animation behavior and keyframes.

12 Press Enter (Windows) or Return (Mac OS) to play back the Timeline, and the word Dance now animates in the same exact way as the word Jam.

13 Repeat steps 11 and 12 for the Skip layer.

Paste the motion from the Jam layer to the Dance and Skip layers. All three now have the same tweens applied (as shown).

Creating Motion Presets

As seen in the previous exercise, the ability to Copy and Paste Motion is a great way to quickly share animation behavior among multiple objects in your movie. However, if you'd like to apply animation behavior across multiple projects, or store an animation behavior for later use, Flash CS6 gives you the ability to capture animation behavior into motion presets.

Now you can save any existing tween (or series of tweens) into a motion preset, which can be recalled and applied from the Motion Presets panel. In addition, motion presets are saved in Flash itself (not to any specific file), and so they can be used across any number of Flash files.

In the following steps, you'll save the animation you designed in the last exercise to a new motion preset, and apply it to other objects in your movie.

1　Choose Window > Motion Presets to open the Motion Presets panel. It contains two folders, Default Presets and Custom Presets. Any new presets you create are added to the Custom Presets folder.

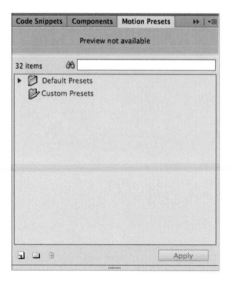

The Motion Presets panel stores saved animation behavior in named presets. You can apply any preset to any object from any file, at any time.

2　On the Timeline, click to select the entire tween span on the Skip layer. This tween contains animation that you copied and pasted from the Jam layer in the previous exercise. If necessary, reopen the Motion Presets panel.

3　At the bottom of the Motion Presets panel, click the Save selection as preset button to create a new motion preset from the selected tween. When the dialog box appears, type **Fade and Focus** for the new preset name, and click OK. The new preset now appears inside the Custom Presets folder.

4　Select the first keyframe of the 65 Trillion layer. This layer contains a graphic symbol with another tag line, and currently has no animation applied.

　　If necessary, reopen the Motion Presets panel and select the new Fade and Focus preset you created, and click the Apply button at the bottom of the panel. The tween behavior is now applied to the 65 Trillion layer!

5　On the Timeline, expand the Everything Else layer. Locate the Logo layer, and turn its visibility back on (it's currently switched off). This reveals the skyPod logo in the middle of the Stage.

6 Select the first keyframe of the Logo layer. Click the skyPod logo in the middle of the Stage to select it. From the top of the Property Inspector, use the pull-down menu to choose Movie Clip. Keep the first keyframe of the Logo layer selected. In the Motion Presets panel, make sure your new Fade and Focus preset is selected, and once again, click the Apply button. This applies the animation behavior to the Logo layer, just like you did with the 65 Trillion layer.

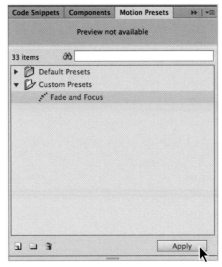

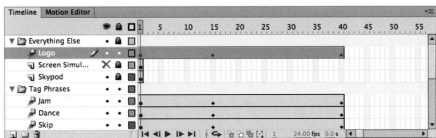

Apply the animation in the Fade and Focus preset to the 65 Trillion and Logo layers with just a couple clicks.

7 Press the Enter (Windows) or Return (Mac OS) key to play back the Timeline and see the new animations you created using Motion Presets.

8 Choose File > Save to save your work.

The Motion Presets panel includes many ready-to-use presets in the Default Presets folder. Try some of these to help you get up-and-running quickly.

Applying Advanced Easing Behavior

Flash CS6 provides many basic and advanced easing behaviors (such as bounces and springs), available from the Motion Editor panel, enabling you to add realistic behavior to your tweens.

In the following steps, you'll apply some of the easing behaviors to a new tween using the Motion Editor panel.

1   Under the Tag Phrases layer folder, locate and select the first keyframe of the Bounce layer.

2   Right-click (Windows) or Control+click (Mac OS) on the selected frame and choose Create Motion Tween from the contextual menu that appears. A 24-frame tween span is created on the Bounce layer.

3   Click and select the tween span, and move your cursor over the last frame of the span. Click and drag to the right, and extend the tween span out to frame 40 (it should end at the same point as the other tweens you've created so far).

4   Move your pointer over frame 40 of the new tween span. Right-click (Windows) or Control+click (Mac OS) and choose Insert Keyframe > Position from the contextual menu that appears. This captures the word Bounce in its current position in the middle of the Stage.

5   Click on keyframe 1 to return the playhead to the beginning of the tween span. Using your Selection tool (▸), drag the word Bounce on the Stage straight upward until it sits directly above the Stage in the pasteboard area.

A motion path appears on the Stage to show the direction the word Bounce will follow.

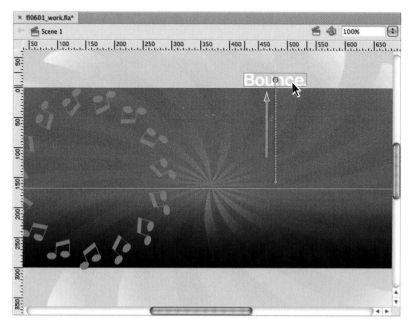

The Motion Tween you created sends the word Bounce from above the Stage back to the middle of the Stage alongside the other tag lines.

6   Press Enter (Windows) or Return (Mac OS) to preview the animation so far. The word Bounce moves from above the Stage and stops next to the other taglines to its left.

7   Now, you'll add some easing behavior to your new tween to make it more exciting. Click and select the entire new tween span you've created. Below the Stage, click the Motion Editor tab to bring the Motion Editor panel forward.

8   Scroll down to the bottom of the Motion Editor, and locate the Eases row, where you can add and modify easing behaviors to use on the selected tween. In the middle of the row, locate and click the Add Color, Filter, or Ease button (⊕). A menu appears with several ease behaviors—select the **Bounce In** ease behavior to add it to your current eases.

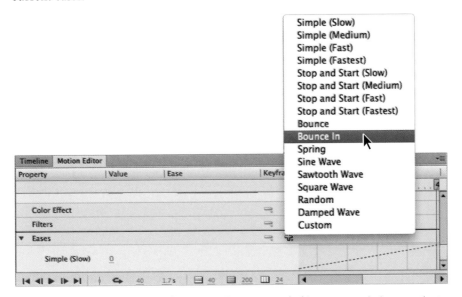

Add the Bounce In behavior to your list of active eases. You can now apply this to any properties in your motion tween.

9 Once you've added an ease, you can assign it to different aspects of your tween, such as motion, filters, and color effects. You can even assign different eases to individual motion properties, such as x and y.

Scroll up in the Motion Editor so that you can see the Basic motion row. Locate the menu on that row that reads No Ease—this allows you to assign easing to all the Motion properties at once. From that menu, select the Bounce In ease you just added.

Apply the newly added Bounce In ease behavior to all the Position properties in your tween at once.

10 Choose Control > Test Movie > in Flash Professional to preview your work so far in the Flash Player. The word Bounce falls in from the top of the Stage and bounces when it reaches its final position in the middle.

11 Close the Flash Player and choose File > Save to save your movie.

Animating Masks

Masking allows you to hide and reveal selected areas of artwork on your Stage using a Mask layer and a chosen shape. You've learned the basics of this common design concept in Lesson 4, "Advanced Tools."

Now, you'll take masks a step further by incorporating tweens to create moving masks that add unique effects to your movies. Animated masks are the key to some common, cool Flash "tricks" that you may have already seen, such as magnifying glass and spotlight effects.

In the following steps, you'll have your skyPod device move across the screen, magnifying your tag line text as it crosses the Stage.

1   On the Timeline, expand the Everything Else layer folder, if necessary. Locate, unlock, and select the Skypod layer, which contains the symbol of the skyPod device you'll be tweening.

2   Click the New Layer button to insert a new layer above the Skypod layer, and rename the layer **Screen Mask**.

3   Return the playhead to frame 1, and drag an instance of the Screen Mask Movieclip symbol from your Library panel to the left of the Stage. Position it so it lines up and obscures the screen on the skyPod graphic below it.

On frame 1 of the Screen Mask layer, add an instance of the Screen Mask movie clip to the Stage, and position it so it overlays the screen on the skyPod device.

4 Select keyframe 1 on the Skypod layer. Right-click (Windows) or Control+click (Mac OS) on the selected frame and choose Create Motion Tween from the contextual menu that appears. A new tween span is created.

5 Move your cursor over the last frame of the span, and click and drag to expand the tween span to frame 40.

6 Click on frame 40 on the Timeline ruler to advance the playhead to the end of the tween span. Drag the skyPod graphic from the left, and position it on the right side of the Stage.

To match the completed demo file, use the Property Inspector to set its final position to X: **650** and Y: **200**. A motion path is created on the Stage to indicate that the skyPod device will be tweened from the left to the right.

A new motion path shows that the skyPod device will be tweened from left to right across the Stage.

To move an object in a perfect, straight path, either vertically or horizontally, hold down the Shift key while dragging it.

7 Press Enter (Windows) or Return (Mac OS) to play back your new tween. The device should glide in from the left side of the Stage and stop on the right. Next, you'll copy the motion from this tween and paste it to the Screen Mask in the layer above, so that it follows the exact same behavior.

8 On the Skypod layer, click on the new tween to select it. Right-click (Windows) or Control+click (Mac OS) on the selected frames and choose Copy Motion from the contextual menu that appears.

9 Select frame 1 of the Screen Mask layer. Right-click (Windows) or Control+click (Mac OS) on the selected frame and choose Paste Motion from the contextual menu that appears. A tween identical to the one on the Skypod layer is now added to this layer.

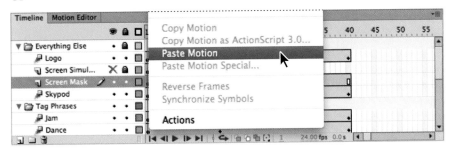

Paste the motion copied from the Skypod layer to the Screen Mask layer. The soon-to-be mask now follows the exact same animation behavior as the skyPod device so that the two move in tandem.

10 Press Enter (Windows) or Return (Mac OS) to play back your movie. The Skypod and Screen Mask layers should both animate exactly the same way. Next, you'll convert your Screen Mask into a mask, so that it reveals artwork as it moves across the Stage.

11 On the Timeline, drag the Screen Mask layer above the Screen Simulation layer. Unlock the Screen Simulation layer, and turn its visibility on. Click on frame 1 of the Screen Simulation layer. This reveals a graphic containing the same tag phrases that are already on the Stage. You'll reveal this behind the Screen Mask as it travels across the Stage.

12 Select and right-click (Windows) or Control+click (Mac OS) on the Screen Mask layer (next to its title). Choose Mask from the contextual menu that appears. This converts the Screen Mask layer, including its animation, to a mask that obscures the contents of the Screen Simulation layer below.

13 To complete the effect, select frame 40 on the Screen Simulation layer. Use the F5 shortcut key to insert a frame here and extend the contents of the layer to the end of the Timeline.

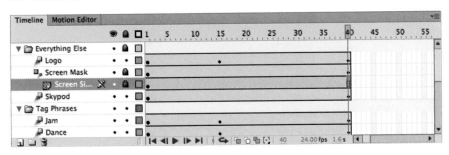

The Screen Mask layer now masks the Screen Simulation layer.

14 Press Enter (Windows) or Return (Mac OS) to preview the animation. The skyPod device moves across the screen, revealing digitized tag lines in its screen as it crosses the Stage!

15 Choose File > Save to save your file.

To enable a masking effect, both the Mask layer and the layer being masked must be locked.

Creating Animation with IK Poses

Two excellent tools for designers and traditional animators are the Bone and Bind tools, which allow you to create poseable, puppet–like Inverse Kinematics (IK) objects that can be animated with the same simplicity that you're accustomed to with motion tweens. You explored these IK tools briefly in Lesson 4, "Advanced Tools," and now you'll put your IK objects into motion by creating *poses*.

Poses are very much like keyframes in a motion tween, and they store positions of connected IK objects at different points along the Timeline. Connected IK objects are grouped together on Armature layers, where you can create poses and animate the changes between each pose.

You'll reveal a pre-created IK object on the Timeline, and create poses to add a funky dancer to your banner.

1 Expand the Notes and Dancer layer folder on the Timeline. Locate and unlock the Dancer layer, and turn its visibility on. Click on the dancer layer and then click on frame 1, if necessary. This reveals a series of connected IK objects on a single Armature layer, indicated by its distinctive icon (✻).

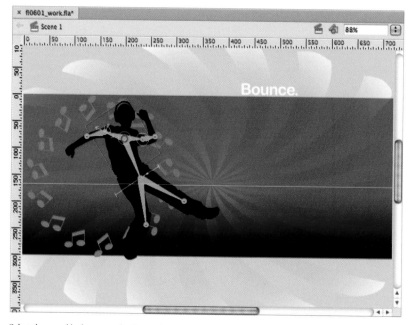

Select the poseable dancer on the Dancer layer to reveal the bones that connect its various pieces.

2 Select frame 10 on the Dancer layer. Right-click (Windows) or Control+click (Mac OS) on the selected frame and choose Insert Pose from the contextual menu that appears. A bullet (that looks much like a keyframe) is inserted at frame 10.

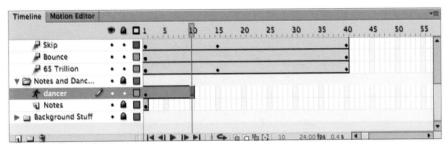

Right-click on a frame in an Armature layer and select Insert Pose to add a new frame where your IK object can be posed and positioned.

3 Choose your Selection tool (k), and click on any part of the dancer; the bones that connect each limb are revealed. Click and drag each limb, and position it to make a new pose for your dancer.

4 Return the playhead to the beginning of the Timeline, and press Enter (Windows) or Return (Mac OS). Flash animates the changes between the original pose on frame 1, and the new one you created on frame 10!

Use Shift+, (comma) to rewind the Timeline and return the playhead to frame 1.

5 Select frame 20 on your Dancer layer. Right-click (Windows) or Control+click (Mac OS) on the selected frame and choose Insert Pose from the contextual menu that appears.

6 Just as you did on frame 10, use your Selection tool to position the limbs of your dancer in a new pose.

7 Repeat steps 5 and 6 to create new poses at frames 30 and 40.

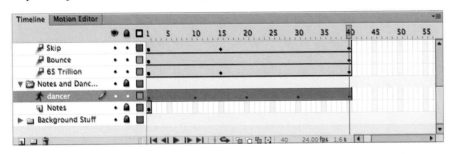

The completed layer, with poses at frames 10, 20, 30, and 40. Flash animates the changes between each pose.

8 Press Enter (Windows) or Return (Mac OS) to play back your animation. Your dancer animates through all four poses.

9 Choose File > Save to save your work.

Sequencing Animation

The true strength of the Timeline lies in the ability to sequence animation, graphics, and sounds across the Timeline to build more complex scenes. Now that you've added several layers of animation to your banner project, you'll work toward sequencing your movie so that every animation falls into its proper place. Think of it as writing a script for your first big movie—you've got the actors, you've got the Stage, and now it's time to orchestrate the scene.

Shifting, Moving, and Extending Tween Spans

Once you've created a tween span, you can easily slide it along a layer to reposition it at different points along the Timeline. This is an essential concept for creating well-planned scenes that get your message across.

You'll now begin to move a few things around to get your banner project closer to completion.

1   Locate the Dance layer on the Timeline (under the Tag Phrases folder). Click anywhere on the tween span to select it.

2   Click and drag the entire span to the right. Release the span when the first keyframe is on frame 15. Fourteen empty frames now exist at the beginning of the Timeline.

3   Repeat step 2 for the Skip, Bounce, and 65 Trillion layers, repositioning their tween spans so they begin at frames 30, 45, and 120, respectively.

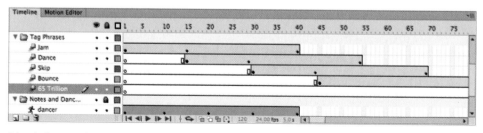

Select the frames on the Dance, Skip, Bounce, and 65 Trillion layers, and sequence them across the Timeline.

4   Under the Everything Else layer folder, reposition the Screen Mask, Screen Simulation, and Skypod layers so all three begin at frame 80. The Screen Simulation layer is not a tween span, in order to move it you should click on the first keyframe and then Shift+click the last frame. This will allow you to move all the frames by clicking and dragging the selection.

Shift the Logo layer so it begins at frame 125.

As you extend the overall Timeline, some layers end abruptly and their contents disappear from the Stage. To remedy this, you'll need to extend those layers by either expanding their tween spans, or adding frames.

5 Locate the tween span at the end of the 65 Trillion layer, which now ends around frame 159 or 160. Move your cursor over the last frame of the tween span until a double-arrow appears; click and drag to extend the tween span to frame 165.

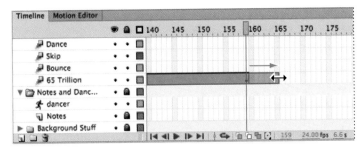

Extend the 65 Trillion layer to frame 165.

6 Locate the Skypod layer (under the Everything Else layer folder). Select frame 165 on the Skypod layer and use the F5 shortcut key to insert a frame at this position. This continues the layer's contents without disturbing the keyframes before it. Repeat this for the Screen Mask and Screen Simulation layers. You may not actually see the additional frames created on the layers contained within the folder unless the folder is expanded.

Keyframes in an existing tween span shift when the span is extended or trimmed. If you want to extend the duration of a tween layer without shifting keyframes, add frames to the layer using the F5 shortcut key.

7 Repeat step 6 for the Jam, Dance, Skip, and Bounce layers. All layers should be extended to frame 165.

A nice shortcut when using layer folders is the ability to extend all included layers at once by extending the layer folder itself. You'll extend the layers within the Background Stuff layer folder using this shortcut.

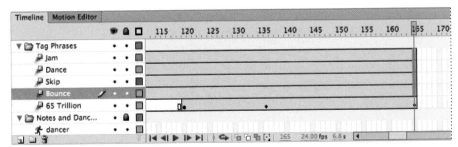

Extend tween layers by adding frames using the F5 shortcut key.

8   On the Timeline, select frame 165 on the Background Stuff layer folder. Press the F5 shortcut key; this extends the included layers (Twirl and Backing Box) so that the background artwork is visible until the end of the scene.

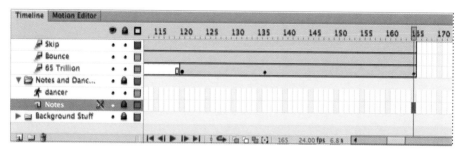

You can extend several layers within a layer folder by adding frames to the layer folder itself.

9   Choose File > Save to save your file.

Rendering and Animating in 3D

Web graphics have advanced a tremendous amount in recent years, with users demanding more than ever before. One aspect of this is the prominent use of 3D graphics across the Web to enhance the overall experience.

The 3D Rotation and 3D Translation tools give designers a way to take two-dimensional artwork and rotate, transform, and animate them in the 3D realm. This opens up the doors for unlimited creative possibilities and stunning effects through the use of movie clip symbols (covered in detail in Lesson 12, "Introducing Movie Clips"), and the 3D Rotation and 3D Translation tools.

Although you haven't yet explored the intricacies of movie clips, keep in mind that at this point, it's simply necessary for an item to exist as a movie clip symbol to take advantage of these 3D tools in Flash. This lesson file gets you started by providing you with several movie clips that you will use.

The 3D Rotation tool

This tool can be used to rotate and transform an object around an x-, y-, and z-axis, rendering 2D objects in the 3D plane. Every aspect of 3D rotation can be included in a motion tween, and modified using the Motion Editor.

The 3D Translation tool

In contrast to the 3D Rotation tool, which rotates movie clips *around* an axis, the 3D Translation tool slides a movie clip *along* a specific axis to change its perceived distance and depth relative to other objects on the Stage. Like the 3D Rotation tool, all aspects of 3D Translation can be tweened.

These two tools can be used together on a single object to add a lot of dimension to your graphics and your tweens.

To add the finishing touches on your skyPod banner, you'll rotate and transform graphics on your Stage using the 3D Rotation and 3D Translation tools, and incorporate those transformations in several new tweens.

1   Locate and unlock the Notes layer (found under the Notes and Dancer layer folder). Right-click (Windows) or Control+click (Mac OS) the first keyframe of the Notes layer and choose Create Motion Tween from the contextual menu that appears.

A new tween span is created on the Notes layer.

2   Move your cursor over the last frame of the new tween span until a double-arrow appears; click and drag to extend the tween span to frame 80.

3   Click on frame 20 of the new tween span to select it. Choose the 3D Rotation tool (⊕) from the Tools panel on the right, and click once to select the ring of musical notes on the Stage. You see a set of handles that resembles a target—these allow you to rotate the selected symbol around the x-, y-, and z-axes (or all at once).

4   Move your pointer carefully over the red beam that appears in the center—you should see a small *x* appear. This handle lets you rotate the symbol around the x-axis—click and drag to the left or right to rotate the symbol around the x-axis. Once you get a feel for this handle, click and drag slightly to the right to achieve the position shown in the figure below. A new keyframe is created at frame 20 to mark the change in rotation.

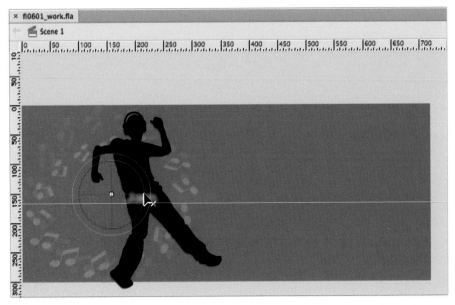

Rotate the symbol around the x-axis on frame 20. The change in position is marked by a new keyframe within the tween span.

5 Click and select frame 40 on the same layer, leaving the 3D Rotation tool active. Locate the blue circular handle that appears in the middle of the symbol; this is your z-axis handle. Click and drag on the handle to the right to rotate the symbol around the z-axis.

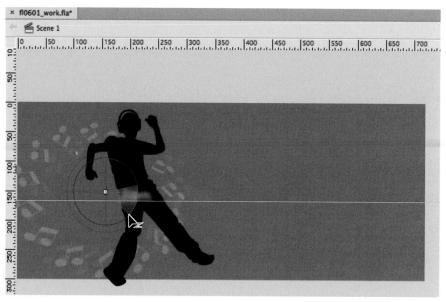

Rotate the symbol around the z-axis on frame 40.

6 Return the playhead back to the beginning of the Timeline (Shift+,) and press Enter (Windows) or Return (Mac OS) to see the tween that has been created so far. The rotations you added on frames 20 and 40 are now tweened from position to position!

7 Click and select frame 60 on the tween span, click and hold down the 3D Rotation tool and choose your 3D Translation tool (⅄) from the menu. Click on the Notes layer, if necessary. The rotation handles on your notes symbol are replaced by three arrows that you'll use to slide your symbol along the x-, y-, or z-axis.

8 Click and drag directly on the head of the red arrow—this moves items along the x-axis. Drag to the right until the notes touch the right edge of the Stage.

9 Click and select frame 80 on the same tween span, leaving the 3D Translation tool active. Click and drag the head of the green arrow, which controls movement along the y-axis. Drag downward until the notes end up in the lower-right corner.

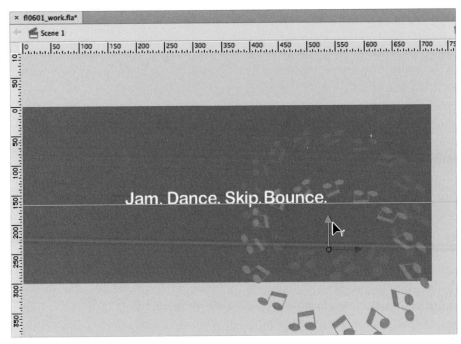

Slide the notes along the z-axis to the lower-right corner as shown.

10 Select frame 165 of the Notes layer, and use the F5 shortcut key to add a frame here—this is simply to extend the contents of this layer to the end of the Timeline.

11 Return your playhead to the beginning of the Timeline (Shift+,) and press Enter (Windows) or Return (Mac OS) to play back the entire tween span on the Notes layer. Your notes should rotate and slide their way to the lower-right corner of the Stage, creating cool depth and 3D effects along the way.

12 Choose File > Save to save your movie.

Fine-Tuning tweens with the Motion Editor

Once you've created a tween, you may want to adjust the degree or timing of how different properties (such as z-axis rotation) animate. The Motion Editor displays a selected tween and all its properties in an intuitive graph, where you can tweak, add, and remove as needed.

You may have noticed that the transformation you created using the 3D Translation tool is active throughout the entire tween span, even though it wasn't applied until around frame 60. Occasional side effects such as these can be easily fixed with the Motion Editor to control when a property changes during a tween span.

1 Click on the Notes layer to make it active and then click on frame 60. Bring the Motion Editor panel forward by clicking its tab.

You can increase the height of the Motion Editor by moving your pointer in between the Stage and the Motion Editor panel—when you see a double-arrow, click and drag upwards to vertically resize the Motion Editor panel. You can also undock the Motion Editor by dragging it out of the panel group by its tab, and resize it from the lower-right corner.

2 Locate and click on the Y row to expand it and view its graph.

Use the scroll bar at the bottom of the Motion Editor to scroll the graph to frame 60. Use the frame ruler shown at the top of the Motion Editor panel for reference.

3 Click the keyframe that appears on the graph line at frame 60 and then move the keyframe up or down to change the Y value at this frame. Watch the Stage to see how your changes affect the appearance of the notes.

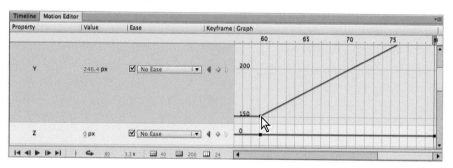

Click and drag a keyframe up or down to change a property's value at that position.

4 Using the vertical scroll bar on the side of the Motion Editor, scroll down and locate the Rotation X row. Click on it (near the title area) to expand it and view its graph.

5 Scroll horizontally until you reach frame 20. Right-click (Windows) or Control+click (Mac OS) and choose Add Keyframe from the context menu to insert a keyframe. Press the Shift key to keep the keyframe from moving left or right, and click and drag the keyframe down to the baseline (0.0) of the Rotation Z row. Then, again holding the Shift key, click and drag it to the right to frame 30. The z rotation now begins at frame 30.

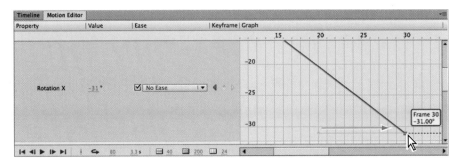

Hold down shift and drag left or right to move a keyframe horizontally without any vertical shift.

6 Bring the Timeline panel forward by clicking its tab, and return the playhead to frame 1. Press Enter (Windows) or Return (Mac OS) to play your movie and see how the edits you made in the Motion Editor have changed your animation on the Stage.

7 Choose File > Save to save your file.

Mastering the Motion Editor: tips and tricks

The Motion Editor is a complex and powerful tool, so it helps to know a few shortcuts to make working with it easier.

Editing Graphs

Hold down Ctrl+click (Windows) or Command+click (Mac OS) on a graph to add a keyframe.

Hold down Ctrl (Windows) or Command (Mac OS) over an existing keyframe to delete it.

Click and drag left or right on a keyframe to change its position (in frames).

Click and drag up or down on a keyframe to change its value.

Changing the Display

Use the three sliders at the bottom of the Motion Editor to change your view of graphs and frames. The icons (in order of display) control Graph Size, Expanded Graph Size, and Viewable Frames.

Undock the Motion Editor by grabbing it by its tab and dragging it out of the panel group at the bottom. You can then resize it by its lower-right corner.

Adding shape tweens and shape hints

To wrap up your banner project, you'll add a basic shape tween to morph a musical note shape into the logo for Pineapple, Inc., the creators of the skyPod device. You explored shape tweens in Lesson 5, "Creating Basic Animation," and you will use the same techniques here. You will also learn shape hinting, a technique for fine-tuning shape tweens.

Before you explore shape hinting, you'll first create a new shape tween on your Timeline using some graphics from your Library panel.

1   Locate and select the Logo layer (it can be found within the Everything Else layer folder on the Timeline). Click the New Layer button to insert a new layer above it. Rename the new layer **Pineapple Inc Logo**.

2   Insert a new, blank keyframe at frame 125 on the new layer using the F7 shortcut key.

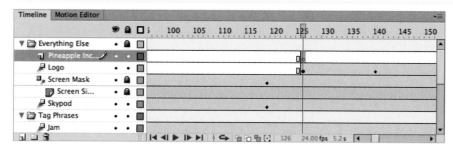

Add a blank keyframe at frame 125 of the new layer to set up for a shape tween.

3   In your Library panel, locate the Shape Tween Art folder and expand it. It contains two graphic symbols that you'll use to build your shape tween. Drag an instance of the skyPod Note graphic to the Stage. Position and center it directly on the screen of the skyPod player that sits on the right side of the Stage.

4   Using your Selection tool (⬧), select the new symbol instance. Choose Modify > Break Apart to break the symbol down to mergeable artwork. This will allow you to include it as part of a shape tween.

Use Modify > Break Apart to convert the symbol instance to basic artwork.
This will make it possible to include the graphics as part of a shape tween.

Shape tweens can't use symbol instances, so in order to use artwork from your library, you need to first break it apart on the Stage by choosing Modify > Break Apart.

5   Select frame 165 of the same layer, and use the F7 shortcut key to insert a new, blank keyframe at this position.

6   In your Library panel, locate the Pineapple Inc. Logo graphic symbol, which is located in the Shape Tween Art folder. Drag an instance of it to the Stage on the new keyframe. As you did with the skyPod Note, position it so it overlaps and centers over the skyPod player screen.

7   Leave the symbol selected, and choose Modify > Break Apart. This breaks the pineapple logo into mergeable artwork so that it can be included in the shape tween you're going to create.

8   Select frame 125 of the current layer. Right-click (Windows) or Control+click (Mac OS) on the selected frame and choose Create Shape Tween from the contextual menu that appears.

A green shaded area and arrow appear between the keyframes, letting you know that a new shape tween has been created.

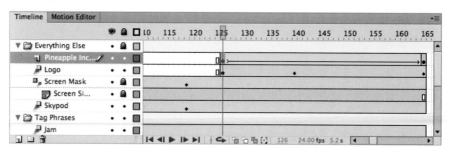

At keyframe 125, create a new shape tween to morph the note into the pineapple.

9   With the playhead positioned at frame 125, press Enter (Windows) or Return (Mac OS) to view the new shape tween. The note now morphs into the pineapple logo!

You may notice that while the shape tween is successful, the transition may not be as smooth as it could be. To perfect this, you'll explore the use of shape hints to finesse the new shape tween.

Creating Shape Hints

Depending on the shapes you choose for your tween, you may find that some transitions are smooth while others need some fine-tuning. For those that need a little help, you can make use of *shape hints*.

Shape hints tell Flash where it can find common points between two seemingly uncommon shapes. To use them, you place a matched set of small markers at important parts of the shapes on the start and end keyframes of a shape tween. The markers tell Flash that the indicated shapes and points are related, and should be preserved through the animation as much as possible. Say, for example, you're morphing a star into a square. You could place shape hints in the upper-right corner of each shape to match those points and keep the transformation as smooth as possible. You can place several shape hints, if necessary, to fine-tune a single shape tween.

Because shape hints are alphabetically labeled, Flash limits you to 26 shape hints per tween.

You'll use shape hints in this exercise to help Flash find common points between the musical note and pineapple logo for a better tween.

1   Select the Zoom tool (Q) from the Tools panel. Click and drag to draw a marquee around the skyPod device on the right side of the Stage. This zooms in so that you can better see the transition between the two shapes.

2   Choose View > Show Shape Hints to make shape hints visible on the Stage. Nothing will appear until you add shape hints.

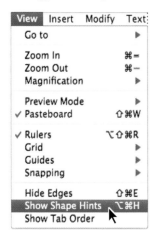

Before making use of shape hints, make sure they are visible by selecting View > Show Shape Hints.

3   Select keyframe 125 of the Pineapple Inc Logo layer. Shape hints must always be added (or removed) from the beginning of a shape tween. Choose Modify > Shape > Add Shape Hint. A new shape hint labeled *a* appears in the center of the note.

4   Click on the shape hint and drag it until it snaps into place at the very top of the musical note. This pins that point in place—you'll now match that point with a similar one on the pineapple shape at the end of the tween.

5   Click to select keyframe 165 (the end of the tween). You see the mate for the shape hint you just created, waiting to be placed. Click and drag the shape hint and snap it into place at the top of the pineapple shape. It should turn green, indicating the pair has been set.

6   Reselect keyframe 125, and choose Modify > Shape > Add Shape Hint. A new shape hint labeled *b* appears on the Stage. Click and drag the shape hint and snap it into place at the end of the note's attached flag.

7   Select frame 165, and locate the matching *b* shape hint. Click and drag it, and snap it into place at the top of the pineapple's right-most leaf.

8 Repeat steps 6 and 7 to add two more shape hints (*c* and *d*), and position them as shown in the figure.

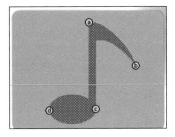 

Position the shape hints on frame 125 (left) and frame 165 (right) as shown.

9 Position the playhead at frame 125, and press Enter (Windows) or Return (Mac OS) to play back your animation. You should see that the new shape hints you added have made a substantial difference in the smoothness and quality of the shape tween.

10 Choose File > Save to save your work.

To remove a shape hint, return to the beginning of the shape tween, right-click (Windows) or Control+click (Mac OS) on a shape hint, and choose Remove Hint from the contextual menu that appears.

Self study

Continue adding shape hints to the same tween you just worked on. Experiment with positioning, adding, and removing shape hints. Use the tips shown in the sidebar to help you get the best possible results. Expand the Dancer layer so that the dancing figure extends to the end of the animation with the other layers.

Hints for successful hinting

Adding shape hints is usually straightforward, but it can get a bit tricky with complex shapes. Follow these tips to create better shape tweens with a little less confusion:

Always enable Snap to Objects (View > Snapping > Snap To Objects). Although you can place shape hints without snapping, it's much more difficult.

Use shape hints in sensible places; although Flash doesn't make associations on its own, it can tell when a shape hint and its counterpart are not matched in a logical way. If the second hint remains red even after you place it, Flash is alerting you to a potential problem.

Avoid shapes that are broken into too many pieces; instead, try to tween between two whole shapes. Although Flash can tween between a single shape and a broken shape, the results are not always what you expect. If you need to tween between two multipart shapes, consider isolating each piece and applying to each its own shape tween.

Use Onion Skin view to assist you in placing shape hints. When you're having a hard time determining exactly what's happening in the course of a shape tween, turn on Onion Skin or Onion Skin Outlines view to follow the action and make better decisions on shape hints.

Sometimes less is more—gradually add shape hints and keep testing your animation as you go. Too many shape hints can sometimes have the reverse effect.

Sometimes it takes a few shape hint passes to get exactly the look you want. Try to fine-tune and complete the note-to-pineapple shape tween by adding some additional hints.

Review

Questions

1   What are three properties of a tween that Copy Motion captures?

2   What type of artwork can be rotated in 3D?

3   Name two useful panels that help you reuse and fine-tune motion tweens.

Answers

1   Position, Scale, and Rotation.

2   Movie clip symbols.

3   The Motion Presets and Motion Editor panels.

Lesson 7

What you'll learn in this lesson:

- Working with guides and the grid

- Creating custom workspaces

- Assigning custom keyboard shortcuts for maximum efficiency

- Fine-tuning with alignment and distribution

Customizing Your Workflow

Those extra few seconds spent hunting for tools or aligning elements can add up. To keep moving smoothly through your project and avoid the distraction of having to locate tools, panels, and menu items, you can customize Flash's interface to your working style. Beyond streamlining its interface, Flash also provides visual aids to help you quickly and accurately place objects on the Stage.

Starting up

Before starting, make sure that your tools and panels are consistent by resetting your workspace. See "Resetting the Flash workspace" in the Starting up section of this book.

You will work with several files from the fl07lessons folder in this lesson. Make sure that you have loaded the fllessons folder onto your hard drive from the supplied DVD. See "Loading lesson files" in the Starting up section of this book.

See Lesson 7 in action!

Use the accompanying video to gain a better understanding of how to use some of the features shown in this lesson. You can find the video tutorial for this lesson on the included DVD.

Customizing workspace layouts

Flash has many different features that enable you to customize your work environment. Although it means spending a little time organizing before you create a document, customizing saves time and headaches later when you're deep in a project. You can strategically place your tools, then save the workspace so the panels you use most often are at hand.

In this lesson, you will learn how to customize the Flash Professional CS6 workspace for a more efficient workflow. You'll also learn how visual aids and keyboard shortcuts can help you work smarter and faster.

Opening the completed file

This exercise involves assembling a small interactive .swf file for a fictional design firm. You'll place logos, text elements, and navigation buttons on the Stage with the help of guides, grids, and the align panel.

1   Launch Flash CS6 Professional, if it is not already open.

2   Choose File> Browse in Bridge to open Adobe Bridge. Use the Folders tab in the upper-left of the Bridge workspace to navigate to the fl07lessons folder that you copied onto your computer. Adobe Bridge is used to navigate and open files in this lesson, but if you prefer, you can choose File > Open.

3   Once you have the fl07lessons folder open, double-click on the file named fl0701_done.fla to open it in Flash. A project file that includes a splash page for a mock design firm appears; you will reproduce this layout in the following exercises.

4   You can keep this file open for reference, or choose File > Close at this time. If asked to save changes, choose No.

5   Choose File > Browse to bring Adobe Bridge to the front. If you are not already viewing the contents of the fl07lessons folder, navigate to it now.

6   Double-click on the fl0701.fla file to open it in Flash.

7   Choose File > Save As. When the Save As dialog box appears, type **fl0701_work.fla** into the Name text field. Navigate to the fl07lessons folder and press Save.

Working with panels

Before getting started choose Workspace > Reset 'Essentials' to reset your workspace and return all panels to their default positions. The right side of the screen contains the Toolbar and two important panels: Library, and Properties. By default, the Property Inspector is in front of the Library. Many of the most common tasks in Flash can be easily achieved with this default layout; however, Flash includes a number of helpful panels that give you more sophisticated options to streamline your workflow.

The Properties and Library panels are open in the default workspace.

Most panels are docked with other panels in the workspace by default. If you have a number of these panels open at the same time, they may become cumbersome to manage. Next you'll explore your options for docking panels in Flash CS6.

1 Choose Window > Color to open the Color panel, which allows you to apply color to fills and strokes of objects in Flash.

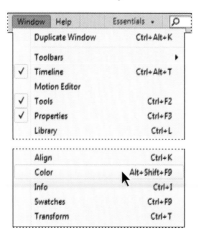

Open the Color panel through the Window menu.

The Color panel is docked with the Swatches panel by default. This prevents you from having both panels open at once, but there are a number of options for repositioning them.

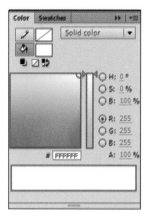

The Color and Swatches panels.

2   Remove the Color panel from the dock by clicking and dragging the Color title bar. Do the same with the Swatches panel to remove it from the dock.

3   Use the dark gray title bar to drag the Swatches to the bottom of the Color panel. When you get close to the bottom of the Color panel you should see the Swatches panel 'snap' into place below the Color panel. This helps you arrange panels in your workspace without overlap or misalignment.

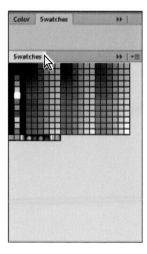

Panels can be separated, positioned and docked back together by dragging them by their title bars.

Collapsing and storing panels

In addition to docking and snapping panels together, Flash CS6 provides a number of flexible options for maximizing screen space. By collapsing panels you can focus on only the features you need at any given moment, but keep within easy reach everything you might need during a session.

1   Double-click on the Color panel's title tab to collapse the panel. This option allows you to maximize vertical space. It's especially useful if you have several panels open at the same time. To expand the panel again, simply double-click the title tab again.

A panel that is docked into an icon bar will not collapse, but will minimize back to an icon in its respective panel group.

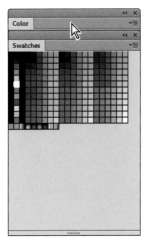

Collapse undocked panels by double-clicking on the gray bar above its title tab.

2   Double-click on the dark gray bar that sits at the top of the Color panel (above its title tab). This collapses the Color panel, as well as the Swatches panel into icon view.

3   Click on each icon to expand and collapse its panel. Notice that only one panel stays open at a time. Once you're familiar with the features of each panel, icon view can be a great way to hide panels when they're not in use.

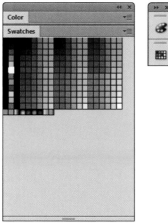

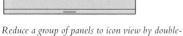

Reduce a group of panels to icon view by double-clicking the bar above its title tab.

4   Click the double arrows at the top of the icon group to re-expand the panels.

5   Using the Color panel's title tab, drag it over the icon bar on the far right of the Stage (from where you originally pulled the color and swatches panels). When you see a blue line indicator at the top of that bar, release it. The Color panel will be redocked and its icon will appear again along with the others.

Redock panels into groups by dragging them back into those groups.

Managing workspaces

Once you arrange a layout that's ideal for your workflow, you can save it as a workspace for future use. You can save as many workspace layouts as you need, customizing them by task, project, or even for use among multiple users. Once you build up a collection of workspaces, Flash also offers controls for managing them.

Let's go ahead and set up your first custom workspace:

1   Choose Window > Workspace > New Workspace.

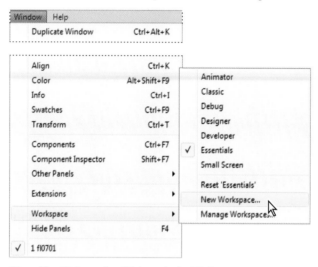

Choose New Workspace from Workspace in the Window menu.

In the resulting dialog box, type **Design Layout** in the Name text field, and press OK.

*Enter **Design Layout** in the New Workspace dialog box.*

2   Choose Window > Workspace > Reset 'Design Layout'. The panels reset to the default Flash workspace layout.

3   To restore your custom workspace, choose Window > Workspace > Design Layout.

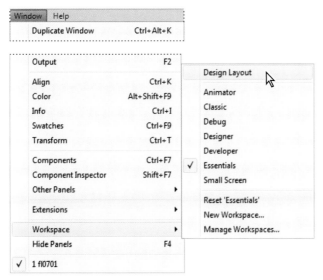

Access your saved workspace through Window > Workspace.

The panels and dock arrangement that you created in the previous exercise is now restored. Having multiple workspaces is very helpful for one person doing different types of projects or for multiple users who use the same machine. If you end up having multiple workspaces, you need a way to manage them.

4   Choose Window > Workspace > Manage Workspaces.

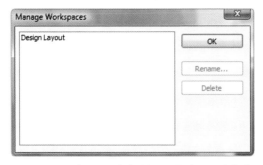

Manage your workspaces with the Manage Workspaces dialog box.

The Manage Workspaces dialog box lists all saved workspaces, including your newly created Design Layout. Even with a single saved layout, you can edit, rename, or delete it from here.

5 Choose the Design Layout and click the Rename button. Rename it **07 Design Layout** and press OK.

6 Press OK again to exit the Manage Workspaces dialog box.

You don't have to go to the menu area to switch workspaces. Click the Workspace drop-down menu on the right side of the main menu bar to see the same options available from Window > Workspace > Manage.

Setting preferences

Sometimes the little things can make the biggest difference in your workflow. Are you tired of seeing the Welcome Screen every time you launch Flash? Would you prefer having more levels of Undo or a different highlight color? You can change these settings, and more, in Flash's Preferences dialog box.

1 Choose Edit > Preferences (Windows) or Flash > Preferences (Mac OS) to open the Preferences dialog box. Select General from the list of categories shown on the left.

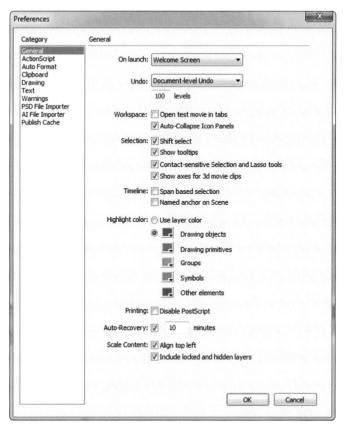

Options available in the General category of the Preferences dialog box.

2 To turn off the Welcome Screen, choose No Document from the On launch drop-down menu. You could also choose to have the application open a new document or even the last document saved.

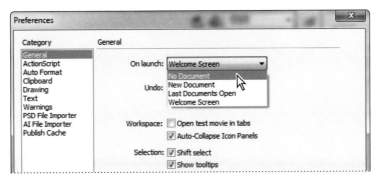

Use the On launch drop-down to turn off the Welcome Screen.

3 In the Undo section of the General preferences, the Undo levels are set to the default of 100. Type **150** in this text field. This increases the number of times you can Undo steps by 50. Flash supports up to 9999 undo levels, but this would likely slow down the performance of your system.

If you change your Undo preferences in the middle of a project, you will lose the history of the work you have done since you started your work session, which means you cannot go back and undo your previous actions. Object undos deal with tracking the separate steps performed on objects like the Stage, or symbols in the Library. Document undos deal with the series of linear actions you made in the current and open document like timeline changes, creating keyframes, and scaling.

4 Farther down in the General Preferences dialog box, you can set your preferred Highlight colors. You can change the default colors used for bounding boxes displayed around drawing objects, groups, or symbols. Click on the color swatch next the Drawing objects option and note that you could choose an alternate color here. Click on the main swatch color to avoid making changes at this time.

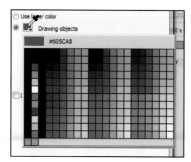

Highlight colors can be customized in the General section of the Preferences dialog box.

If you're a dedicated layer user, click the Use layer color button. This automatically sets bounding boxes to match the color assigned to each layer, so you'll know for sure to which layer a selected object belongs.

5 Press OK to commit the small changes made in this exercise.

Keyboard shortcuts

If customizing your workspace streamlines your workflow, then using keyboard shortcuts adds speed. Flash provides a window for you to view all the keyboard shortcuts in one location. You can do more than just identify shortcuts, however; you can also add, remove, and reassign shortcuts in one location, allowing you to truly customize the way Flash Professional CS6 functions.

Access the Keyboard Shortcuts dialog box.

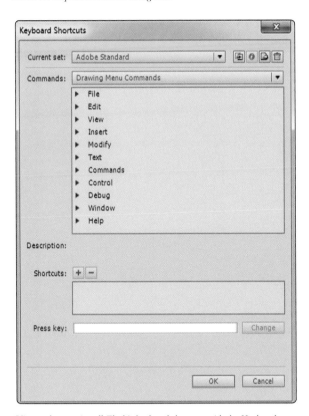

View and customize all Flash's keyboard shortcuts with the Keyboard Shortcuts dialog box.

1 Choose Edit > Keyboard Shortcuts (Windows) or Flash > Keyboard Shortcuts (Mac OS). In the Keyboard Shortcuts dialog box, choose Drawing Menu Commands from the Commands drop-down menu if it is not already selected. Flash displays a list of all the commands specific to the Drawing menu below.

2 Scroll through the commands and locate Modify, then click the arrow to the left to expand the available menu commands. Flash indicates whether or not a keyboard shortcut is assigned to any given command already. In this case, Ctrl+B (Windows) or Command+B (Mac OS) is assigned to Modify > Break Apart. You're going to change this in the upcoming steps.

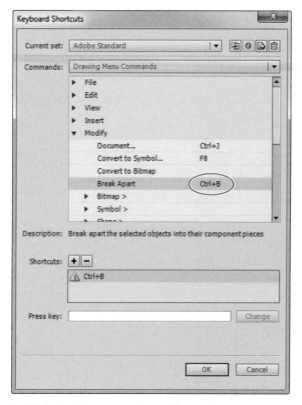

Find the keyboard shortcut assigned to Modify > Break Apart.

3 Before you can customize the shortcuts, you must first make a copy of your current set of shortcuts and save it with a new name. Immediately to the right of the Adobe Standard menu are four buttons. The first button is the Duplicate Set button (⊞). Press this now to duplicate the current keyboard shortcut set.

4   In the Duplicate dialog box, type **Mine** as the name for the duplicate set and press OK.

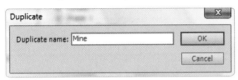

Name your new set of keyboard shortcuts.

5   Your new set, Mine, should appear selected in the Current set menu at the top, but if not, reselect it from the Current set drop-down menu.

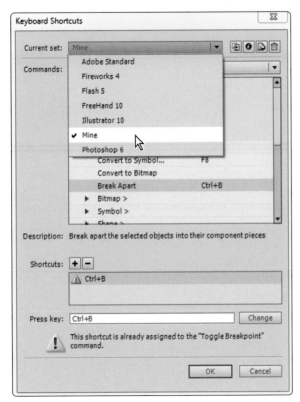

If necessary, select Mine from the Current set menu.

To rename a set of shortcuts, click the Rename Set button (○) in the top-right corner of the Keyboard Shortcuts dialog box. To generate an HTML file listing every shortcut in the program, click the third button, Export Set as HTML, and then save the file to the desktop. You can open the file for reference at any time, or edit it with any standard text editor.

6 After saving the new shortcut set, let's edit the shortcut for Modify > Break Apart. Select the Break Apart command under Modify. Click once inside the Press key field at the bottom of the window to activate the field, and press Ctrl+Shift+9 (Windows) or Command+Shift+9 (Mac OS) on your keyboard.

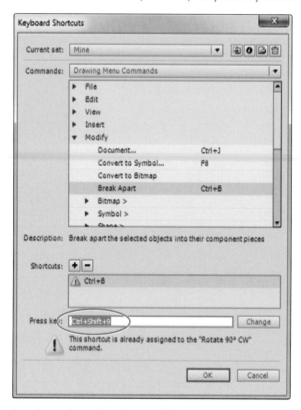

Enter the new shortcut in the Press key field.

The application can determine if the key combination you choose is available. For obvious reasons, you can only have one key combination for any given shortcut. You will now test this by trying different combinations.

7 Click inside the Press key field again and press Ctrl+M (Windows) or Command+M (Mac OS). You will receive no warning, therefore that combination is available. Now press Ctrl+K (Windows) or Command+K (Mac OS). A warning triangle appears, because that combination is the Align command's shortcut.

8 Press the Cancel button; you will not be modifying this keyboard shortcut right now.

To thoroughly customize your shortcuts, export the shortcut list as HTML, print it out, grab a pen, and circle the commands you use frequently. Choose the Shortcuts menu and try running a sequence of command keys until you find one that's usable, assign it to one of your frequently used commands, jot it down on your list, then try again for the next command.

Visual aids for alignment

Flash's visual aids streamline how you work on the Stage, whether it's drawing, placing objects, or aligning items in a layout. Rather than determining locations by eye, or placing graphics through trial and error, you'll take advantage of guides, rulers, grid, guide layers, and advanced alignment tools.

Rulers and guides work together to let the user place an item on the Stage at specific locations, while guide layers change artwork into a device that can be used for alignment and reference purposes. The grid functions much like graph paper, and appears superimposed on the Stage so that you can precisely place objects on the Stage. The Align feature and Flash's various visual aids allow for very precise positioning. To put these visual aids to use and explore their benefits, you'll put together a sample home page for a design firm.

Rulers and guides

Rulers and guides work together to provide more precise placements in less time. Here's how they work.

1   Choose the View menu. If there is a checkmark to the left of the Rulers option, the rulers are currently displayed. If there is no checkmark, select the Rulers option now. When activated, rulers appear on the top and left side of your work area.

Rulers can be toggled on and off from the View menu.

By default, measurements on the rulers are displayed in pixels. You can easily change the unit of measurement in Flash CS6 Professional.

2   Choose Modify > Document, then click on the Ruler units pull–down menu. You have the option to select inches, centimeters, millimeters, points, or pixels. Web pages and web graphics are typically designed using pixels, so select pixels if necessary and press OK.

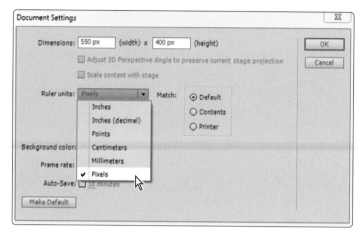

Change measurement units from the Document Settings dialog box.

3   Place your cursor on the horizontal ruler at the top of the Stage and then click and drag downwards. This pulls out a horizontal guideline from the ruler. Drag the guide to the 350-pixel mark displayed on the vertical (left-side) ruler. Click and drag the guide again to fine-tune its position, if necessary.

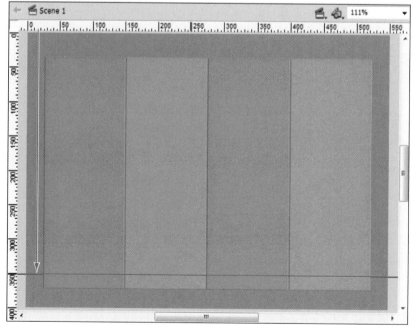

Drag a new guide from the top ruler.

4 Click on the Library tab to bring the Library panel forward, and click on the graphic symbol named logo from the list.

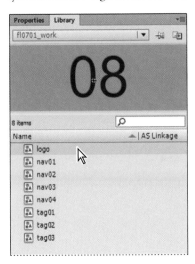

Select the logo graphic symbol.

5 Drag an instance of the logo symbol from the Library panel onto the Stage and drop it above the guide in the first orange column shown on the left. In the exact center of the logo is a small circle. This is the registration point, and you will now align it to the guide.

Drag the logo symbol from the Library.

6 Using the Selection tool (♦), grab the logo by its registration point and drag it downward. When the registration point approaches the guide, it snaps to it.

The symbol's centered registration point snaps to the guide.

So, what if you wanted the bottom of the logo to snap to the guide instead of the center? To do this, you need to edit the registration point. In order to permanently change the registration point of any library item, you need to edit the original symbol.

If you're finding that objects aren't snapping into place as you expected, check to make sure Snapping is enabled for your document. Choose View > Snapping and make sure Snap Align, Snap to Guides, and Snap to Objects are all checked.

7 Double-click on the icon of the logo graphic in the library to edit it in place. Once you are in the item's edit mode, select the text box with the Selection tool (↖).

In the symbol's edit mode, use the Selection tool to select the text box.

The registration mark, shown as a crosshair, appears to be centered, so you'll need to move the content relative to the registration point (the registration point itself cannot be moved).

8 If it's not already visible, choose Window > Align to open the Align panel, and check the Align to stage checkbox at the bottom of the panel. The Align panel's icon should appear on the right in the default "Essentials" workspace.

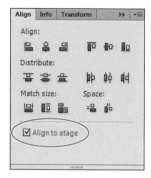

Click the Align to stage checkbox on the Align panel.

The top row of buttons grouped under Align heading are all the alignment choices available to you. Place your cursor over the first button and a box appears, indicating that this is the Align left edge option.

9　Place your cursor on the last button in the Align row, make sure the Align bottom edge box appears, and click once. The text box will move upward and the registration mark is now aligned to the bottom of the text box. Close the Align panel.

By default, the alignment, sizing, and distribution options on the Align panel work by comparing two or more selected objects on the Stage. Selecting the Align to stage checkbox sets the Stage itself as the ultimate point of reference, so results will be very different with this option enabled.

10　Click the Scene 1 link above the Stage to exit the symbol and return to the main Timeline. You'll see that the logo now properly sits with its lower edge resting on the guide. By default, guides always snap to the registration mark of an object.

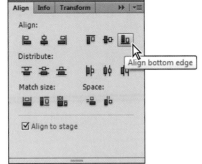

Change the symbol's alignment so that it sits properly on the guide.

If you prefer, you can change the default snapping behavior of guides. Go to View > Snapping > Edit Snapping, and uncheck Snap to Guides to prevent objects from snapping to guides.

Guide layers

Unlike standard layers, the contents of Guide Layers only appear during the design process, and are not published to your final movie

Important information to consider is that objects on guide layers will not export with your final movie; objects on a guide layer are only visible within the authoring environment.

Before you work with guide layers, however, you will first add the content to your current document.

1   Press the Insert Layer button (⊐) at the bottom left of the Timeline. Double-click the
    new layer name to rename it and type **Text**.

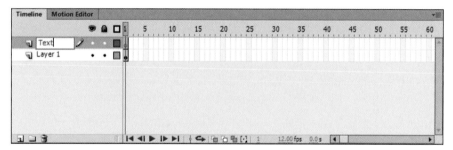

Create a new layer and name it **Text**.

2   Double-click on the existing layer 1 name, and rename this layer **Background**. You
    will now move the logo you added in the previous exercise to the Text layer

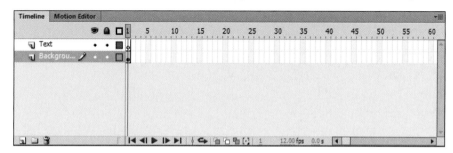

Rename the bottom layer **Background**.

3   Select the *08* logo on the artboard, then choose Edit > Cut.

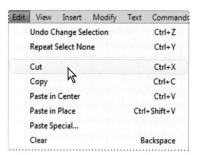

Select the logo and choose Edit > Cut.

4 Select the Text layer, then choose Edit > Paste in Place.

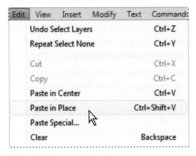

Move the logo to the Text layer.

The logo is placed on the new layer in the exact location it occupied on its original layer.

You are now going to convert the orange Background layer to a guide layer. This will allow you to use the structure of the columns to align the text you will be adding shortly.

5 Click the dot below the padlock column on the Background layer. This locks the orange columns so they can't be moved accidently. You will now remove the guide you added in the previous exercise. Part of the benefit of guide layers is that they remove the need to add multiple guides to your document. Instead of aligning to a guide, you align to an object.

6 Click the guide at the bottom of your document and drag it back to the ruler on the top. It is removed from the page.

7 Right-click (Windows) or Ctrl+click (Mac OS) on the Background layer in the Timeline, and choose Guide.

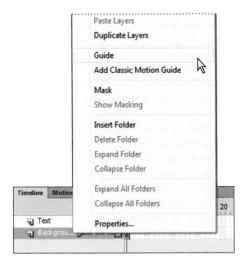

Choose Guide from the Background layer's contextual menu.

The standard layer icon converts to a T-square icon (✎), indicating that this is now a guide layer.

8 On the Text layer, select and drag the logo down to the bottom of the first orange column until the registration point snaps to the bottom of the column.

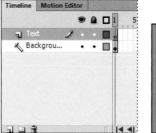

Drag the logo down to the bottom of the orange column.

Sensitivity

You can adjust how close a graphic needs to be to a guide before it snaps by choosing View > Snapping > Edit Snapping.

In the resulting dialog box, you can use the checkboxes at the top to set the type of snapping behavior you'd like to use.

A number of options are available for snapping behavior.

To change the pixel distance, or tolerance, click the Advanced arrow to access the Advanced options. Stage Border is how close the graphic needs to be before it snaps; increase or decrease that number according to your feel for moving elements around the Stage.

The good thing is that you can save these settings by clicking Save Default just under the Cancel button on the top-right side of the dialog box. Your new settings become the standard setting for the entire program; not just the current document.

9 Now you'll continue using the guide layer to position more graphics on the Stage.

Select the Text layer so it's active. Select the nav01 graphic symbol in the Library panel and drag an instance of it onto the Stage within the first orange column on the left. Do the same to place nav02, nav03, and nav04 in the second, third, and fourth columns, respectively.

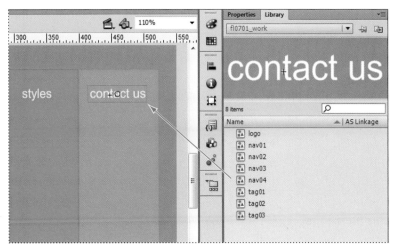

Drag and place the nav symbols onto the Stage.

10 To align the graphics, click and drag each one until its bounding box baseline is on top of its respective column, as shown below.

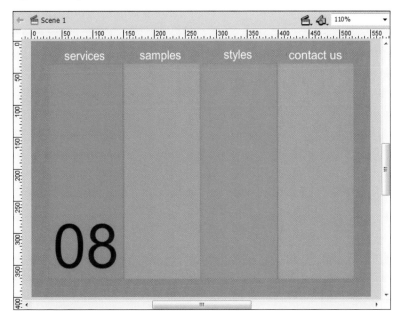

Place the nav symbols above their orange columns.

You will now convert the Background layer back into a standard layer.

11 Right-click (Windows) or Ctrl+Click (Mac OS) on the Background layer and deselect the Guide option. This converts this layer back to a standard layer.

12 Choose File > Save to save your work.

Advanced alignment

Because all four navigation elements are at the top of the columns, you will now properly align them, not just across the columns but also in spatial relation to each other.

1 Select the instance of nav01 (services) on the Stage and make sure it's centered above the column.

You can cycle through and select symbols on the Stage by using the Tab key.

2 Click on the padlock icon (🔒) to the right of the Background layer to unlock it. You will be aligning the navigation to the column and you need to be able to select the column.

3 Shift+click to select the orange column underneath the nav01 symbol instance you already have selected, so that both the symbol instance and the column are selected. Open the Align panel (make sure the Align to stage checkbox is unchecked), then click Align horizontal center to center the nav01 symbol above the column.

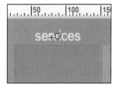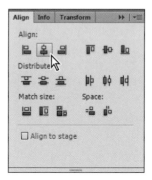

Align the nav symbols with their respective columns.

4 Click on the last navigation element (contact us) and then Shift+click on the column beneath it. Click on the Align horizontal center button in the Align panel to center it.

Now that the first and last navigation elements are aligned with their respective columns, you will work with the Distribute feature. Distribute is designed to evenly distribute the space between objects, and doesn't necessarily have anything to do with alignment.

5 Shift+click the four navigation elements to select them all at once, then click the Distribute horizontal center button. The first and last objects are fixed and the second and third objects are now evenly distributed between them. Each element should be centered over its assigned column.

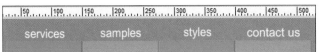

Select and distribute all four nav symbols.

Distribute looks at the registration point, not the bounding boxes, of each graphic. So, when you look at the four graphics, the centered registration marks are evenly distributed.

6 With all four items still selected, click the Space evenly horizontally button (⬚). Notice how nav02 and nav03 shift a bit. It's the space between the bounding boxes, and not the center points, that becomes even. Distribute distributes the center points of graphics, while Space distributes the spacing between the bounding boxes of graphics.

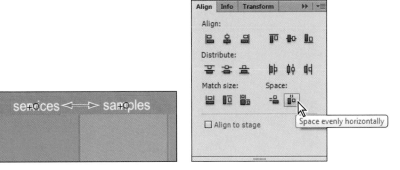

Choose settings that even the spaces between the symbols' bounding boxes.

7 The last few items you need to place on the Stage are the tag graphics. Drag the tag01 symbol from the Library panel to the Stage and position it in the top third of the third column.

8   Click and drag the tag02 text and place it in the third column beneath the tag01 text you just added. Drag tag03 and place it in the middle of the fourth column. You will now be using the Align panel to center these.

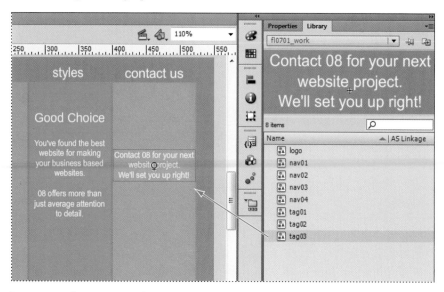

Drag instances of tag01, tag02, and tag03 into the second and third columns.

9   Shift+click tag01 and tag02 to select both graphics, press the Align panel button on the right to open it, then press the Align horizontal center button in the Align panel to center the two graphics. You will now group these two graphics so you can align all the text inside the third column.

10   Choose Modify > Group to group tag01 and tag02 together. Grouping two objects together allows you to align the entire unit within the column.

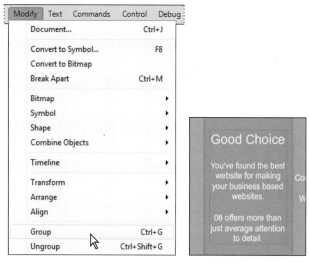

After centering tag01 and tag02, select Group from the Modify menu.

11 Shift+click the third orange column to select both it and the grouped text, then press Align vertical center and Align horizontal center buttons in the Align panel.

12 Click on tag03 in the fourth column and then Shift+click the fourth column to select it as well. In the Align panel, press the Align vertical center button and the Align horizontal center button. Aligning your text in this fashion is much more precise than doing it by hand.

Refining your aligned objects

The devil is always in the details. Although you have been able to align tag03 within its own column, what if you wanted to align the top of the paragraph in column four with the top of the paragraph in column three? You could use a guide, but there is a more efficient method using the align techniques you have been learning.

1 Select the group that contains tag01 and tag02, and choose Modify > Ungroup to ungroup the two symbols. Now you can freely align the tag02 and tag03 symbols without including tag01.

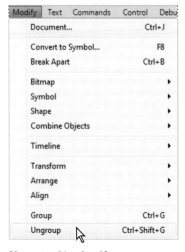

Ungroup tag01 and tag02.

2 Select tag03, then Shift+click tag02 to select both graphics. Press the Align top edge button in the Align panel; tag03 jumps upward to align itself with tag02.

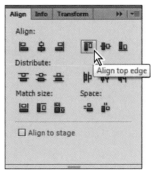

Select tag02 and tag03 and press the Align top edge button in the Align panel.

3 Choose File > Save, then File > Close.

Congratulations! You have finished the lesson.

Grids

If you find that rulers and guides become too time-consuming for you, consider setting up a grid system to assist in placing graphics on the Stage. To turn on the grid behind the Stage, choose View > Grid > Show Grid.

To edit the grid details, such as color or increments, choose View > Grid > Edit Grid.

Grid options can be accessed by choosing View > Grid > Edit Grid.

In the Grid dialog box, you can choose to show or hide the grid, change the grid line color, and adjust snapping accuracy. It can be very frustrating to move a graphic onstage and see it randomly jump to a guide or grid line. Change snapping accuracy to suit your working style, and you'll have fewer surprises during layout.

Self study

Try adding some additional graphics to your movie, and use the Align panel to position them within one of the columns you already have on the Stage.

Set up a new keyboard shortcut set that includes at least three custom shortcuts to help you work faster and better. Become familiar with the keyboard shortcut alternatives to the Align panel located at Modify > Align. If there are a few you use often, it may help to know these when the Align panel is not visible in the workspace.

Review

Questions

1   How do you add or modify keyboard shortcuts to work more efficiently?

2   How can you increase the sensitivity of snapping to guides on the Stage?

3   How do you determine whether Flash tracks object- or document-level changes for the Edit > Undo command?

Answers

1   Go to Edit > Keyboard Shortcuts (Windows) or Flash > Keyboard Shortcuts (Mac OS) and choose an element to make a shortcut from the Commands drop-down menu.

2   You can set the tolerance to be higher or lower from this menu: View > Snapping > Edit Snapping. If you need to change the pixel distance or tolerance, click on the Advanced button.

3   From the Preferences menu, go to the General tab. Change the Undo drop-down menu to either Object or Document.

Lesson 8

What you'll learn in this lesson:

- Importing bitmap images
- Working with layered artwork from Photoshop and Illustrator
- Editing and updating imported artwork
- Working with the Bitmap Properties dialog box
- Converting artwork to symbols on import

Working with Imported Files

Even after you've learned to create vector artwork and text directly in Flash, you may still need a little help from the outside. Fortunately, Flash can import a wide variety of file formats into Flash documents. With this capability, you can create raster and vector images, audio files, and video in other applications, and then import them for use in your movies and applications.

Starting up

Before starting, make sure that your tools and panels are consistent by resetting your workspace. See "Resetting the Flash workspace" in the Starting up section of this book.

You will work with several files from the fl08lessons folder in this lesson. Make sure that you have loaded the fllessons folder onto your hard drive from the supplied DVD. See "Loading lesson files" in the Starting up section of this book.

See Lesson 8 in action!

Use the accompanying video to gain a better understanding of how to use some of the features shown in this lesson. You can find the video tutorial for this lesson on the included DVD.

The project

In this lesson, you will work with a series of bitmap and vector images to practice importing and manipulating external files. First, you'll import a flat bitmap image and learn the techniques for modifying and updating it. Then, you'll move on to artwork in Adobe Photoshop and Illustrator native formats (.psd and .ai, respectively) to take advantage of Flash CS6's import features for these files.

Import formats

One of the strengths of Flash is its ability to import a wide variety of file formats. Flash can read and import a wide variety of common file types, including:

- Adobe Illustrator (.ai)
- Adobe Photoshop (.psd)
- Bitmap (.bmp)
- GIF and animated GIF (.gif)
- JPEG (.jpg)
- PNG (.png)
- Flash Player (.swf)

Adding the QuickTime Player plug-in (a free download for both Windows and Mac OS) adds the ability to import QTIF and TIFF images as well.

- For a full list of supported import (and export) file formats, refer to the Adobe knowledge base article located at *http://kb2.adobe.com/cps/402/kb402701.html*.

Import options

Flash offers four separate commands that enable you to import a variety of external media and control how they are treated once they're in Flash. Import to Stage, Import to Library, Open External Library, and Import Video all perform slightly different, but equally important, operations:

Import to Stage: Automatically places an instance of the imported file on the Flash Stage at the time of import.

Import to Library: Places the imported file in your library and allows you to manually place it onto the Flash Stage.

Open External Library: Allows you to open the library of any Flash file (.fla) and use its assets.

Import Video: Opens the Import Video wizard to walk you through the steps needed to bring your video files into Flash.

If you select a video file while in the Import dialog box for Import to Stage or Import to Library, Flash automatically opens the Import Video dialog box. The option you choose depends on how you want to work with Flash. Some users prefer to import everything into the library at once and then pull the content from there, while others prefer to import assets onto the Stage as they are needed.

Importing still images

Still images, such as photographs, scanned artwork, and graphics created in Photoshop, are some of the most common types of files that users want to bring into Flash. You can choose how to import images, and how you work with them once they are in Flash. Imported bitmap images can even be directly edited in an external application such as Fireworks or Photoshop. The images are then updated automatically without having to be reimported. In the following exercises, you'll explore some of those choices.

Viewing the completed lesson file

1   If you don't already have Flash Professional CS6 open, launch it now.

2   Choose File > Open and locate the file named fl0801_done.fla within the fl08lessons folder that you copied to your desktop. Press Open. This is the completed file that you will make in this lesson.

3   Choose Control > Test Movie > in Flash Professional to preview the final movie. Once you've taken a look, close the preview window and return the Flash CS6.

4   Keep the file open for reference, or close it by choosing File > Close.

Import a bitmap image

One of the easiest ways to import a bitmap image is with the Import to Stage command.

1   Create a new Flash file by choosing File > New, or pressing Ctrl+N (Windows) or
    Command+N (Mac OS). When the New Document dialog box appears, choose
    ActionScript 3.0. Press OK.

2   Select File > Save As. In the Save As dialog box, navigate to the fl08lessons folder, and
    then type **fl0801_work.fla** into the Save As text field. Press Save.

3   Choose File > Import > Import to Stage to open the Import dialog box.

Import to Stage can be found under Import in the File menu.

The keyboard shortcut for Import to Stage is Ctrl+R (Windows) or Command+R (Mac OS).

4   In the Import dialog box, select the fl0801.jpg file from the fl08lessons folder. This is
    a black-and-white version of the final photo you will use as the background for this
    greeting card. Later you'll learn how to swap stand-in graphics for finalized artwork.
    Press Open.

5 Flash detects that the file you are trying to import may be a part of a sequence of images, and displays a dialog box asking if you want to import them all. Press No to import the selected image only.

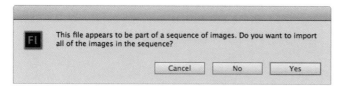

This file appears to be part of a sequence of images. Do you want to import all of the images in the sequence?

Cancel   No   Yes

Flash detects a sequence of images in the folder containing fl0801.jpg.

When using Import to Stage, you can import individual still images or image sequences that have been manually created or exported from video editing and animation programs. If Flash detects that a sequence exists, it gives you the option to import the entire series of images. Flash can then place these images sequentially in consecutive frames on the Timeline.

The imported item appears in your Library panel, and Flash places an instance of it on the Stage.

The library stores .jpg files as well as symbols.

The library doesn't store just symbols. All imported items, whether bitmap graphics, sound files, or video clips, appear in the Library panel.

6   Now that you have your stand-in image in Flash, you can begin to build the e-card around it. The graphic and the Stage are very different sizes, so the first order of business is to change the Stage to match the size of your image. Choose Modify > Document from the main menu. In the resulting Document Settings dialog box, type **600 px** in the (width) text field and **490 px** in the (height) text field. Press OK.

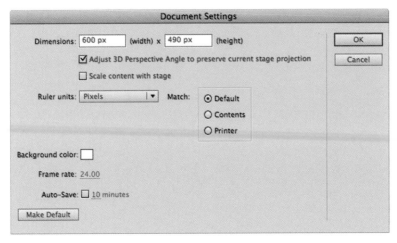

Change the dimensions of your document in the Document Properties dialog box.

7   Your image may not be centered on the Stage. To fix this, select the image with the Selection tool (✸). Choose Window > Align, or press the keyboard shortcut Ctrl+K (Windows) or Command+K (Mac OS), to open the Align panel.

8   Make sure the Align to Stage checkbox is selected and select the Align horizontal center and Align vertical center buttons to center the image on the Stage.

The Align panel allows you to align and distribute artwork on the Stage.

9   Choose File > Save to save your work.

Adding text

1 In the Timeline, double-click on Layer 1 to rename it **background**. It is always a good idea to change the default layer names to more descriptive names that help you identify content at a glance.

2 Click the space under the Lock or Unlock All layers button (⚿) to the right of the background text to lock this layer. This will make moving the rest of the objects you will use in this lesson much easier.

3 With the background layer selected, press the Insert Layer button (⬇) below the Timeline to add a new layer. Double-click on Layer 2 and rename it **text**. This layer is where you will insert and animate the words Happy Halloween for your e-card.

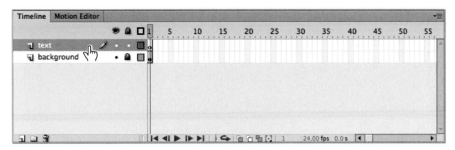

Layers can be renamed by double-clicking them.

The text you'll be using has been formatted, broken apart to a shape, and then saved as a movie clip. Flash provides a number of options for sharing symbols between .fla files. In this case, you'll use the Open External Library feature to access a movie clip that has been saved into the library of another file.

4 In the Timeline, select frame 1 of the text layer. Choose File > Import > Open External Library from the main menu. In the Open as Library dialog box, navigate to the fl0801_library.fla file located in the fl08lessons folder. Choose this file and press Open.

5   Drag the text movie clip from the external library onto the left side of the Stage, as shown below. Afterwards, close the external library by clicking the X in the top-right corner (Windows) or the top-left corner (Mac OS) of the Library panel. It's important to realize that using symbols from an external library copies those symbols into your local library. After you copy them, it's good practice to close the external library to avoid confusion.

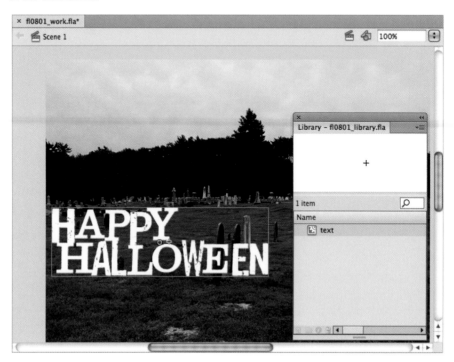

Drag the text movie clip onto the Stage.

6   Choose the Selection tool (⬉) from the Tools panel and select the text movie clip. In the Property Inspector, type **185** in the X text field and **265** in the Y text field to position the text to the left of the Stage.

Next you'll animate the text with a motion tween.

7   Right-click (Windows) or Ctrl+click (Mac OS) the Happy Halloween text movie clip. From the contextual menu, choose Create Motion Tween. The Stage appears to go blank, but try not to panic. Flash adds 23 frames to the text layer when you add a motion tween. You'll adjust this in a moment, and then extend frames on the background layer to make the white text visible again.

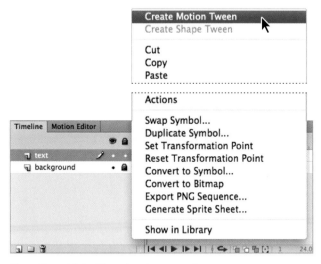

Choose Create Motion Tween from the contextual menu.

 If you can't seem to get the contextual menu when you right-click (Windows)/Ctrl+click (Mac OS) on the text movie clip, make sure you're clicking on the letters. It's easy to click the background through the letters by mistake.

8   In the Timeline, scroll over to frame 120. Click on frame 120 of the text layer and choose Insert > Timeline > Frame to extend the text layer for 120 frames. Select frame 120 of the background layer and choose Insert > Timeline > Frame to extend this layer as well.

9   Now that you've got a little more room on the Timeline, click on frame 1 of the text layer. If you remember from previewing the finished file, this greeting card will feature text that shrinks down and snaps into place at the start of the animation.

10 Click on the Happy Halloween text movie clip. Make sure the Property Inspector is visible, and then make sure the link icon (∞) next to W and H is unlinked. Type **800** in the H field and press Enter (Windows) or Return (Mac OS) to commit the change.

*Make sure the width and height are not locked together, and type **800** in the H field of the Property Inspector.*

11 Move the playhead to frame 15. Click on the Happy Halloween text movie clip on the Stage and then type **20** in the H text field of the Property Inspector.

12 Finally, move the playhead to frame 18, and with the Happy Halloween text movie clip still selected, set the H text field in the Property Inspector to **102.7**, which is the original height of the movie clip.

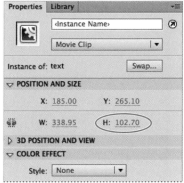
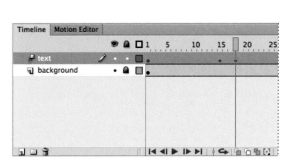

The Timeline after animating the text movie clip.

13 Select File > Save to save your work, then press Ctrl+Enter (Windows) or Command+Return (Mac OS) to preview your animation in the Flash Player.

Swapping out an imported file

The Library panel has the ability to replace one imported image with another. This is a very helpful feature when, for example, you want to use a stand-in image as a placeholder while the final artwork is still being developed.

Now you will swap out the basic image you imported from Photoshop with the image you will use in your final e-card.

1 Click the Library tab to bring the Library panel forward. Select the fl0801.jpg file in your Library panel and click the Properties button (●) at the bottom of the panel.

2 In the Bitmap Properties dialog box that appears, choose Import.

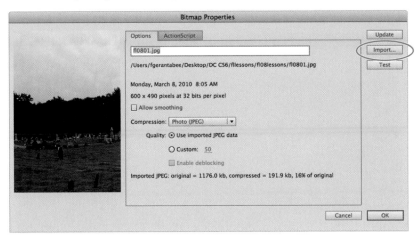

Use the Import button to swap the selected target file for another image.

3 In the Import Bitmap dialog box, select fl0802.jpg from the fl08lessons folder and press Open.

4 In the Bitmap Properties dialog box, press OK. The new image replaces the original fl0801.jpg wherever it occurs in your project.

A color-tinted image replaces the black and white image on the Stage.

5 Choose File > Save to save your work.

Modifying imported artwork

One of the advantages of working in Flash is that you can easily modify imported artwork using an external editor, and have the changes take effect in Flash. When you want to modify imported artwork, Flash gives you the option of opening the external editor directly from the Library panel. In this exercise, you will use Adobe Photoshop CS6. If you do not currently have Photoshop CS6 installed, you can download a trial version from *adobe.com,* or you can skip this step and jump ahead to the next exercise in this lesson.

1 If necessary, open your Library panel by choosing Window > Library. Right-click (Windows) or Ctrl+click (Mac OS) on the fl0801.jpg file shown in the Library panel.

2 From the contextual menu that appears, choose Edit with.

If Flash recognizes that you have Adobe Photoshop installed, then Edit with Photoshop appears above the Edit with option. You can use Adobe Photoshop to edit any standard bitmap image.

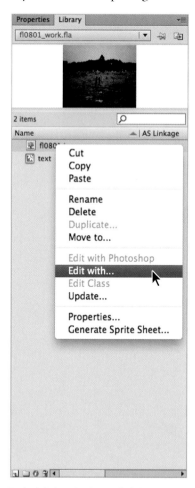

Right-click (Windows) or Ctrl+click (Mac OS)
to use Edit with.

3 If necessary, from the Select External Editor dialog box that appears, navigate to the Photoshop CS6 application and press Open.

Photoshop CS6 allows users to create and manipulate artwork.

Except when using Photoshop, Adobe Flash Professional CS6 requires that you browse for your image editing application each time you want to edit a file.

4 In Photoshop, select Image > Adjustments > Curves to open the Curves dialog box. In Photoshop, curves are used to adjust the shadows, mid-tones, and highlights of an image. You will use curves here to darken the image to make it a little spookier.

5　Place your cursor at the middle point of the diagonal line, then click and drag down to create an arc. As you drag the curve deeper, the image becomes darker. Adjust the curve to your liking, remembering that you want it to look spooky but not so dark that you can no longer make out the image's details. Press OK.

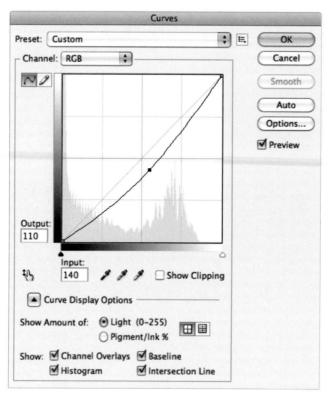

Make the image darker by adjusting the curves as shown here.

6　Select File > Save. If the JPEG Options dialog box appears, click OK to accept the default settings and choose File > Close to close the image. Choose File > Exit to close Photoshop. Return to Flash. Your image has been updated automatically.

7　In Flash, select File > Save. Do not close this file.

Updating imported files

What if you forget to use Edit with, and you simply open Photoshop (or another external editor) and modify previously imported images? You may want to update those files in the Flash library without the time and trouble of reimporting them. Flash offers an easy solution.

1 Select the fl0801.jpg file in the Library panel.

2 Press the Properties button (●) at the bottom of the Library panel to open the Bitmap Properties dialog box.

3 In the Bitmap Properties dialog box, press Update. Changes you made to the imported image outside of Flash now become visible.

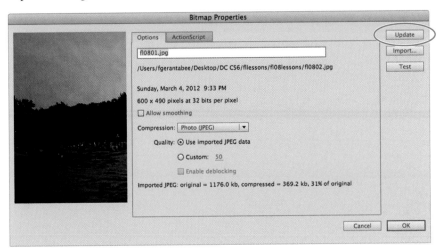

The Update button refreshes images modified in external editors.

4 Press OK to exit the Bitmap Properties dialog box. Keep this file open for the next part of this lesson.

Importing Photoshop files

In addition to importing standard bitmap image formats, Flash offers native import of Photoshop .psd files. This means you can import layered Photoshop files (including full support for Layer Comps), and choose which layers to import and how to treat each one as it's placed in Flash.

Importing a layered Photoshop file

To see how these settings work, import a layered .psd file:

1   With fl0801_work.fla still open, choose File > Import > Import to Library.

2   In the Import to Library dialog box, select fl0803.psd from the fl08lessons folder and press Open. The PSD Import Options dialog box opens.

Photoshop import options

When you import a .psd file, Flash automatically opens the Photoshop Import dialog box, which is divided into two main areas: On the left, you choose which layers to bring into Flash from your Photoshop document (by default, all layers are selected for import). On the right, you set the import options for each layer. When you highlight a layer on the left, its options appear on the right. The layer options are:

Import this image layer as: Specifies whether to import the layer as a flat bitmap image or with layer styles as editable sections of the image.

Create movie clip for this layer: Creates a movie clip symbol from the imported bitmap layer at import, and adds it to your library.

Publish settings: Defines the compression setting with which each bitmap image is published. Flash uses two types of compression: the Lossy setting, which applies JPEG compression, and Lossless, which applies PNG compression. By default, the compression setting is the same setting as in your Flash file's Publish settings.

3   In the PSD Import dialog box, uncheck the checkbox next to the layer named sky_bg. Because you are importing this Photoshop document into a Flash movie, you do not need the background layer.

4   Shift+click on the three remaining layers: moon_highlights, moonshadows, and moon_base.

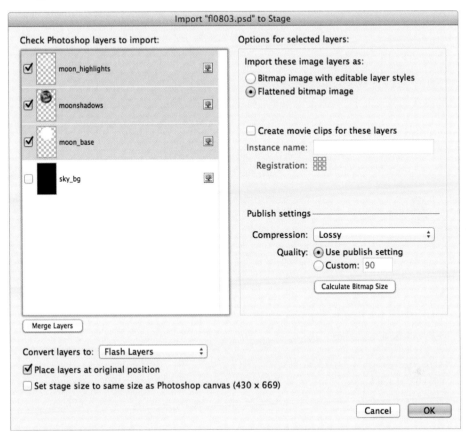

Select all three layers.

5 Click the Merge Layers button at the bottom of the list of layers. This allows Flash to treat all three layers as if they were one. You will use this to create a new movie clip directly from the PSD Import dialog box.

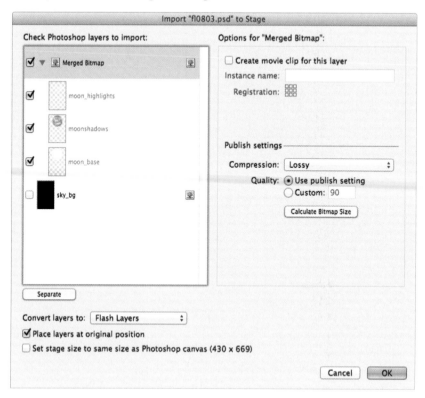

Import "fl0803.psd" to Stage

Check Photoshop layers to import:

☑ ▼ 🖼 Merged Bitmap 🖼

☑   moon_highlights

☑   moonshadows

☑   moon_base

☐   sky_bg 🖼

Options for "Merged Bitmap":

☐ Create movie clip for this layer

Instance name: [   ]

Registration: ⊞

Publish settings ─────────

Compression: [Lossy ↕]

Quality: ⦿ Use publish setting
         ○ Custom: 90

[Calculate Bitmap Size]

[Separate]

Convert layers to: [Flash Layers ↕]

☑ Place layers at original position

☐ Set stage size to same size as Photoshop canvas (430 x 669)

[Cancel] [**OK**]

Merge the top three layers.

Selecting multiple layers is a great way to apply the same operation to all layers at once, or to merge layers into one object within the Flash environment.

6 Double-click on the name of the new Merged Bitmap layer and rename it **Moon**.

7 With the Moon layer selected, select the checkbox next to Create movie clip for this layer. Center the movie clip's registration point. Leave all other settings as you find them, and press OK.

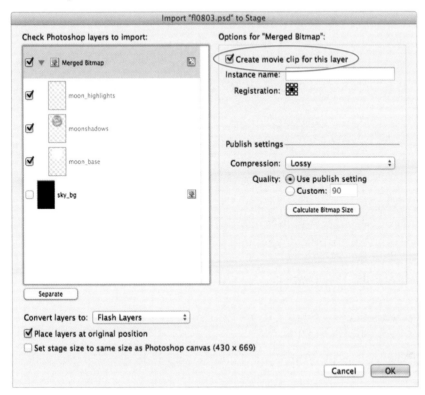

Select the Create movie clip for this layer checkbox and center the registration point.

8 You now have two new items in the library: a graphic symbol named fl0803.psd and a folder named fl0803.psd Assets. The graphic symbol contains all the objects that were in the Photoshop file in their original positions and their relation to each other, while the folder contains the individual imported bitmap layers (located in the Assets sub-folder) and the movie clips created during import.

In the Library panel, double-click on the fl0803.psd Assets folder to open it.

9 Click on the Insert Layer button (⬚) below the Timeline to create a new layer. Double-click on the layer name and rename it **moon**. Select the first frame of the new moon layer.

10 Drag the Moon movie clip symbol from the fl0803.psd Assets folder within the Library panel to the Stage. Do not worry about where you place it; you will deal with that in a few moments.

11 Right-click (Windows) or Control+click (Mac OS) on frame 1 of the moon layer and choose Create Motion Tween from the contextual menu. You'll use this tween to animate a filter applied to the moon.

Working with the Moon

Once a PSD has been placed into Flash, it can be edited like any natively created content. In addition, Flash has a variety of built-in filters that can be used to add style to your artwork.

1 With the Selection tool (➤), select the moon image on the Stage and click on the Properties tab to bring this panel forward.

2 Check to make sure the the Lock width and height values together button on the left of the W and H fields is activated. Type **100** into the W text field and press Enter (Windows) or Return (Mac OS) to reduce the moon to a more reasonable size.

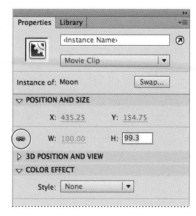

Use the Property Inspector to resize the moon.

3 In the Property Inspector, change the X position of the moon to **530** and the Y position to **65**. This positions it in the upper-right corner of the Stage.

4 With the moon still selected, expand the Display options in the Property Inspector and choose Hard Light from the Blending drop-down menu. You may be familiar with Blend modes from Photoshop. They're very similar in Flash.

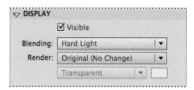

Choose Hard Light from the Blending drop-down menu.

5 With the moon still selected, click the Add Filter button (⊒) at the bottom of the Filters section of the Property Inspector. Choose Glow from the resulting menu. The default red filter is a bit too spooky even for this project. Select white for the color, and set the Blur X and Blur Y values to **100**.

Setting up the glow for the moon graphic in the Filters panel.

6 A glowing moon is nice, but you could have done that in Photoshop just as easily. Fortunately, in the previous exercise, you created a motion tween for this moon. Let's put it to good use in the next step.

7   Choose frame 60 of the moon layer, and click on the moon to access the Filter options in the Property Inspector. Type **250** in the Strength field.

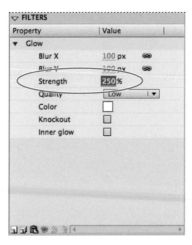

Change the Filter setting to animate the moon's glow.

8   Choose frame 120 of the moon layer, select the moon, and then type **100** in the Strength field you adjusted in the last step. This creates a loop where the glow gets more intense between frames 1 and 60 and then returns to its original strength on frame 120.

9   Choose Control > Test Movie > in Flash Professional to preview your Flash animation, then choose File > Save. The moon animation is subtle, but it's those little things that make your animation seem interesting without being obnoxious. Keep the file open for the next part of this lesson.

Importing Illustrator artwork

As with .psd files, importing and using native Illustrator .ai files in Flash is enhanced with a variety of features to make integration with Illustrator as seamless as possible.

Import options available in the AI Import dialog box give you the flexibility to build your layered projects in Illustrator, and then determine how the artwork on individual layers should be handled on import. In the following part of this lesson, you'll also explore the option of mapping Illustrator layers to keyframes in a movie clip. This can be a powerful option for quickly building frame-by-frame animations.

Let's import an Illustrator file to see these features in action:

1 With fl0801_work.fla still open, select Insert > New Symbol. In the Create New Symbol dialog box, rename the symbol **bat**, and choose Movie Clip from the Type drop-down menu. Press OK.

Create a new symbol named bat.

2 Don't be alarmed by the blank Stage. You may remember from Lesson 5 that creating a new symbol from scratch automatically places you in symbol editing mode for that new symbol. Notice the indication in the Navigation bar.

The Navigation bar indicates that you are editing your new bat movie clip.

3   Choose File > Import > Import to Stage.

4   In the Import dialog box, select fl0804.ai from the fl08lessons folder and press Open.

The AI Import dialog box opens with each layer and sub-layer of your Illustrator document represented. The AI Import dialog box is divided into two main areas. On the left you select the layers or sub-layers you want to import, and on the right you specify the options for how Flash treats each layer.

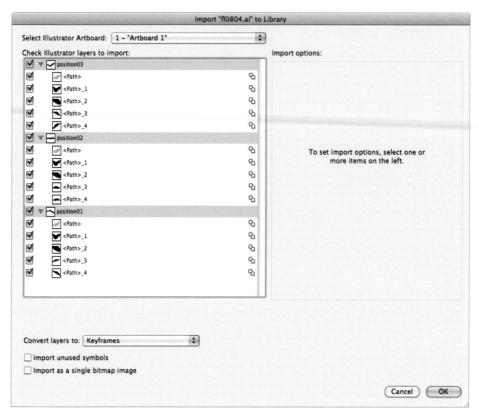

Every layer and sub-layer in your Illustrator file is visible in the Import dialog box.

5   To make viewing more manageable, collapse all the sub-layers by clicking the triangle icon to the left of the following three layer names: position03, position02, and position01.

To easily collapse or expand all layers at once, right-click (Windows) or Ctrl+click (Mac OS) inside the layer view on the left side of the dialog box and choose Collapse All/Expand All from the contextual menu that appears.

6   Select the Illustrator layer named position01. On the right, click the checkbox next to Create movie clip, and choose a centered registration point.

Setting the registration point of a movie clip is very important. The registration point determines how a movie clip is scaled, rotated, or otherwise transformed.

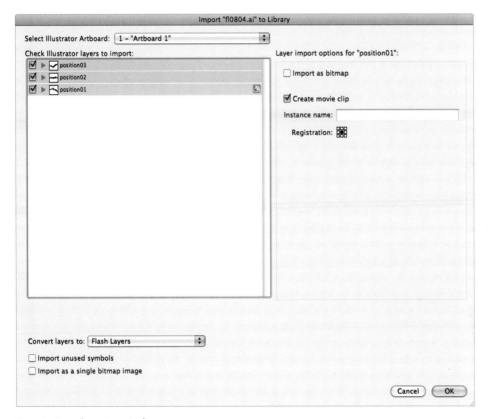

Convert primary layers to movie clips.

7   Repeat step 6 for the layers named position02 and position03.

What's in an instance name?

When you import the contents of a layer as a movie clip, you have the option to specify an instance name. Instance names are used by ActionScript (Flash's built-in scripting language) to programmatically manipulate and animate movie clip instances on the Stage. This name serves as a unique identifier that ActionScript can use to target a specific movie clip instance on the Stage. Instance names for a movie clip instance can be set at any time from the Property Inspector.

8   At the bottom-left area of the dialog box, click on the Convert layers to drop-down menu and choose Keyframes. This imports each individual Illustrator layer as a separate keyframe. Because you used the Import to Stage command here, each keyframe is positioned on your movie clip's Timeline, providing you with a ready-made animation straight from Illustrator.

More Illustrator import options

The AI Import dialog box offers three additional options:

Import as bitmap: Converts vector artwork from Illustrator into a bitmap image on import.

Import as a single bitmap image: Converts all vector Illustrator layers into a single bitmap image on import.

Import unused symbols: Imports any unused objects from the Illustrator symbols panel into Flash.

9   Press OK to import the Illustrator file. The Illustrator layers should now occupy the first three frames of the bat Timeline.

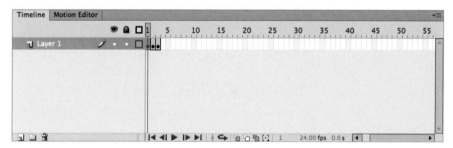

The Timeline now shows three keyframes for each layer added to the Stage.

10 Select the Scene 1 link on the Navigation bar above the Stage to return to the main Timeline. Click on the moon layer, and press the Insert Layer button (⥍) on the Timeline to insert a new layer. Double-click the new layer name and rename it **bat**.

11 Drag an instance of the bat movie clip onto the Stage from the Library panel. Don't worry about the position of the movie clip just yet.

12   Choose File > Save to save your work.

Animating the bat

Movie clips can be animated using basic motion tweens, just as the Happy Halloween text was animated.

1   Select frame 1 of the bat layer. With the Selection tool (k), select the instance of the bat movie clip that is on the Stage. Right-click (Windows) or Ctrl+click (Mac OS) and choose Create motion tween.

2   Bring the Property Inspector forward by clicking on its tab. Make sure that the link next to W and H is set to constrain proportions. Type **200** in the W field to size the bat down.

3   Set the X position to **600** and the Y position to **0**. The bat will start offstage, and then fly onto the scene after the text animation finishes.

4   Hover over the first frame of the bat layer in the Timeline. When your cursor turns into a double-headed arrow, click and drag the beginning of the bat animation to frame 20. Now that you've given the viewer some time to read the text, you can animate the bat.

5   Select frame 60 of the bat layer. Using your Selection tool, drag the bat to the center of the Stage. Switch to the Free Transform tool (⊞) and resize the bat as shown below.

Move the bat to the center of the Stage.

6 Select the Free Transform tool, and hover over the corner of the bat movie clip until the cursor turns into a diagonal two-headed arrow. Hold down the Shift key to constrain proportions and drag toward the center of the bat movie clip to size it down. When the animation is finished, this will give the appearance of the bat flying away from the viewer.

Resize the bat with the Free Transform tool.

7 Select frame 120 of the bat layer. Drag the bat off the Stage, and then size it up with the Free Transform tool as shown below.

Reposition and resize the bat again to complete the animation.

8   Choose File > Save to save your work. Choose Control > Test Movie in Flash Professional to preview your Flash animation. The bat will swoop across the screen. It will appear to fly away from the viewer for the first half of the animation, and toward the viewer during the second half.

If you think the bat is moving a bit more gracefully than bats frequently do, feel free to add a few more positions inside that motion tween. In addition to scaling the bat, the Free Transform tool makes it easy to rotate the bat to put some pretty wacky daredevil flying into your animation.

Congratulations! You have finished the lesson. Choose File > Close.

Self study

Import a variety of bitmap images into your Flash file and then practice replacing and updating them.

Import a Photoshop or Illustrator file into Flash, and practice combining the layers together to create different parts of the image that are editable in different fashions. Experiment with Import to Stage to see how the layer contents can be distributed among Flash layers and keyframes.

Review

Questions

1   What is the advantage of importing layered Photoshop and Illustrator files?

2   What is the advantage of being able to update an imported bitmap image?

3   What are the four options in the Import sub-menu, and what do they do?

Answers

1   Each individual layer of a layered file can be imported as a separate object in Flash. In addition, you can pick and choose which layers you want to import.

2   Updating an imported image allows you to make changes or corrections to the original image without having to reimport it into Flash. When you update an image, all occurrences of that image in your Flash movie are also updated.

3   Import to Stage automatically places an instance of the imported file on the Flash Stage at the time of import. Import to Library places the imported file in your library and allows you to manually place it onto the Flash Stage. Open External Library allows you to open the library of any Flash file (.fla) and use its assets. Import Video opens the Import Video wizard to walk you through the steps needed to bring your video files into Flash.

Lesson 9

What you'll learn in this lesson:

- Exploring the Actions panel
- Getting up-and-running with Script Assist mode and the Code Snippets panel
- Creating stop and goto actions
- Controlling movie clip behavior

Introducing ActionScript

When it's time to do more with your movies, Flash's built-in scripting language, ActionScript, puts you in the driver's seat. In addition to controlling Timelines and enabling buttons for navigation and user controls, ActionScript can handle dynamically generated animation, connectivity to other web applications, and real-time loading and control of images, sound, and video.

Starting up

Before starting, make sure that your tools and panels are consistent by resetting your workspace. See "Resetting the Flash workspace" in the Starting up section of this book.

You will work with several files from the fl09lessons folder in this lesson. Make sure that you have loaded the fllessons folder onto your hard drive from the supplied DVD. See "Loading lesson files" in the Starting up section of this book.

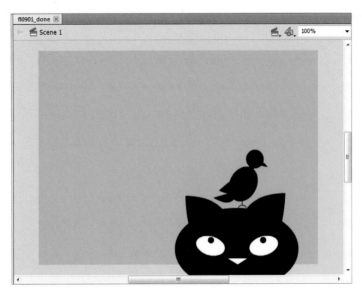

> ### See Lesson 9 in action!
>
> *Use the accompanying video to gain a better understanding of how to use some of the features shown in this lesson. You can find the video tutorial for this lesson on the included DVD.*

The project

You will learn how to stop, play, and loop an animation, using ActionScript to control the Timeline. To view the finished file, Choose File > Open and select the fl0901_done.fla file from within the fl09lessons folder. Choose Control > Test Movie > in Flash Professional to see how the finished movie behaves. Close the preview, and then close the file when you are finished, or keep the original FLA open as a reference if you'd like.

The finished file.

Exploring the lesson file

The lesson file features animation of a bird hopping across the Stage and onto the head of a cat. The scene is rife with tension. The bird animation uses the same techniques you explored in Lessons 5 and 6. In this lesson, you'll be using ActionScript to adjust the flow of this animation by starting and stopping the Timeline. While it would be possible to achieve a similar result with additional movie clips and a more complex Timeline, ActionScript allows you to streamline the process. Also, using ActionScript will increase the flexibility of your finished file and, in certain cases, decrease the size of your published movie.

1   Choose File > Open, and navigate to the fl09lessons folder.

2   Select the file named fl0901.fla and press Open.

3 Before you get started, choose File > Save As, type **fl0901_work.fla** in the Save As text field, navigate to the fl09lessons folder, and press Save.

4 Leave the file open, as you'll be using it in the next exercise.

What is ActionScript?

ActionScript is Flash's built-in scripting language and your way of sending instructions to the Flash Player and exerting more control over your movie. Using Flash's Actions panel, you can create and place lines of ActionScript code (often referred to as *actions*), in keyframes on the Timeline, or in external files. This code is interpreted and carried out by the Flash Player during playback. If the idea of typing code seems a little overwhelming, don't worry; you can use the Actions panel's Script Assist mode or the handy Code Snippets panel to help you create your first lines of code.

At its most basic level, ActionScript can control the playhead to fine-tune the behavior of animations or enable user controls for navigation of the Timeline (such as Stop and Play buttons). Beyond this, ActionScript is a powerful language that can manage virtually any object or piece of information in (and in certain cases, out of) your movie. It can even retrieve and display real-time data from databases, files, and web services.

Which version of ActionScript should you use?

Since you can work with several versions of ActionScript in Flash, the first step is sometimes deciding which version to use. Flash comes with both ActionScript 3.0, the latest version (and recommended), and 2.0, the previous version which was used predominantly with Flash Player versions 8 and earlier. You are also able to publish much older movies with ActionScript 1.0, but this is no longer recommended unless there's a good reason to do so.

The Flash Player continues to run ActionScript 2.0 and 3.0 side-by-side using two virtual machines (VM1 and VM2), with one dedicated to each version. At the time of this writing, ActionScript 2.0 is still in use (although much less frequently) and continues to be supported in both Flash CS6 and Flash Player 11. Version 3.0, however, not only adds many features and improvements in speed and performance but is considered the preferred standard for most movies.

ActionScript 3.0 is built upon object-oriented programming (OOP) concepts that make it modular and performance-oriented, which is essential for building large-scale Flash applications. In this book, you'll be working exclusively with ActionScript 3.0. It's important to note that if you are publishing to Flash Player 8 or earlier, you cannot use ActionScript 3.0.

If you are unsure which version to use, it's recommended that you stick with ActionScript 3.0. However, make sure that your project has no special requirements that would require you to publish for a much earlier version of Flash Player. Versions of Flash Player earlier than 9.0 do not support ActionScript 3.0.

Where Do I Place ActionScript?

ActionScript is placed on keyframes along the timeline using the Actions Panel or the Code Snippets panel. Just as you would create a keyframe and place graphical content on it, you can add ActionScript code to a keyframe to have your movie do something at a specific point along the timeline.

In some more advanced and complex scenarios, you can also place ActionScript in external files that can be then referenced from your movie. Older versions of ActionScript (2.0 and earlier) also support placing ActionScript directly on symbol instances (although this widely considered to be a bad practice). For all the exercises in this lesson, you'll be placing ActionScript along the timeline as ActionScript 3.0 requires.

The Code Snippets Panel

While the capabilities of ActionScript are something every Flash designer should take advantage of, there is often a learning curve associated with any coding language, especially if you have limited scripting or interactive design experience. Flash CS6 helps to get you up-and-running quickly with the Code Snippets panel, which gives you one-click access to pre-created code blocks that handle everything from timeline navigation and animation tasks to loading and controlling audio and video.

These code snippets can be easily added to the timeline, saving you time as well as the need to create code by hand. You'll learn how to use the Code Snippets panel later in this lesson, and use it again in later lessons to help accelerate some common coding tasks. As you become more experienced with ActionScript, you can even add Code Snippets of your own.

An important note about Publish settings

You must adjust the ActionScript version as part of your Publish settings to match your preferred version of ActionScript.

1   Make sure that no objects on the Stage are selected, and choose File > Publish Settings.

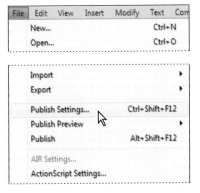
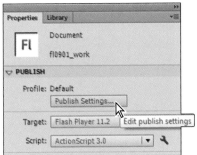

Access your Publish settings through the File menu or Property Inspector.

2 From the Script drop-down in the top right corner, make sure that ActionScript 3.0 is selected and press OK.

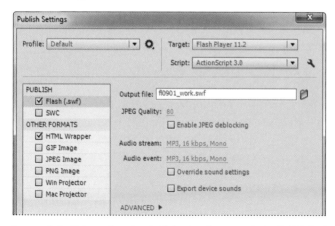

Set your ActionScript version using the Script drop-down menu in the Publish Settings panel.

You can also access the Script drop-down menu from the Property Inspector when nothing on the Stage is selected.

The Actions panel at work

The Actions panel is a script wizard, text editor, and code-checker, all in one. To open the Actions panel, choose Window > Actions, or press F9 (Windows) or Option+F9 (Mac OS). Note: On many laptops, you will need to add the function (fn) key: Fn+Option+F9.

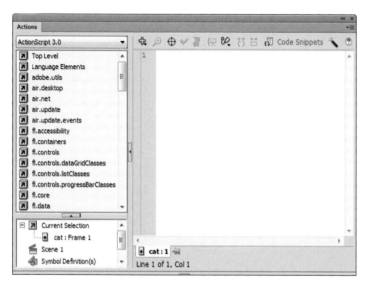

Open the Actions panel by choosing Window > Actions.

Here you build scripts (groups of actions) and place them in your movie. You can type scripts directly into the panel, choose scripts from drop-down menus, or use the Actions toolbox, which is a categorized menu of actions on the left side of the panel. To use the toolbox, double-click the script or click and drag it to the window on the right. You can use actions from the toolbox and drop-down menu in either standard or Script Assist mode.

Standard (default) script editing mode

By default, the Actions panel opens up in a standard editing mode that lets you type freely in the Script window on the right. In this mode, you can still insert scripts from the Actions toolbox on the left, or by using the Add a new item to the script button (⊕) at the top. This mode is generally recommended for users who are more experienced with ActionScript or comfortable with typing code in general.

Using Script Assist

For the novice user, the thought of dealing with a new scripting language can be overwhelming. Because ActionScript is very sensitive to both case and spelling, trying to type code freely before you're comfortable with the language can result in errors. To spend more time working and less time troubleshooting, try the drop-down menus or the Actions toolbox in Script Assist mode, which function together like a wizard that lets you pick, modify, and apply scripts without the need to type directly into the script window. After choosing your ready-made actions, you can tweak them with a series of form and menu controls at the top of the Actions panel.

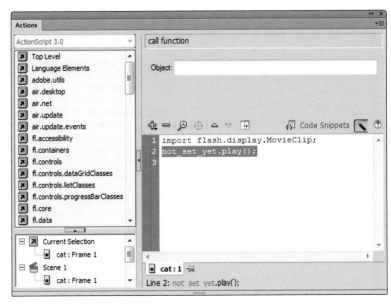

Script Assist mode lets you modify scripts with menus and type-in boxes.

Adding and removing actions

You can enter Script Assist mode at any time by pressing the Script Assist button in the upper-right corner of the Actions Panel. When in Script Assist mode, clicking Add a new item to the script button (⊕) at the top of the script window adds actions, and clicking Delete the selected action(s) button (⊖) removes them. If you need to reorder scripts, use the Move the selected action(s) up (▲) and Move the selected action(s) down (▼) buttons. You'll learn more about this mode later in this lesson.

As you highlight lines of code in the script window, menus will appear at the top of the Actions panel that let you adjust and set options for the selected action.

Adding actions to frames with the Code Snippets Panel

With a firm grasp of ActionScript fundamentals, you're ready to do some real work on the project. In this exercise, you'll use ActionScript to prevent the animation from looping, which is the default behavior of the Flash Player. Since you are most likely new to ActionScript, you'll get up-and-running quickly using the new Code Snippets panel to handle the heavy lifting for you.

Adding a stop() action

To stop a Timeline at a specific point, or prevent an animation from looping when it reaches the end, you use the stop() action. A stop() action halts playback at the frame upon which you place it. When you test, preview, or publish a movie, the default behavior of the Flash Player is to loop playback; stop() actions override that behavior to ensure that the movie doesn't loop unnecessarily.

1   If it's not already open, choose File > Open and open the file named fl0901_work.fla, which you saved earlier.

Although you aren't required to place actions on their own layer, it's a good practice to help avoid accidentally selecting a script versus an object on the Stage (and vice versa). Common practice is to keep a layer named actions at the top of the layer stack.

2   Select the cat layer in the Timeline, and click the New Layer button (⌐) to add a new layer above this one. Double-click on the layer name and type **actions** to rename the layer. It's considered a good practice to create a dedicated layer just for ActionScript.

3   Test the movie using Control > Test Movie > in Flash Professional. Notice that the animation continues to loop back to the beginning. Let's change that.

4 Like any object on the Stage, actions can be placed on keyframes only. Select frame 42 on the new Actions layer, and create a new keyframe by pressing the F6 shortcut key.

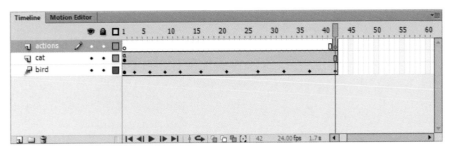

As a matter of good practice, always create a dedicated layer for your ActionScript.

5 Select the new keyframe, and open the Code Snippets panel by pressing the Code Snippets button ( ) on the right side of your workspace or by choosing Window > Code Snippets.

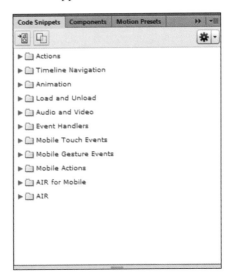

Once you've created a new keyframe, open the Code Snippets panel.

6   Within the Code Snippets panel, you'll see snippets organized into several named folders. Locate and double-click the Timeline Navigation folder to expand it. Locate the snippet named Stop At This Frame, and double-click it.

The Actions Panel will launch, and the code from the selected snippet will be automatically added to Actions Panel at this keyframe. You should see a comment with some descriptive text and the statement `stop()`; directly below it.

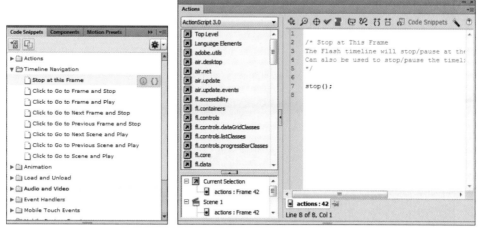

Placing a `stop()` *action using the Stop At This Frame code snippet.*

You may notice descriptive text in the Actions panel above or below certain lines of code. These are referred to as comments and are flanked by the characters /* and */ to separate them from real code and prevent them from being interpreted. You can use comments to annotate your code and describe its purpose and functionality.

7   Close the Actions panel and look at the frame. The icon that looks like a lowercase *a* indicates that the frame contains actions that will run when the playhead passes it during playback.

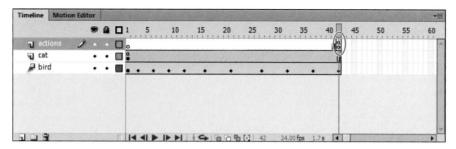

The lowercase a icon indicates that actions exist on frame 42.

8 Test your movie by choosing Control > Test Movie > in Flash Professional. The animation should play and stop abruptly at frame 42, exactly where you placed the action. The bird hops across the Stage and then perches on the cat. Close the preview.

9 Choose File > Save to save your work.

Placing a goto action using the Actions Panel

To make the playhead jump forward or backward to a specific frame, turn to the *goto* actions. The two variations—gotoAndStop() and gotoAndPlay()—jump to a specific frame, then stop playback and resume playback from that point, respectively. In this exercise, you'll explore these actions and get a little practice adding and subtracting actions.

This time, you'll be using the Actions Panel, and more specifically the Script Assist, which will help you build actions without hand-typing any code. This is a slightly different approach from the Code Snippets panel in the sense that you'll be building your own actions rather than using pre-created ones.

1 Select frame 42 on your Actions layer, and launch the Actions panel (Window > Actions). You must first remove the stop() action and comment created by the Code Snippets panel.

2 When the Actions Panel appears, press the Script Assist button in the upper-right corner. The top of the Actions Panel expands to indicate that you are in Script Assist mode.

3 Click in the Script window to select the comment above the stop() action. Click the Delete the selected action(s) button (⊖) to delete the comment. Click the button twice more to remove the last two lines remaining in the Actions panel, including the stop(); action, until the Script window is clear.

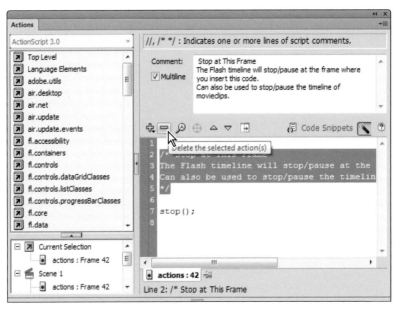

Remove comments and stop() *action on frame 42.*

4   Keep the Actions panel open. Press the Add a new item to the script button (⊕) and choose flash.display > MovieClip > Methods > gotoAndStop. You may notice that `gotoAndStop()` and `stop()` are found in the same location. These are both methods of the MovieClip class. It's not too important to know exactly what that means, but simply put, it means that MovieClips can do things like stop, play, and go to specified points on their Timelines. Because ActionScript 3.0 is an object-oriented programming language, all the actions you add will be found grouped with the objects they relate to.

If you would like to further your knowledge of the key differences and new features in ActionScript 3.0, check out the articles and tutorials on Adobe's Developer Network site at adobe.com/devnet/.

5   In the Object text field, type **this**. Just like the `stop()` action from earlier, the this keyword tells Flash which Timeline you are referring to. A little later, you'll see how useful this field can be.

6   Right below the Object text field, type **20** in the frame text field. ActionScript is very logical. If you're telling the Timeline to go somewhere and stop, you have to tell it where to go and stop. You can use frame numbers, or add labels to your frames. Close the Actions panel.

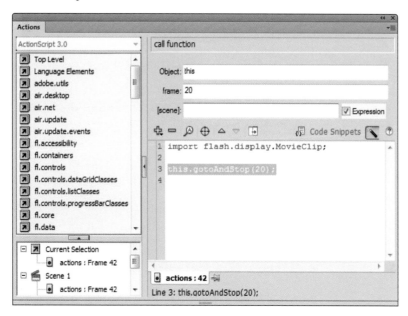

Your script window with the `gotoAndStop()` *action added.*

7   Choose Control > Test Movie > in Flash Professional to preview your movie. The bird jumps onto the cat's head and then quickly changes his mind and jumps back to a safe distance. Close the preview.

8   Choose File > Save and keep this document open for the next section.

Definition: Parameters

You may see the word *Parameters* a lot in the Actions panel. Parameters are additional pieces of information you feed to ActionScript functions to make them work. For instance, `gotoAndPlay()` requires you to specify a frame number, a parameter it uses to complete its task. Many functions in ActionScript take parameters, some that are required and some that are optional.

You enter parameters for selected actions using the menus and type-in fields that appear at the top of the Actions panel in Script Assist mode.

Controlling Movie Clip Timelines

1   Open the Actions panel by choosing Window > Actions from the main menu. Click on frame 42 of the Actions layer to make sure you're adding actions to this frame. The `gotoAndStop()` action you added in the last section should still be hanging around here.

You may remember from the finished file that this animation will feature an intense and indefinite standoff between cat and bird. Let's swap out that `gotoAndStop()` action with a simple `stop()` action and then move on to some finer points of this animation.

2   Press the Delete the selected action(s) button twice to clear out the actions panel. Now click the Add a new item to the script button and choose flash.display > MovieClip > Methods > stop. Hopefully this enigmatic menu is getting a bit more familiar at this point. You'll use it pretty frequently.

3   Type **this** in the Object text field. The Actions panel should look like the figure below when complete. Close the Actions panels when you are done.

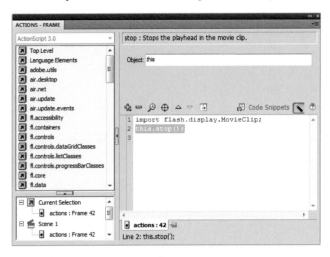

Swap out the `gotoAndStop()` *action for a* `stop()` *action.*

4   You may not have noticed, but the bird and cat are twitching and blinking respectively throughout the movie. It may be nice to hold off these movements until the bird has alighted atop the cat. You can stop and play the bird and cat Eye timelines the same way you stop and play the main timeline. But first you'll need a way to refer to each of these objects.

5   Using the Selection tool (↖), click on the bird Movie Clip on the Stage. Click on the Properties tab to make sure the Property Inspector is accessible.

The Actions panel often interferes with your access of objects on the Stage. Refer to Lesson 7 for tips on managing your workspace. Most Flash users who rely heavily on scripting create custom workspaces to help manage this sometimes cumbersome panel.

6   At the very top of the Property Inspector, type **bird_mc** in the Instance Name text field. Instance names are the way you refer to objects like Movie Clips and Buttons on the Stage. Remember that there can be multiple instances of these symbols in a movie. This is how you can tell one apart from another. Instance names are very important for writing ActionScript, in fact, you won't get very far without them.

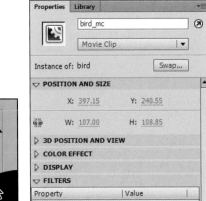

*Select the bird Movie Clip and give it the instance name **bird_mc**.*

7   Select Frame 1 of the Actions layer. If you closed the Actions panel to see the bird better, open it back up by choosing Window > Actions. Click on the Add a new item to the script button (⊕) and choose flash.display > MovieClip > Methods > stop.

In the Object text field, type **bird_mc**. In this case you're not stopping the main timeline, you're stopping the bird timeline. For more information on Movie Clips and managing their timelines, refer to Lesson 12, "Introducing Movie Clips."

8   Choose Control > Test Movie > in Flash Professional. The bird no longer twitches. In the next section, you'll start the twitching animation at the end of the hopping animation on the main Timeline; first, get some practice by stopping the eye animation. In this case there are two eyes, so you'll have to do it twice.

9 Click on the cat's left eye and type **leye_mc** in the Instance Name text field of the Property Inspector. Then click on the cat's right eye and type **reye_mc** in the Instance Name text field of the Property Inspector.

10 Click the first frame of the actions layer. In the Actions panel, click the Add new item to the script button and choose flash.display > MovieClip > Methods > stop. Type **leye_mc** in the Object text field. Press Enter (Windows) or Return (Mac OS).

11 Click on the code section first to exit the cursor from the Object text field. Click the Add new item to the script button and once again choose flash.display > MovieClip > Methods > stop. This time, type **reye_mc** in the Object text field.

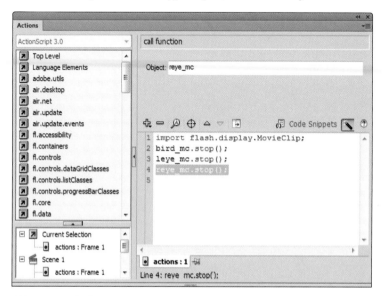

Add stop actions for the cat's eyes.

12 Choose File > Save, and then Control > Test Movie > in Flash Professional to see the results. The twitching and blinking should be all in the past.

Functions

In the next section, you'll use ActionScript to trigger the bird and eye animations after the bird hops onto the cat's head. There are a number of ways to make this happen, but in this case, you'll explore creating a reusable function to take care of this task.

Functions are one of a handful of elements that are common to almost every programming language. They allow you to group a number of statements together and then run them when needed. Imagine teaching someone how to change the toner in a copy machine. There are probably a handful of steps that never really change. Instead of posting your telephone number on the copier and walking people through the process every time it needs to be done, you could write up a set of instructions that they could follow on their own. The key to this concept is reusability. It may take a bit longer at the onset, but it will save you a lot of time in the long run.

In this exercise, you'll be removing the safety net by disabling the Script Assist, and coding this task entirely by hand. It's important to remember to follow the instructions carefully, and be conscious of case and spelling (ActionScript is pretty touchy about those things!).

1   Make sure the Actions panel is open with frame 1 of the Actions layer selected. You should see the actions you added in the last section. For this section, you'll turn off Script Assist and get your feet wet with a little hand coding. Don't worry, it won't hurt that much. You might even find it a bit easier than wading through the menus in Script Assist.

2   Click on the Script Assist button to turn off Script Assist. Writing in the ActionScript panel is just like writing in a text editor.

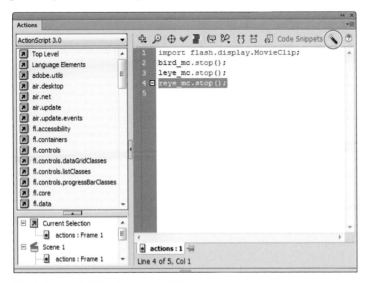

The Actions panel with Script Assist disabled.

3   Click at the end of line 4, after the semi-colon, and press Enter (Windows) or Return (Mac OS) twice. With the cursor blinking on line 6, type:

```
function playClips(){

}
```

Be sure to include the space between function and playClips, the opening and closing parenthesis characters after playClips, and the opening and closing curly braces after the parentheses.

```
import flash.display.MovieClip;
bird_mc.stop();
leye_mc.stop();
reye_mc.stop();

function playClips() {

}
```

Add a function named `playClips` *in the Actions panel.*

4 Place the cursor at the end of line 6 and press Enter (Windows) or Return (Mac OS). Your cursor should be blinking and indented on line 7. Indenting the code inside functions is helpful for reading it later. Type the following lines to make the bird twitch and the cat's eyes blink:

```
bird_mc.play();
leye_mc.play();
reye_mc.play();
```

The Actions panel should look like the figure below when you're finished.

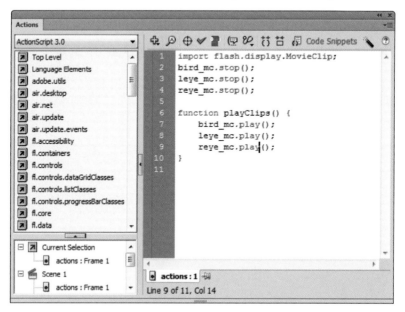

Add three statements inside the new playClips function.

Curly braces define the beginning and end of one or more lines of grouped, or related code. The placement of curly braces on the same or following line after a function name is up to you, and is more a personal decision than anything. The code will work exactly the same regardless of whether you choose to keep curly braces and code on the same line or on dedicated lines, but in some cases spreading them out may result in more readable code.

5   Choose File > Save and then Control > Test Movie > in Flash Professional. It's a bit anticlimactic, but nothing has changed. This is an important lesson about functions. They must be called in order to run. Going back to the copy machine analogy, the instructions for changing toner only get used when the toner needs changing. In this case, you'll call the playClips function when you want the clips to play.

6   Click on frame 42 of the Actions layer. Place your cursor at the end of line 2 in the Actions panel and press Enter (Windows) or Return (Mac OS) twice to get to line 4. Type the following line:

```
playClips();
```

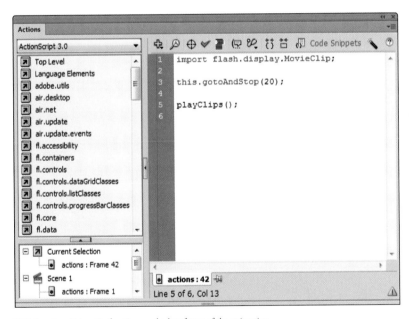

Call the playClips() function on the last frame of the animation.

Calling a function isn't so hard. Choose Control > Test Movie > in Flash Professional to see the fruits of your labor. The bird hops onto the cat's head and then they proceed to blink and twitch, caught in the immemorial struggle between the two noble species.

7   Choose File > Save, then File > Close.

Congratulations! You have finished the lesson.

Wrapping up

ActionScript offers a world of possibilities. Lesson 10, "Creating Navigation Controls," demonstrates how you can apply ActionScript to buttons to create controls and navigation. There you'll learn the power of another ActionScript staple: event listeners, and event handlers. Event handlers are specific functions that tell your movie what to do in response to a button or keyboard action. Because a button can be clicked, rolled over, released, or pressed and held down, event listeners help the button sort out when to perform which action, whether it's jumping to a frame on the Timeline, stopping playback, or launching a website in a browser window. Unlike frame-based actions, button-based actions can occur at any time, or not at all, based on what the user chooses to do.

Self study

Create a new, blank Flash file by choosing File > New > Flash File (ActionScript 3.0). Create a basic motion tween on the Timeline using a graphic of your choice. Add actions on the last frame to stop, loop, and play your movie from different locations on the Timeline. Create at least two different keyframes along the Timeline and assign the frame labels. Modify your ActionScript on the last frame to jump to and play from these points using `gotoAndPlay()`.

Review

Questions

1   On what items can actions be placed in ActionScript?

2   Which action is used to jump to a specific frame and stop playback?

3   What menu command should you use to preview actions applied to your movie?

Answers

1   In ActionScript 3.0, scripts can be placed on keyframes on the Timeline or in external files.

2   `gotoAndStop()`.

3   Control > Test Movie.

What you'll learn in this lesson:

- Creating buttons that change during user interaction

- Using buttons to navigate between frames

- Using buttons to control the movie playback

- Linking to an external website

Creating Navigation Controls

Flash is a great tool for creating highly interactive navigation controls for websites, applications, banners and just about any type of interactive project. Button symbols let you put your users in control when viewing your movies or web pages. In this lesson, you'll learn how to create button symbols and utilize them for full control of your movies. You'll also learn some new ActionScript code to get your buttons up-and-running right away.

Starting up

Before starting, make sure that your tools and panels are consistent by resetting your preferences. See "Resetting the Flash workspace" in the Starting up section of this book.

You will work with several files from the fl10lessons folder in this lesson. Make sure that you have loaded the fllessons folder onto your hard drive from the supplied DVD. See "Loading lesson files" in the Starting up section of this book.

See Lesson 10 in action!

Use the accompanying video to gain a better understanding of how to use some of the features shown in this lesson. You can find the video tutorial for this lesson on the included DVD.

The project

In this lesson, you'll be designing a mini-site project for the talkShop retail cellphone store. You'll build a few buttons, then link them to key points within the Flash movie and a sample website. For a preview of the final result, open the fl1002_done.fla file in the fl10lessons folder. Close the file when you are finished, or keep it open as a reference.

Working with button symbols

Buttons are one of three symbol types in Flash, and, like all symbols, they live in the library and are managed from the Library panel. Buttons are designed specifically to react to the user's mouse and keyboard actions. Like other symbol instances, each button instance can have its own transformation and color characteristics. In addition, button symbols have filter effects applied from the Property Inspector, and can be assigned instance names for ActionScript control.

To understand the anatomy of a button, you'll now open a sample file with a button instance so that you can explore a button symbol and its different components:

1   Choose File > Open. In the Open dialog box, navigate to the fl10lessons folder and open the file named fl1001.fla.

2   On the Stage, you see a single button. Double-click this button to enter its Edit mode, and to view its Timeline.

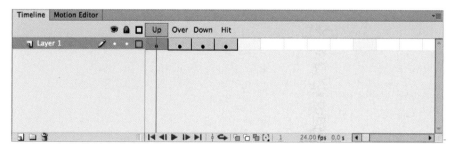

Button symbols have a unique, four-frame Timeline.

3 You'll see here that a button symbol has a unique Timeline featuring four main frames in each layer—Up, Over, Down, and Hit. Each represents a button's appearance in different states of use. Navigate through a button's frames by clicking on the frame ruler, or by using the < and > (comma and period) keys.

The **Up state** is the button's default appearance when it's just sitting on the Stage without any user interaction. By default, when you convert Stage graphics to a button symbol, they are automatically placed on the Up frame.

The **Over state** displays when the mouse pointer moves over a button. This indicates to the user that the button is a control that can carry out some action in your movie. You can characterize the Over state with anything from a simple color or text change to an animation or sound.

When the user presses down on the mouse button, the button symbol changes to its **Down state**. It remains in its Down state until the user releases the button. Because the Down state is visible only briefly during a typical mouse click, customizing a button's Down state with a long animation or sound is not the best idea.

The **Hit area** defines the *hot spot* where the button becomes active when the user moves over it. This state is never visible, and content placed on the Hit frame defines only the active area.

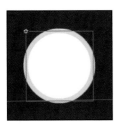

The contents of the Hit frame define the clickable, or 'hot,' area of a button.

This is especially crucial for buttons that are small, have an irregular shape, or contain only text with no underlying shape. Because the Hit area defines the active area of the button and is not visible, the size and shape of the content on the Hit frame matters most—color choice, for instance, has no effect on the button's operation.

What makes a good Hit state? The best Hit states are solid shapes that are generally as big as, or slightly bigger than, the visible states of the button. If your button changes shape from state to state, consider choosing a shape for the Hit state that is fairly neutral and encompasses as much of the visible area of the button as possible.

4 Choose Control > Test Movie > in Flash Professional to preview the button in the Flash Player. Move your mouse pointer over the button, and then click it to see how it switches between its various states as the mouse interacts with it. Then close the preview window.

Button symbols display a hand cursor
when the user moves their pointer over them.

5 Choose File > Close to close your movie. If asked to save changes, choose Don't Save.

Building buttons

With a solid introduction to button symbol theory, you're ready to begin work on the project. The first step is to create a new button symbol and design its Up, Over, and Down states.

1 Choose File > Open and navigate to the fl10lessons folder. Select the fl1002.fla file and choose Open. Here you see a mini-site project for the talkShop retail cell-phone store.

The talkShop project file you will be working with.

2 Before you modify this file, choose File > Save As. When the Save As dialog box appears, type **fl1002_work.fla** into the Save As text field. Navigate to the fl10lessons folder and press Save.

First, you'll create a button very much the same way you'd create any other symbol—from existing graphics on the Stage.

3 Click on the rounded rectangle and the arrow on the right side of the Stage under the talkShop logo. Choose Modify > Convert to Symbol. In the Convert to Symbol dialog box, type **Products Button** as the name, and set the Type to Button. Set the registration point to the upper left, and click OK to create the new symbol.

Select graphics on the Stage and use Modify > Convert to Symbol to convert them to a button symbol.

4 The next step will be to add to your button by designing the additional states (Over, Down, Hit). Double-click on your new button to enter its Edit mode.

5 The first state you'll design is the Over state, which is how the button will appear if and when the user rolls their mouse pointer over it.

Select Over frame directly on the layer. As with any other Timeline, you need to create a keyframe to put content here. Use the F6 shortcut key or choose Insert > Timeline > Keyframe to insert a keyframe here.

The graphics from the Up keyframe will be duplicated; take a moment to make some changes, such as color, to this copy, to make it distinctive from the Up frame. You may need to ungroup the box and the arrow graphics to change their colors individually. Select the graphics and ungroup by choosing Modify > Ungroup. Click anywhere in the background to deselect, then click on the button to select it. Click on the Fill color swatch and choose a grey color.

Add a keyframe to the Over state to design a unique look for your button when the mouse pointer rolls over it.

6 Next, you'll design the Down state, which is how your button appears when the mouse pointer is clicked and held down on it. Select the Down frame, and use the F6 shortcut key to insert a keyframe here.

Again, click anywhere in the background to deselect, and then click on the grey button to select it. Click on the Fill color swatch and choose an orange color.

7 Finally, select the Hit frame, and use the F6 shortcut key to create a keyframe here. The Hit frame is not visible, but determines the clickable area of your entire button.

For this reason, you should generally use a solid shape (color is unimportant) that is the same size as, if not bigger than, your button. In this case, you can use the graphics themselves to set the Hit state, as they accurately represent the size and shape of the button. Leave the duplicated graphics on this keyframe as-is.

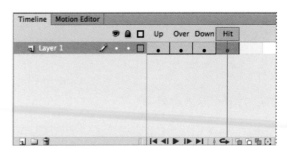

Create a keyframe on the Hit state and use the duplicated graphics from the Down state to set the Hit area.

8 Exit your new button by clicking the Scene 1 link above the Stage to return to the main Timeline.

9 Choose Control > Test Movie > in Flash Professional to preview your new button. Roll over and click with your mouse button to see the different states at work.

Test your button design by choosing Control > Test Movie > in Flash Professional.

10 Close the preview window, and choose File > Save to save your file.

Button design tips

When designing buttons, keep your users in mind and follow these guidelines:

- Aim for an interesting design that makes the navigation process easy for users to understand. An interesting-looking button may entice users to click on it.

- Make a button's purpose clear. Although you already know what all your buttons do, and where they'll lead, users aren't as familiar as you are with what's going on. Design buttons with familiar shapes (for example, a Play button that looks like a forward arrow), or label buttons with text if necessary.

- Make buttons easy to find. If the buttons are hard to pick out on the interface, or if their functions are unclear, your interactive project becomes a frustrating experience for the user.

Also, let the content drive the need for buttons. Know the sections you want to include in your project before you start to design the buttons. Developing content as you design your buttons can slow you down. A flowchart is a simple way to plan basic layout and navigation, and gives you a blueprint to work from when setting up your movie in Flash.

If a hit keyframe is not created (or empty), a button uses the contents of the last available keyframe as the Hit area. This works across all layers, so be cautious not to let your button use a non-graphic keyframe for its Hit area (such as an empty keyframe or one that contains a sound). The result may be a non-clickable button!

Adding text to a button

Like other symbols, and like the main Timeline itself, buttons can have multiple layers. Using layers helps you to create more complex designs and add more information while keeping everything carefully organized. In this exercise, you'll add a new layer to incorporate text into your button.

1 Double-click your new button on the Stage to enter its Edit mode.

2 Press the New Layer button below the Timeline to add a new layer to your button. Rename the layer **Text**.

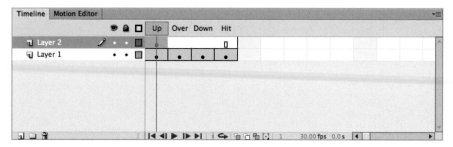

Add a new layer and name it Text. You can layer graphics and content in button Timelines just like you can on the main Timeline.

3 Select your Text tool (T) from the Tools panel. Make sure the new layer is selected, and click slightly to the right of the white arrow on your button. Type the word **Products**, and switch to your Selection tool (k).

4 Leave the text frame selected, and locate the Character options on the Property Inspector on the right. Choose Arial from the Family drop-down menu, and set the Size value to 18 pt, and the color to White (#FFFFFF).

If necessary, use your Selection tool (k) or the arrows keys on your keyboard to reposition the text on the button.

5   The text should extend across all four frames of your button's Timeline. If not, select the Down frame on the Text layer and press the F5 shortcut key to extend the first keyframe and your text. This ensures that your text will appear across all three visual states.

Add text to the new layer and style it using the Property Inspector. Your text can (and should) extend across all frames on the button's Timeline.

6   Click the Scene 1 link above the Stage to return to the main Timeline.

7   Choose File > Save to save your file, and then choose Control > Test Movie > in Flash Professional to preview your movie. The new text should appear across all three states of your button as you interact with it. Close the preview window. That's one button down. The next button will be much faster and easier to create because you can build on what you've already done.

Duplicating and modifying buttons

Why build a completely new button when you can copy and modify an existing one? Using the Library panel's Duplicate command is faster, and it ensures that new buttons are consistent with those you've already created.

1   In the Library panel, select the Products Button symbol. If necessary, choose Window > Library to open the Library panel.

2   Choose Duplicate from the Library panel menu.

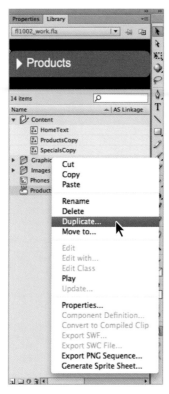

Make a copy of your Products Button symbol in the library using its panel menu's Duplicate command.

When the Duplicate Symbol dialog box appears, type the name **Home Button**. Leave the Type set as Button and press OK. A new copy of your original button, named Home Button, now appears in the Library panel.

3   Drag an instance of the Home Button to the Stage, and place it directly below your Products Button on the same layer. Double-click it to edit it in place.

4 Once inside the button, select your Text tool (T) from the Tools panel, then click on your existing text until you get the I-Beam. Replace the word Products with the word **Home**. Click the Scene 1 link above the Stage to return to the main Timeline.

Edit the text on your button copy to read Home.

5 Repeat steps 1 to 4 to create a new duplicate of your button named Specials Button, and edit the text to read **Specials**.

6 Choose File > Save to save your work, and choose Control > Test Movie to preview your movie. You should now have three identical buttons with different text labels, completing your navigation menu.

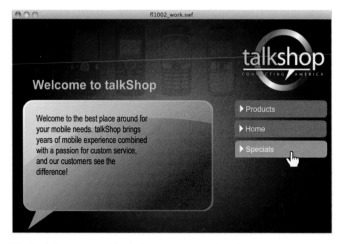

The finished menu, created by duplicating your original Products Button.

Use your Align panel (Window > Align) to evenly align and space the three buttons on the Stage.

Testing buttons on the Stage

Once you've added buttons to the Stage, you can conveniently test their behaviors and appearance directly within the authoring environment using the Enable Simple Buttons command. Enable Simple Buttons lets you quickly test button behavior without launching the Flash Player, and prevents you from selecting, moving, or editing buttons on the Stage.

To use Enable Simple Buttons:

1   Choose Control > Enable Simple Buttons.

2   Roll over and click your buttons as you normally would, to test their behavior.

3   When finished, choose Control > Enable Simple Buttons to toggle it back off.

Keep in mind that most ActionScript behavior is limited in this mode, and requires you to preview your movie using Control > Test Movie > in Flash Professional instead. In addition, you cannot move or edit button instances until Enable Simple Buttons is toggled back off.

Creating text-based buttons

Text-based buttons work differently because they are formed only from the character outlines that form your text, with no significant solid area or shape that defines them. A problem with text buttons is that if the mouse pointer is not precisely on a type character, the button remains inactive, appearing not to work. This is where the Hit area comes into play. By defining a hot spot in the Hit frame of your button, you create a solid and easy target for users to click.

1   Choose Insert > New Symbol.

2   When the Create New Symbol dialog box appears, name the symbol **Learn More**, and set the symbol Type as Button. Press OK. The main Timeline disappears, and you are brought into the edit mode for your new symbol. The Stage appears empty for now.

3   Choose the Text tool (T) from the Tools panel, then click on the Stage and type **Learn how to create sites like this**.

4   Highlight the text and use the Character options on the Property Inspector to set the text to Verdana, 10pt, white (#FFFFFF) type. Note that you can use the Zoom tool to zoom in on the Stage to make working with small text easier.

5   Choose the Selection tool (▶) in the Tools panel and select the text you just created. Open the Align panel (Window > Align) and click the Align to stage checkbox, if it's not already checked. Click the Align Horizontal Center (⊜) and Align Vertical Center (⊛) buttons in the Align panel to align the text to the symbol's registration point.

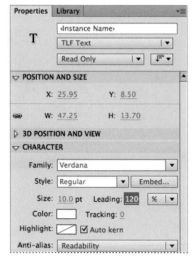

Use the Property Inspector to set its formatting, then use your Align panel to align the text to the symbol's registration point on the Stage.

6   Select the Over frame and use the F6 shortcut key to create a keyframe. Using the Text tool, select the text and use the color swatch on the Property Inspector to set the color to light orange (#FFCC33).

7   Insert a keyframe in the Down frame. Select the text, and use the color swatch in the Property Inspector to set its color to pale grey (#CCCCCC).

8   Finally, you will need to set a Hit area for your button. Because the Hit area relies on solid areas, type will only be clickable on the characters themselves, making it difficult to interact with your button. Instead, you'll use a solid shape (such as a rectangle) to set the Hit area.

Select the Hit frame of your button, and use the F6 shortcut key to insert a keyframe there.

9   Select the Rectangle tool (▭) from the Tools panel, and use the Property Inspector to set a fill color for it (the color is unimportant). Click and drag to draw a rectangle on the Hit frame that is larger than the text itself. Use the text duplicated on this keyframe as a reference, drawing the rectangle around it.

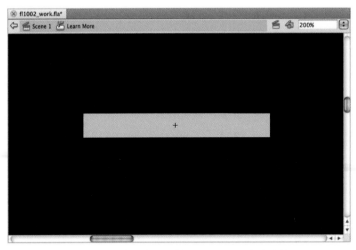

Draw a solid, filled box larger than the actual button text to set the clickable area.

10 Click the Scene 1 link above the Stage to return to the main Timeline. Locate your new Learn More button in the library, and drag an instance to the Buttons layer on the Timeline. Use your Selection tool to position it at the bottom center of the Stage.

Drag an instance of your new button to the Buttons layer, and position it at the bottom of the Stage.

11 Choose Control > Test Movie > in Flash Professional to preview your movie. Move your pointer over your new button, and you should see it change colors.

12 Close the Flash Player and choose File > Save to save your work.

Creating frame labels for ActionScript

Now that you've built your navigation buttons, you'll learn to use ActionScript to have those buttons jump to different points on the Timeline that represent your different sections, such as Home, Products, and Services. To help you easily accomplish frame-to-frame navigation, you can name individual keyframes using *frame labels.*

Frame labels are a convenient alternative to using frame numbers for navigation, as they allow you to assign casual names (such as *home*) to a keyframe, and use that within ActionScript. Using frame numbers in ActionScript means that if you change the location of a piece of content along the Timeline, you'll likely have to change the frame number you're referencing.

Frame labels, however, travel with their respective keyframes, so it doesn't matter where the keyframe is along the Timeline, as long as the frame label remains the same. You can also use labels to add comments or notes for yourself directly on a layer in the Timeline.

1   Make sure you have the Buttons layer selected, and click the New Layer button (⬏) to add a new layer. Rename the new layer **Labels.**

2   Insert keyframes at frames 5 and 10, using the F6 shortcut key—this lines up with the placement of the different content sections on the Timeline.

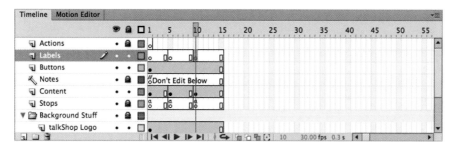

Create a new layer named Labels, and add keyframes at frames 5 and 10, where you'll be creating frame labels.

3   Click and select keyframe 1 on the Labels layer. In the Property Inspector, type **home** in the Name text field in the Label options area to set a frame label for this frame. Press Enter (Windows) or Return (Mac OS). You should see a red flag icon (▸) appear inside the keyframe.

Type a frame label of home for keyframe 1 on the Labels layer. You'll add frame labels for keyframes 5 and 10 as well.

4   Repeat step 3, this time add the label **products** at frame 5 and the label **specials** at frame 10.

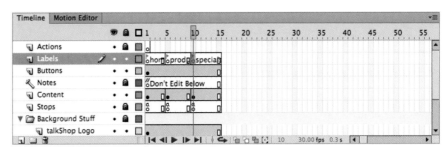

The finished layer, which now contains three frame labels that you can later navigate to.

Later on, you'll reference these frame labels in ActionScript to tell your navigation buttons where to send the playhead to view different sections of content across the Timeline.

The Notes layer is created using a frame label set as a comment. Comments place text across the layer itself and are useful for making notes directly on the Timeline, just like the lesson file does here. Please note, however, that comments cannot be used for navigation like frame labels. To set a frame label as a comment, type text in the Property Inspector's Frame text field and choose Comment from the Type menu.

Adding ActionScript: Events and event handlers

You've already explored basic ActionScript in Lesson 9, "Introducing ActionScript," and learned to navigate the Timeline using frame-based actions. While working with buttons involves some similar code, there are some new concepts you'll need to familiarize yourself with to get your buttons up-and-running.

The process of scripting buttons revolves around two important items: events and event listeners.

Understanding events

Simply put, an *event* is an occurrence that triggers something else to happen. In the case of ActionScript, events occur, and blocks of ActionScript known as *event handlers*, run in response to those events.

If you are an employee at a company, you respond to events each day. When you receive phone calls, e-mails, or direct requests from managers and other staff, you respond to those events by carrying out certain tasks. Very often, those tasks are outlined ahead of time (for example, *file an expense report* or *design a logo*) so you're ready to respond when the time is right.

Some events you've become accustomed to during typical website navigation include mouse clicks, rollovers, and keyboard presses.

Responding to events with event handlers

An event handler is a block of ActionScript code that runs in response to an event. Event handlers are essentially ActionScript *functions*, or named blocks of code that can be reused over and over again throughout a movie. Any block of code that is designed specifically to respond to an event, however, always falls into the category of event handlers.

Once you've chosen an event, and created an event handler, you assign the pair to a specific button or control on the Stage using an *event listener*.

A detailed exercise on creating and using functions is included in Lesson 9, "Introducing ActionScript."

Tying it all together with event listeners

Event listeners assign a trigger event (such as a click) and an event handler to a specific button or control on the Stage. Every item in a Flash movie capable of triggering events (such as Button or Movie Clip symbols, and even the Stage) can be assigned an event/event handler pair using the addEventListener() method.

You can call this method from a specific button instance, and tell it what type of event to listen for, and what event handler to use if that event occurs:

```
mybutton_btn.addEventListener("click", myEventHandler);
```

To use the employee metaphor from earlier, you could think of your workflow represented in pseudo-code like this:

```
employee.addEventListener("boss calls", submitExpenseReport);
```

To code your buttons in the next exercise, you'll create an event listener function, and then attach that function to your button instances using the *addEventListener( )* method.

New Term: Method

A method is something that an object, or any copy of that object, is capable of doing. For example, a Movie Clip symbol, or any instance of any movie clip, can use its gotoAndStop() method to jump the playhead to a specific frame and stop.

Using metaphors once again, you can say that every human being has a sleep() and eat() method, and that methods can be called from any instance of a human being.

Linking buttons to specific frames

Now that you've set up frame labels across the timeline, you'll use ActionScript to link each button to a specific section within your movie. Each frame label corresponds to a specific section of the site, and the end result is when each button is clicked, users will be sent to that specific section within your movie.

1   Click to select frame 1 of the Actions layer in the Timeline. Choose Window > Actions to open the Actions panel. Make sure that Script Assist mode is not active; you can disable it by clicking the Script Assist button in the upper-right corner of the Actions panel.

2   First, you'll build the event handler that will advance the playhead to the Products section. Type the following code on Line 1 in the right side of the Action panel to build the framework of your new event handler:

```
function gotoProducts() {

}
```

Here the function keyword is followed by an arbitrary name, creating a new block of code that you can call later on. The parentheses are a mandatory part of the language and the curly braces are used to group several lines of ActionScript together. You'll add code inside of these braces, which the function will run when called.

All ActionScript is case-sensitive. Be conscious of entering code exactly as it's shown in the steps here, including the same casing.

3   You'll now add the code necessary to instruct the playhead to jump to the Products section when called. On Line 2, in between the two curly braces, add the following line of code:

```
gotoAndStop("products");
```

The gotoAndStop action should be familiar to you already, except here you are adding it to an event handler that may be called at any time. The entire event handler should now read:

```
function gotoProducts() {
    gotoAndStop("products");
}
```

You may remember that "products" was the frame label you assigned to keyframe 5 on your Timeline, where the Products information is displayed. You could have also typed gotoAndStop(5), but using the frame label is more flexible in the event that you decide to move content around on the Timeline.

4   Any function that will serve as an event handler (like your gotoProducts function) needs a few specific pieces of code to be fully complete. The first item you add lets ActionScript know that your function will not return any type of information, but will instead perform an action and shut down until it's next called.

Directly after the parentheses (no spaces), type **:void**, as shown here:

```
function gotoProducts():void {
    gotoAndStop("products");
}
```

The :void return type is just like saying *gives back nothing*. While your event handler will work without it, it's a good practice to include it. If nothing else, this visually distinguishes this function as an event handler, which can never return a value.

Watch your quotes. It's important to use only straight quotes and not curly quotes, sometimes called typographer's quotes. Only the straight quotes function properly.

5   Next, add the following code within the parentheses themselves:

```
evt:Event
```

The entire event handler should now appear like this:

```
function gotoProducts(evt:Event):void {
    gotoAndStop("products");
}
```

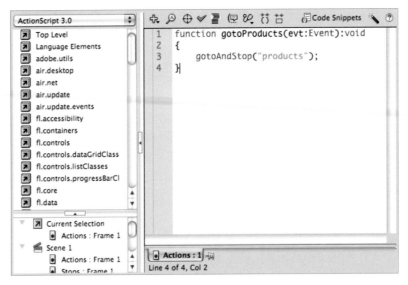

The code in the Actions panel should now display as shown above.

This little piece of code is referred to as a parameter, or parameter placeholder. It is designed to act as a container for any information passed into your event handler when and if it's called. While functions can generally be designed to take any number of parameters, event handlers are allowed only one, which is reserved to catch the event information itself.

Here, you've created a parameter named *evt*, which is designed to catch Event-type information.

The Event parameter passed to an event handler contains a number of pieces of useful information, such as the button/control that captured the event and the type of event (such as click) that occurred. At this stage, you won't use this information, but later on in your ActionScript travels, it may prove to be very useful.

6   You've completed your event handler for this one section, Close the Actions panel, then choose File > Save to save your file. In just a moment, you'll add more code to tie it all together.

Adding an event listener to a button

Once you've created an event handler, you'll need to assign it to a control within your movie, such as a button instance. This assignment first tells a button when to run an event handler, and then which event handler to run.

This assignment is created by the `addEventListener()` method.

1   To target any button instance from ActionScript, you first must assign it an instance name. Using the Selection tool (⬚), click once on the Products Button to select it on the Stage.

2   At the very top of the Property Inspector on the right, locate the instance name text field box, which sits directly to the right of the symbol icon.

3   Type **products_btn** as the instance name for the selected button and press Enter (Windows) or Return (Mac OS) to commit the change. You can now refer to this button by this new name anywhere in ActionScript.

Before you can assign ActionScript to a button instance, you first must assign it an instance name in the Property Inspector.

4   Press Alt (Windows) or Option (Mac OS), then double-click on the first frame of the Actions layer in the Timeline to open the Actions panel.

5   Below the event handler you created in the last exercise, make a line of space, and add the following code:

```
products_btn.addEventListener();
```

```
1   function gotoProducts(evt:Event):void
2   {
3       gotoAndStop("products");
4   }
5   product_btn.addEventListener();
```

Insert a new, full line below your existing code and add the code that ties it all together.

Here, you've targeted the Products Button by the instance name you just assigned to it, and called its `addEventListener` method. This method can be called from any button instance to assign it an event/event handler pair.

6   Next, you'll fill in the blanks and tell `addEventListener` two important things: first, what type of event this button has to receive to respond, and second, which event handler to use as its response.

Inside of the parentheses following `addEventListener`, type **"click"** (including the quotes), like so:

```
products_btn.addEventListener("click");
```

This lets the button know it's listening for a single click as its event, or trigger.

7   Finally, you will add one more piece of information inside of the parentheses, which is the name of the event handler the button should use as its response when and if it is clicked.

Within the parentheses, but after the click, add a comma and the name of the event handler you created earlier:

```
products_btn.addEventListener("click",gotoProducts);
```

```
1   function gotoProducts(evt:Event):void
2   {
3       gotoAndStop("products");
4   }
5   product_btn.addEventListener("click",gotoProducts);
```

The completed code as it appears in your Actions panel.

8 Close the Actions panel, and choose Control > Test Movie > in Flash Professional to preview your movie. Clicking on the Products Button should now advance you to the Products section within your movie.

Close the Flash Player and keep the file open.

Your button should now advance you to the Products section when clicked.

Troubleshooting events, event handlers, and event listeners

Casing or spelling errors in your code may generate errors when you try and test your movie, and ultimately prevent your movie from working properly. If the Compiler Errors panel appears on preview or publish, and lists any errors, check first for the following:

1 Pay careful attention to the line numbers referenced in any errors that come up—they can be essential in finding out exactly where the error lies.

2 Use the Check Syntax button at the top of the Actions panel to check for any code errors on the spot. This will display a warning dialog if your code is not correct.

3 Review the code shown in the lesson steps to check for spelling, casing, or naming errors.

4 Make sure that the instance name you assigned your button exactly matches the instance name you're targeting in ActionScript. Even with instance names, a discrepancy in casing or spelling will be a problem.

5 Look for missing parentheses or curly braces. Curly braces and parentheses always work in sets—if you see a starting or ending brace or parenthesis without a mate, this could be your problem.

Linking buttons to a website

In addition to linking buttons to specific frames within your movie, you can instruct them to jump to a local web page, external website address, or file download.

In this exercise, you'll use the Code Snippets Panel to add the necessary code to have your button jump to an outside website. You worked with the Code Snippets panel in Lesson 9, "Introducing ActionScript." In this exercise, you'll work with it again as an alternative to coding this task by hand.

Introducing navigateToURL() and URLRequest()

The `navigateToURL` method was introduced in ActionScript 3.0, and is used to instruct your movie to open a local or remote web page in a browser or download a file. You can place `navigateToURL` directly on a keyframe to have it run at a specific moment in time or, like you're about to do here, add it to an event handler so a URL is opened in conjunction with a button click.

Experienced Flash users please note: `navigateToURL` *replaces ActionScript 2.0's* `getURL()` *method.*

When feeding a URL to just about any ActionScript 3.0 method, that URL first needs to be wrapped inside of a new `URLRequest()` object. Think of *URLRequest* as a fancy container that a URL must be placed in before handing it to ActionScript methods such as `navigateToURL`.

While `URLRequest` has many uses that go beyond the scope of this book, you'll get to use a single `URLRequest` object to get one of your buttons to launch an external web page in your system's default web browser. You'll see how the Code Snippets panel uses these two actions to make it all happen.

1   First, you'll need to select a button on the Stage and assign it an instance name so
    you can reference it in ActionScript. Click to select the Learn button instance at
    the bottom of the Stage. At the top of the Property Inspector on the right, type
    learn_btn in the instance name text field. Note that if you do not create an instance
    name for your button, the Code Snippets panel will do it for you.

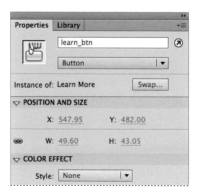

*Assign the text-based button at the bottom of
your Stage an instance name of learn_btn.*

2   Make sure the Learn button is still selected, and expand the Code Snippets panel. If
    the Code Snippets panel is not visible, choose Window > Code Snippets to open it.
    Note that in the default workspace, the Code Snippets panel is collapsed into icon
    view on the right side of your workspace.

3   Within the Code Snippets panel, locate and expand the Actions folder. Locate and
    double-click the Click to Go to Web Page snippet.

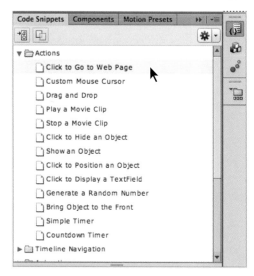

Add a new code snippet to open a web page.

The Actions panel will appear, and the new code will be placed below the existing code in the Script window.

```
function gotoProducts(evt:Event):void {
    gotoAndStop("products");
}
products_btn.addEventListener("click", gotoProducts);
/* Click to Go to Web Page
Clicking on the specified symbol instance loads the URL in a new brows

Instructions:
1. Replace http://www.adobe.com with the desired URL address.
   Keep the quotation marks ("").
*/

learn_btn.addEventListener(MouseEvent.CLICK, fl_ClickToGoToWebPage);

function fl_ClickToGoToWebPage(event:MouseEvent):void
{
    navigateToURL(new URLRequest("http://www.adobe.com"), "_blank");
}
```

Add a new event handler to open a web page.

Now, you'll use some of your experience creating code by hand to modify the code created by the Code Snippets panel. Specifically, you'll need to adjust the URL that you want the button to go to when clicked.

Be careful of the parentheses at the end. You should have two closing parentheses as shown here: one for navigateToURL *and the other for* URLRequest.

4 In the Actions panel, locate the line that reads:

```
navigateToURL(new URLRequest("http://www.adobe.com"), "_blank");
```

In the double quotes, change the URL from *http://www.adobe.com* to *http://www.wiley.com*. The resulting code should appear as follows:

```
navigateToURL(new URLRequest("http://www.wiley.com"), "_blank");
```

```
function fl_ClickToGoToWebPage(event:MouseEvent):void
{
    navigateToURL(new URLRequest("http://www.wiley.com"), "_blank");
}
```

Modify the code created by the Code Snippets panel.

Close the Actions panel.

5 Choose File > Save to save your work, and choose Control > Test Movie > in Flash Professional to preview your movie and try out the button. If you have an active Internet connection, the Wiley website should launch in your system's default web browser.

6 Close the browser window.

Self study

Use the new skills you've learned to add event handlers for the Home and Specials Buttons on the Stage. Assign them instance names, and build event handlers to navigate to their respective frame labels on the Timeline. Add event listeners to each one to assign it an event handler in response to a mouse click.

Review

Questions

1 What are the three button states that can be used to change the appearance of the button during user interactivity? Which state controls the clickable area of a button?

2 What do you call a block of ActionScript code used to carry out a task in response to an event?

3 What is the significance of instance names?

Answers

1 Up, Over, and Down. The Hit state controls the clickable area of a button. Because this state is not visible, however, it has no effect on the actual appearance of a button.

2 An event handler function.

3 Instance names can give a symbol instance a unique name by which ActionScript can identify (and control) it.

What you'll learn in this lesson:

- Preparing and importing sound files

- Placing sounds on the Timeline

- Editing sounds and creating effects

- Controlling sound behavior and performance

Adding Sound to Your Movies

You've honed your design and animation skills; now you'll put some finishing touches on your movies by including sound effects, narration, and background music. Flash's ability to import, manipulate, and place sound files offers many creative and practical possibilities for creating immersive experiences, and adds a level of accessibility for users with visual impairments. You'll even learn to leverage some ActionScript commands to control sound playback in your movie.

Starting up

Before starting, make sure that your tools and panels are consistent by resetting your workspace. See "Resetting the Flash workspace" in the Starting up section of this book.

You will work with several files from the fl11lessons folder in this lesson. Make sure that you have loaded the fllessons folder onto your hard drive from the supplied DVD. See "Loading lesson files" in the Starting up section of this book..

See Lesson 11 in action!

Use the accompanying video to gain a better understanding of how to use some of the features shown in this lesson. You can find the video tutorial for this lesson on the included DVD.

The project

In this lesson, you will build an interactive slide show with background music to keep the listener engaged, narration to walk the user through the various slides, and sound effects to make the navigation feel more interactive and tactile. You will complete the slide show by importing and placing sounds included with the lesson files. You will also explore how Flash lets you optimize the use of long- and short-form audio for great performance, without sacrificing quality or presentation. To view the finished file, choose File > Open and select the fl1101_done.fla file within the fl11lessons folder. Choose Control > Test Movie > in Flash Professional to preview the movie, and when done, close the Flash player, and then close the .fla file.

You'll use sounds in your Flash movie to enhance this photo gallery for the Brooklyn Arts Cafe.

Preparing sound files for Flash

Before bringing your audio files into Flash, you need to understand some of the characteristics and settings for digital audio files. The more pre-production work you do on files before importing them into Flash, the more likely it is that you'll get the results you want the first time around. In the next few sections, you'll explore the key properties of digital audio files along with some recommendations for preparing your files for import and use in your Flash movies.

Sample rate and bit depth

Digital audio is sound that has been converted from analog sound waves into a series of bits and bytes. The conversion takes place through the use of an A/D (analog-to-digital) converter. Your computer microphone jack contains a very basic converter; audio professionals use high-end units capable of reproducing sound at a much higher level of quality and accuracy. The quality of digital audio is determined by two important factors: sample rate and bit depth.

The *sample rate* refers to the number of samples of an audio waveform that the converter digitizes in one second, and it is analogous to the resolution of a digital photo. The more samples (or pictures) captured in each second, the more accurately the waveform is represented. Although the sample rate is specified when the sound file is recorded or converted, you can adjust it down or up later. As with digital images, however, if the detail wasn't in the original file, increasing the sample rate (or resolution) will not improve it.

Always capture audio at a higher sample rate than you think you'll need. If necessary, you can downsample later to a lower sample rate, which reduces audio file size.

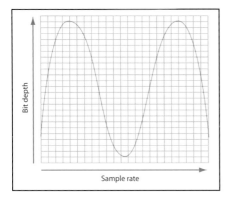

An audio waveform representation of sample rate and bit depth.

Bit depth determines the amount of information that each sample contains; think of it as similar to a digital photo's bit depth setting. The higher the bit depth of a photo, the wider the range of shades available to reproduce the original colors and details. In the audio world, bit depth is responsible for reproducing the amplitude (loudness) and dynamic range of an audio waveform. Low bit depth settings, such as 8 bits or less, produce poor recordings of limited quality, akin to a telephone answering machine. In contrast, a bit depth of 16 bits is sufficient for reproducing the wide range of instruments and vocals found in professionally recorded music.

For reference, audio on a commercial compact disc has a sample rate of 44.1 kHz (or 44,100 samples per second) and a bit depth of 16.

If you plan to record your own audio, pay attention to the sample rate and bit depth settings in your software and consider what they'll mean to the quality of the original sound. Mid- to professional-level audio applications, such as Avid Pro Tools, Steinberg's Cubase or Nuendo, Apple Logic, and Adobe Soundbooth all provide a range of options and tools for recording, importing, editing, and exporting digital audio into a variety of formats. If you'd prefer to let someone else do the recording, you can find many royalty-free sound effects and loops online in a variety of formats and quality settings.

Editing your audio

Although you can perform basic editing and trimming in Flash, to conserve space you should edit your sound files to some degree before importing them. Large audio files sitting in your library can bloat your Flash document (.fla file) unnecessarily. Why import unwanted, extra audio that you know will never be used in your movie?

If you need a basic sound-editing application, your choices range from low-cost shareware to full-featured professional programs. If you are creating original audio for your movie, consider an application that at least lets you trim, cut, copy, and paste, as well as export a variety of popular file formats. (You'll learn about Flash's built-in editing controls later in the lesson.)

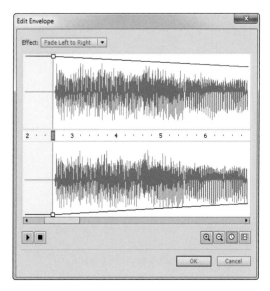

Flash's Edit window provides basic trimming, pan effects, and volume editing.

Mono or stereo

The nature of your source audio will determine whether you should stick with mono or stereo channels for your final output. Single-channel mono audio is a suitable choice for a solo recording of narration or voice. If you are working with prerecorded music or sound effects that pan from left to right, stereo is the best choice; with mono recording, you may lose a great deal of the perspective and placement (this is especially true with music). Keep in mind that stereo files include two channels (left and right), and will often take up twice as much storage space as a mono sound file at the same settings. Whether you record in mono or stereo, Flash has a series of built-in effects, such as fades and stereo effects, which you can apply to any sound you import.

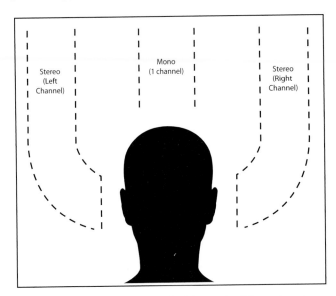

Mono reproduces audio in a single channel, while stereo does it in two channels.

Audio file formats

Flash imports three common file formats: Windows .wav, Mac OS .aiff, and .mp3. If you have QuickTime installed, you can also import additional audio file formats such as Avid's Sound Designer II format. The .mp3 format differs slightly from the others because it compresses audio to facilitate file exchange and streaming over the Web. In addition, .mp3 files use a system of Kbps (kilobits per second) to determine overall quality. The average is 128 Kbps, but you can encode at a much higher level if your software supports it. For the highest quality, keep your source .mp3 files within the 128 to 192 Kbps range.

Which file format is the right one? The answer largely depends on your operating system, as well as the software you use to create and export audio. No matter which file format you start with, Flash performs its own compression on audio included in your movies and converts all the audio in your final .swf file to .mp3 format. You can set specific quality parameters in the Publish settings for your movie.

Importing sounds

To use a sound in Flash, you first must import it using the Import menu's Import to Library command. You'll import this lesson's sound files, so that you can begin to explore and place them on the Timeline.

1   Choose File > Open and navigate to the fl11lessons folder. Select the file fl1101.fla and press Open.

2   Choose File > Save As. When the Save As dialog box appears, type **fl1101_work.fla** into the Save As text field. Navigate to the fl11lessons folder and press Save.

3   Choose File > Import > Import to Library. The Import to Library dialog box opens and prompts you to locate the desired files.

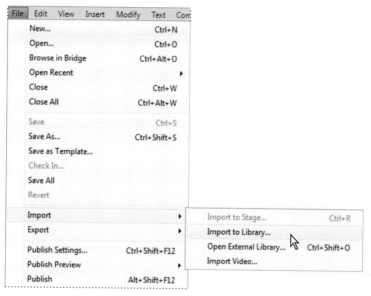

Use the Import to Library command to select and add sound files to your Flash movie.

4   Open the Sounds folder inside the fl11lessons folder. Hold down the Shift key, select the folder's nine .wav sound files, and choose Open to import the files directly to your Library panel.

5   If it's not already open, launch the Library panel by choosing Window > Library. The nine sound files appear as assets marked with a speaker icon.

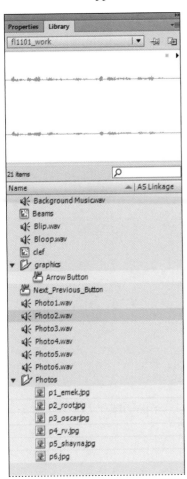

Each imported sound file appears in the Library panel with a speaker icon.
You can use the Play button in the Preview pane at the top to listen to a sound.

6 In the Library panel, select the Blip.wav sound file. Notice that the Preview window at the top of the panel now shows the sound as a waveform and also features small Play and Stop buttons in the upper-right corner.

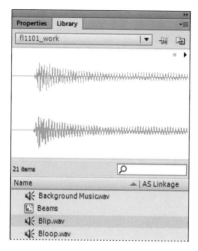

The Preview window displays the sound's waveform when selected.

7 Click the Play button to listen to the sound. Try this with the other sounds to get an idea of what each file contains.

8 Choose File > Save to save your work.

Use the techniques you learned in Lesson 3 to organize your imported sound files into a new folder if you'd like.

Placing sounds on the Timeline

To play a sound at a specific point in your movie, you place the sound on a keyframe on the Timeline. When the playhead reaches the frame where you placed the sound, you'll hear it. To place a sound, you'll select a keyframe and use the Sound options found in the Property Inspector.

You'll see in the following lessons how additional options in the Sound menu can loop sounds or create effects such as fades and pans. There are a few simple rules: sounds must be placed on keyframes, and you can place only one sound per keyframe (on a single layer).

Adding sound to your slide show project

The lesson file contains a photo slide show with six photos and captions arranged across the Timeline. Two buttons on either side of the photo let the user move forward or backward through the photos. You'll enhance this photo slide show by adding background music, a vocal narration for each photo, and subtle sound effects for the Next and Previous navigation buttons.

To begin, make sure your Property Inspector is visible by choosing Window > Properties.

1 Locate and expand (if necessary) the Sound layers folder on the Timeline. Locate the empty layer titled Sounds. Select keyframe 1 on this layer.

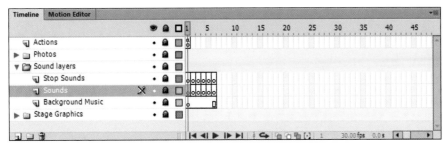

A layer folder and individual keyframes are already created for you so that you can place sounds on the Timeline.

2 With the keyframe selected, locate and expand the Sound options located in the Property Inspector. Click on the Name drop-down menu, which lists all the sounds available in the library. You should see all the sound files listed that you imported earlier.

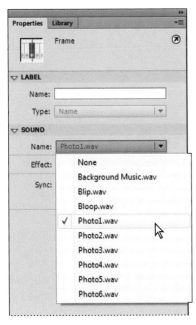

Place a sound on the selected keyframe from the Name menu (located under Sound options).

3   Select the sound named Photo 1.wav from the Sound menu to place that sound on the selected keyframe.

4   From the Sync drop-down menu right below, make sure Event is selected, which should be the default option. For an explanation of Sync options, see the sidebar, "Sync options and sound types."

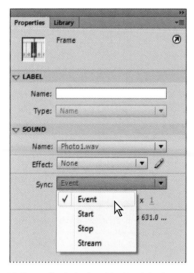

Each sound's playback and loading behavior can be controlled with the Sync menu.

By default, each new sound added to the Timeline has the Repeat option selected and set to 1. You will learn how to change this later on.

5   Press Ctrl+Enter (Windows) or Command+Return (Mac OS) to preview the movie in the Flash Player. You should hear the Photo1.wav sound play when the movie appears. Close the Flash Player and return to the main Stage.

6   Choose File > Save to save your work.

Adding a sound on the Timeline is that easy. There's more to explore, however. Next, you'll take a look at some of the sound options that help you control sounds on the Timeline.

Adding the remaining narration

You'll now add the remaining pieces of narration to their respective photos on the Timeline. Remember that these sounds should occur right when the playhead moves and the new photo is shown, so you'll need to set each one as an Event sound. The steps should be familiar to you.

1 In the Timeline panel, select keyframe 2 of the Sounds layer. Use the Name drop-down menu in the Property Inspector's Sound options to assign the Photo2.wav sound from the list.

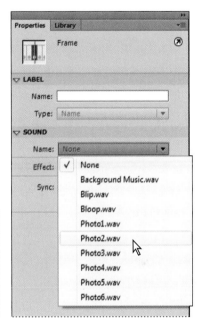

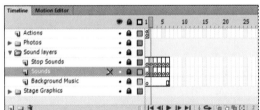

Begin assigning a sound to each sequential keyframe for all six photos.

2 Make sure Event is selected in the Sync drop-down menu. By default, Flash uses the last Sync settings chosen, so it's often unnecessary to reselect this option.

3 Repeat steps 1 and 2 for the remaining four photos, setting the sound Photo3.wav on frame 3, Photo4.wav on frame 4, and so on, until you finally place Photo6.wav on frame 6.

Add the last of the six pieces of narration to the photo on frame 6.

4 Preview your movie by pressing Ctrl+Enter (Windows) or Command+Return (Mac OS). Use the buttons to move among the photos. You may notice that if you move too quickly, the narration audio clips blend into each other. You'll fix this later on in the chapter. Close the Flash Player.

Sync options and sound types

From the Sync menu, you can tell Flash how to handle a sound. Sync options can be used to control sound overlap, stop sounds, and control how sounds work along with content on the Timeline.

Event sounds must fully load before they play back, and they respond to events (such as the playhead reaching a certain frame, as in the previous exercise) or actions (such as a button click, as in the *Adding sound effects to buttons* section). Because you want the slide show narrations to occur in tandem with the user clicking the Next and Previous buttons, be sure to set them to Event sounds, as you did in the previous exercise.

Stream sounds work best for long-form animation, as the audio is matched to the playback, like a soundtrack. Flash does everything it can to keep the sound in sync with the animation, including dropping frames if necessary. A continuous sound (such as a soundtrack or one continuous piece of dialog) that needs to sync with the Timeline from start to finish would be ideally set as a Stream sound.

Start plays a sound so that no other instance of that same sound file can be playing at the same time. This makes Start sounds a great choice if you want to prevent unwanted overlap. A Start sound will play all the way through to the end, and can only be stopped by an instance of the same sound whose Sync is set to Stop.

Stop sounds don't play a sound, but rather stop a specific sound. When choosing Stop for a selected sound, you will stop any instance of that sound that's already playing. Stop sounds can only stop instances of the same sound whose Sync is set to Start.

Adding sound effects to buttons

Sounds are a great way to enhance navigation, and they can make interacting with buttons feel more *real*. You learned about button symbols in Lesson 10, "Creating Navigation Controls." You know that buttons contain four frames, three of which correspond to the buttons' different visual states. The Over and Down frames of the slide show navigation buttons are the perfect locations to place Event sounds that will trigger on a rollover (the Over state) and click of the mouse (the Down state), respectively.

Placing Event sounds on button frames

Event sounds work independently of the Timeline and must be fully loaded before they can play back. The best example of this is a short sound placed on a button frame. Your user can click a button at any time, so an Event sound will be ready to respond to that click without any relation to other content on the Timeline. In this exercise, you'll place some sounds from your library on your Next and Previous buttons for both rollover and click actions. Both the Next and Previous buttons are instances of the Next_Previous_Button symbol in the library, so you'll only need to edit one to add sounds to both instances.

1   Expand the Stage Graphics layer folder on the Timeline, and, if necessary, unlock all layers under the Stage Graphics folder. Double-click the oval portion of the Previous (left) button to edit it directly on the Stage.

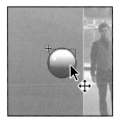

Edit your buttons in place by double-clicking them. Both buttons are instances of the same symbol in your Library.

In the button's Edit mode, you will see its four frames: Up, Over, Down, and Hit.

You'll be placing sounds on the Over and Down frames, so that sounds will go off when a user rolls over or clicks on the buttons.

2 On the Sounds layer, select the Over keyframe and make sure the Property Inspector and Sound options are visible on the right.

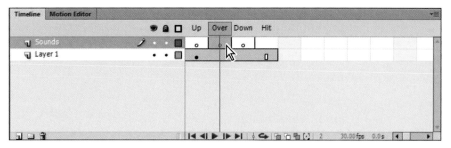

Assign the Blip.wav sound to the Over frame of your buttons.

3 From the Sound options on the right, choose the Blip.wav sound from the Name menu. In the Sync drop-down menu, leave Event selected.

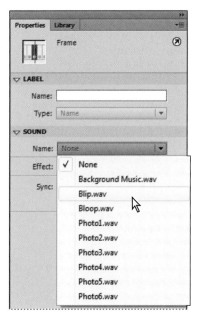

Assign the Blip.wav sound to the Over frame of your buttons.

4   On the Sounds layer, select the Down keyframe, and select the Bloop.wav sound for this frame. In the Sync drop-down menu, leave Event selected.

Assign the Bloop.wav sound to the Over keyframe of your buttons.

5   Exit the button by clicking the Scene 1 link above the Stage, and return to the main Timeline. Because both buttons are instances of the Arrow button symbol, it's not necessary to edit the *Next* button on the right side of the Stage.

6   Press Ctrl+Enter (Windows) or Command+Return (Mac OS) to preview your movie. Rolling over the buttons should trigger a different sound than clicking them.

7   Close the Flash Player, and choose File > Save to save your work.

Editing sounds

If you find you need to adjust imported sounds, Flash offers some very useful tools for basic editing, effects, and sound manipulation. You'll explore these tools' options while adding the background music loop to your photo slide show.

Little audio dynamite: the Edit Envelope panel

When your sounds still need a little something extra, Flash's Edit Envelope panel offers you many ways to trim, fade, and pan your audio for the best possible soundtrack. The Edit Envelope panel is opened using the Edit button that appears on the Property Inspector when a sound on the Timeline is selected.

The Edit Envelope panel displays your sound as a waveform, or visual representation, of the length and volume of the sound. Each channel of a sound displays its own waveform in the panel; a line above the waveform indicates the sound's current volume. You can edit volume by adding handles to the volume envelope to move the line up or down. By default, the line is all the way up (full volume).

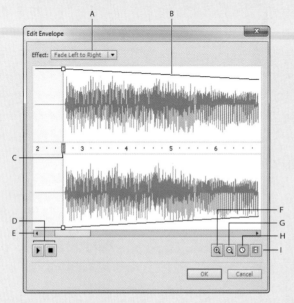

A. Volume/Pan Presets. B. Volume Envelope and handles. C. Trim handle.
D. Stop and Play buttons. E. Scroll bar. F. Zoom In. G. Zoom Out.
H. Seconds. I. Frames.

The lower-left corner features simple Play and Stop buttons so that you can preview your sound as you edit it. Scroll bars let you move through the waveform, and two magnifying glasses at the bottom-right corner let you zoom in or out to see more or less of the waveform in the window at one time.

The clock and filmstrip icons in the right corner let you toggle the Timeline between your waveforms to display in seconds or frames. Use the sliders on your Timeline (there are two) to trim the beginning and end of the sound to eliminate unwanted dead space or set specific in and out points for longer pieces of audio.

In the upper-left corner, a drop-down menu lets you choose from preset envelope and pan settings such as Fade In and Fade Out, Pan Left or Right, or Sweeping Left To Right (and vice versa). Any custom volume (envelope) edits automatically display as Custom in the Preset menu.

Trimming sound

Sometimes a sound contains a certain amount of silence or *dead air* before or after the material you need. Usually you want to minimize or eliminate this dead space to make playback as seamless as possible, especially if a sound needs to loop. Flash lets you trim sounds by adjusting their starting and ending points. This type of trimming can also be useful for selecting a small portion of a longer sound file for use. To edit a sound's starting or ending point, you'll first need to place it on the Timeline.

1 Under the Sound layers folder, locate the Background Music layer and select the first frame.

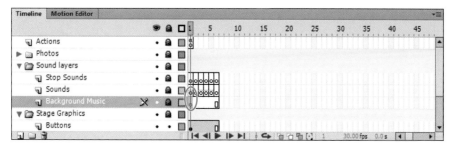

Locate the layer that will contain background music that you'll add in a moment.

2 With frame 1 of the Background Music layer selected, make sure the Property Inspector is visible. From the Sound menu on the Property Inspector, choose the sound called BackgroundMusic.wav.

3 Click the Edit button (⌀) to the right of the Effect drop-down menu to open the Edit Envelope dialog box.

Use the Edit button for a selected sound to edit that sound instance.

Press the Zoom Out button (🔍) until the waveform becomes visible. Listen to the sound by clicking the Play button in the lower-left corner of the dialog box.

4 Click and drag the marker in the Edit Envelope dialog box's middle ruler toward the right. The farther you drag it, the more you trim the beginning of the sound. Drag it as shown below, so that the sound starts when the waveform truly begins, eliminating the dead space at the beginning.

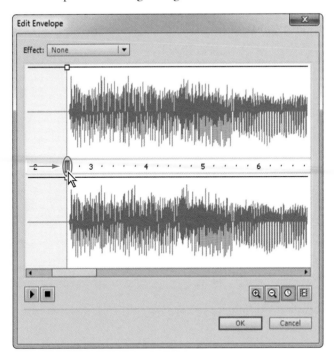

Use the slider between the waveforms to set the start and end points for your sound.

5 Use the scroll bar or arrows at the bottom of the Edit Envelope dialog box to move forward to the end of the sound, if necessary, where you'll find another marker. Click and drag this marker left to trim the end of the sound and adjust its length. Click and drag it so that the sound ends just before the waveform stops, at about 24 seconds.

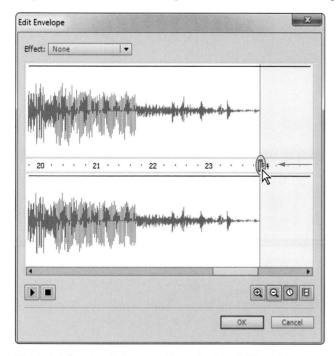

Trim dead air from the end of your sound by moving the end slider as close to the end of the waveform as possible.

6 Click the Play button to preview the sound. The sound plays between the adjusted start and end points.

7 Next, you'll bring down the overall volume of the track so the narration is heard clearly above it. Each waveform displays a line that represents the level of the track. Each time you click on this line, break points are created that can be dragged.

Scroll back the beginning of the sound, and grab the existing break point on the top (left) channel, and drag it so the line is close to the bottom but running straight across. Do the same thing for the bottom (right) channel, as shown in the figure below:

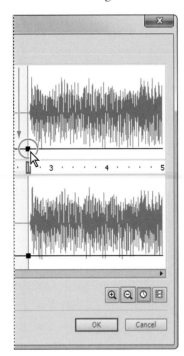 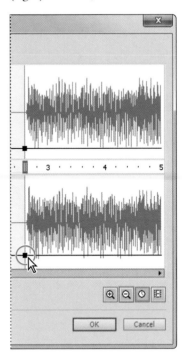

Drag the breakpoints shown to reduce or increase the volume of each channel in your sound.

8 Press OK to close the Edit Envelope dialog box.

Now preview your entire movie. Press Ctrl+Enter (Windows) or Command+Return (Mac OS) to see how the music plays out. Don't use the buttons to navigate; just sit back and listen. The sound should play once without repeating.

9 Choose File > Save to save the file.

There have been reported issues of edits not behaving as expected when using imported .mp3 files. Where possible, use uncompressed (.wav or .aiff) audio for best results. Remember that all sounds imported in your movie and placed on the Timeline are compressed as .mp3 during the Publish process.

Controlling sounds

Once you've placed some sounds, you'll want to make sure you take the extra step to control the behavior of those sounds. Flash doesn't know when one sound should start and another should stop—it plays what you ask it to until the sound is done. This can result in a cacophony of sounds playing all at once if you don't set things up right. Sound control should be an essential part of adding sound, not simply an afterthought. One example is the narration that plays as you shuffle through photos in your slide show. If a user jumps to the next (or previous) photo before the current narration is done, the two overlap. The best solution here is to use a bit of ActionScript to stop any other sounds before playing the next one.

Repeating and looping sounds

When you want a sound to repeat more than once, you can use either the Repeat or Loop options under the Sound portion of the Property Inspector. Experiment with both options with your newly placed background music:

1   Select frame 1 of the Background Music layer, if it's not already selected, and locate the Sound options in the Property Inspector.

2   Under the Sound options, you will see the Repeat drop-down menu and text field. This option allows you to specify the number of times you want your sound to play before it stops. By default, all sounds are set to repeat at least once.

3   Drag over the Repeat value slider, or click and type **3**, to set the number of repeats to 3.

Set the number of repeats for your sound.

4   Preview your movie by choosing Ctrl+Enter (Windows) or Command+Return (Mac OS). The background loop should play three times and stop. Close the Flash Player.

Looping sounds

The Repeat option can be useful in situations where the sound needs to repeat in tandem with events on the Stage, or if you want to put a limit on the number of times a piece of music can repeat. If you are certain you want a piece of music or a sound to repeat continuously, you should choose the Loop option, which plays the sound repeatedly until the movie is closed down. This is a good choice for your background music loop, because you don't want the music to stop while the visitor is enjoying the slide show. Try Loop instead of the Repeat option to hear the difference.

1   Select frame 1 of the Background Music layer, if necessary, and locate the Sound options under the Property Inspector.

2   Select Loop from the Repeat drop-down menu.

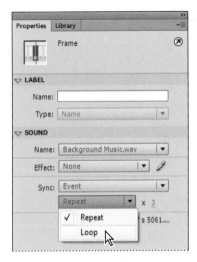

Set the Loop option to repeat forever.

The Repeat text field disappears, as a loop is infinite and has no set number of repeats.

3   Preview your movie by choosing Ctrl+Enter (Windows) or Command+Return (Mac OS). The background loop should play continuously as long as the movie is open. Close the Flash Player.

4   Choose File > Save to save the file.

Introducing the SoundMixer and stopAll()

Introduced in ActionScript 3.0, the SoundMixer class controls the master sound output from your Flash movie, giving you global control over any and all sounds.

In this lesson, you'll focus on the use of one of the SoundMixer's many useful methods, `stopAll()`. This method does exactly what it says—stops all sounds in your movie—and serves as a quick-and-easy way to stop a sound before you begin playback of another.

In the following steps, you'll add the code necessary to stop the current narration from playing before starting a new one on the next photo. To do this, you'll add some code to your Next and Previous buttons to target the SoundMixer's `stopAll()` method.

1   Select the first keyframe of the Actions layer and open the Actions panel by choosing F9 (Windows), Option+F9 (Mac OS), or Window > Actions.

Add the function (fn) key to these shortcuts if you are on a laptop.

2   Look for the comment that reads, `//Moves backwards`, and locate the event handler below it named `prevPhoto`.

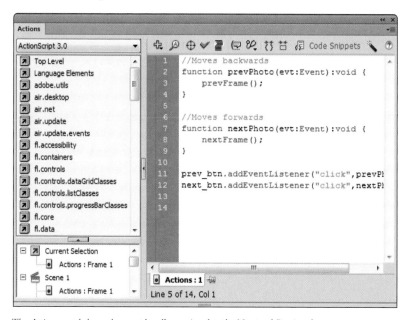

The Actions panel shows the event handlers assigned to the Next and Previous buttons.

3 Click to place your cursor at the beginning of the line that reads `prevFrame()`. Press Enter (Windows) or Return (Mac OS) to make a line of space and add the following script:

```
SoundMixer.stopAll();
```

The event handler should now read:

```
function prevPhoto(evt:Event):void {
SoundMixer.stopAll();
prevFrame();
}
```

As with all ActionScript code, this command is case-sensitive. Make sure you enter it exactly as shown above to avoid errors.

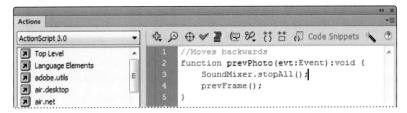

Add the `stopAll()` *statement to the* `prevPhoto` *event handler.*

4 Further down in the ActionScript panel, locate the comment line that reads, //Moves forwards. Directly below it, you should see the nextPhoto event handler. Make a line of space above the line that reads, nextFrame(); and enter the following:

```
SoundMixer.stopAll();
```

The code should now read:

```
function nextPhoto(evt:Event):void {
SoundMixer.stopAll();
nextFrame();
}
```

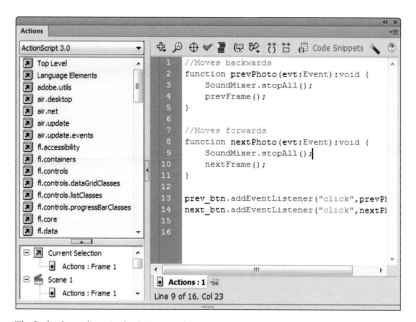

The final code, as shown in the Actions panel.

5 Close your Actions panel and preview your movie by pressing Ctrl+Enter (Windows) or Command+Return (Mac OS). The narrations should now properly stop and start without blending together when you move back and forth between photos.

If you are more comfortable using the toolbox on the left side of the Actions panel to add code, you can find the SoundMixer and its stopAll method under flash.media > SoundMixer > Methods > stopAll.

It's all about the order

Ordering the ActionScript commands correctly on the mouse buttons is essential, because ActionScript executes sequentially from top to bottom. The sounds for each slide show photo are triggered when the playhead reaches their respective frames, so the current sound must stop before Flash advances to the next one. Had you reversed the command order in the exercise, the button would have moved you to the next photo, and played the new sound but immediately stopped it, because the `SoundMixer.stopAll()` function was called after the new sound began. Remember, although it seems that several lines of ActionScript run almost simultaneously, they are actually executed in order.

More sync menu controls: stop and start

You may notice that using the Previous and Next buttons stops your background music from playing. This is because both buttons contain a `SoundMixer.stopAll()` command, which is designed to stop any sound playing in a Flash movie at once. In the following lessons, you'll learn how to selectively stop the narration without affecting the background music.

Beyond Event and Stream, the Sync menu offers two more behavior options for sounds: stop and start. These options allow very fine control over the playback of specific sounds in your movie. You will use them now to fine-tune and complete your slide show. ActionScript allows for more powerful and granular ways to control individual sounds, but those techniques are beyond the scope of this book.

Start sounds

Because sounds placed on a frame are triggered when the playhead reaches that frame, you run the risk that a sound may overlap itself at some point. Consider your background music: you want to ensure that a user returning to the first frame to view the photo doesn't retrigger the background loop and cause it to overlap. To avoid this, set the Sync option for the sound to Start. Start sounds play only one instance of themselves at a time, thus preventing overlap. A Start sound also plays until the end and can only be stopped by a matching Stop sound (more on this in a minute). By setting the background loop as a Start sound, you can make sure it will not be retriggered unintentionally if it's already playing elsewhere in your movie.

---

1   Select frame 1 of your Background Music layer.

2   Choose Start from the Sync drop-down menu under the Property Inspector's Sound options. Leave the Loop options as they are.

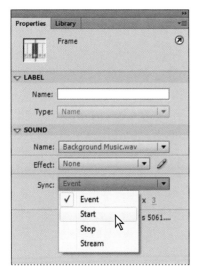

Switch the background music's Sync setting from Event to Start to avoid overlap.

3   Preview your movie by pressing Ctrl+Enter (Windows) or Command+Return (Mac OS), and return to the first photo using the Previous button. The background music should play properly without overlap. Close the Flash Player to return to the Timeline.

Stop sounds

The Sync menu's Stop option works with a single sound you specify through the Sound menu, stopping only that sound, if it is already playing. Stop is a great way to terminate any piece of audio narration without affecting the background music at all. As you've seen with the SoundMixer.stopAll action, it stops all sounds including your background music, which is probably not the intended effect. Let's put Stop sounds into practice for the slide show:

1   Select keyframe 1 of the Actions layer, and open the Actions panel. Locate the two lines that read SoundMixer.stopAll();, and put a double backslash before each one to disable them, like so:

```
// SoundMixer.stopAll();
```

Close the Actions panel.

At the time of this writing, sounds using the start sync option would not playback when previewed or published in Flash Player 10. The issue has been noted and reported to Adobe, and future notes and workarounds will be posted on the Digital Classroom books website at digitalclassroombooks.com as they become available.

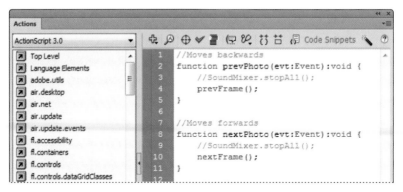

Disable the `SoundMixer.stopAll()` action on the Next and Previous button event handlers.

2   Under the Sound layers folder on the Timeline, locate the Stop Sounds layer. Select keyframe 2 on this layer.

3   In the Property Inspector, use the Name menu (under Sound options) to select Photo1.wav. Although you are on the second photo, the goal is to stop the Photo 1 narration when switching to this frame so that the Photo2.wav sound can play.

4   With Photo1.wav selected, choose Stop from the Sync menu. Rather than play the Photo1.wav sound at this frame, it will stop any instances of this sound only, leaving other sounds unaffected.

Set a Photo1.wav Stop sound on keyframe 2.

5 Choose Control > Test Movie to preview your movie. Move quickly from the first photo to the second. The Photo 1 narration should stop and the Photo 2 narration should begin, without interrupting other sounds in your movie.

6 Use the same methods outlined in steps 1 to 3 to place a Stop sound on each remaining keyframe in the Stop Sounds layer for Photo 2.wav through Photo 5.wav. These will stop any animation from the previous photo from running as you move ahead.

7 Choose Control > Test Movie to preview your movie.

You will notice that moving backward to previous photos, you will still experience overlap. There are a number of ways to alleviate this problem, but the limitations of Stop sounds may make this a better fit for an ActionScript solution.

8 Close the Flash Player, and choose File > Save to save the file.

Sound publishing options

When you publish your movie for final delivery to the Web, mobile, or other destination, you can adjust how Flash exports the audio and packages it with your movie. By default, Flash compresses sounds in your movie into the .mp3 format, regardless of the original file format. However, you can set the sound quality for both Stream and Event sounds in the Publish Settings dialog box at File > Publish Settings. You'll learn more about this, as well as other techniques related to publishing your final Flash movie, in Lesson 14, "Delivering Your Final Movie."

1 Choose File > Publish Settings to open the Publish Settings dialog box. Click on the Flash publish option on the left side of the dialog box to display the Flash publishing settings on the right side.

2 You will see some settings for Audio Stream and Audio Event. Click on the Audio Event settings to open the Sound Settings dialog box.

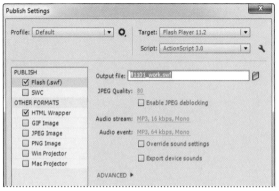

You can set the quality and compression settings for sound in your movie from the Publish Settings panel.

3 Leave or set the Bit Rate to 64 Kbps. MP3 quality is determined by bit rate. The higher the quality, of course, the higher the file size. Press OK to close the Sound Setting dialog box, then press OK again to close the Publish Settings dialog box.

MP3 applications such as Apple's iTunes encode MP3 files at a default bit rate of around 128 Kbps.

Remember that, just like quality settings for bitmap images, sound quality settings have a direct effect on the final file size. Before making a final decision, experiment with different quality settings for Audio Stream and Audio Event until you reach an acceptable quality level.

4 Choose File > Save to save the file, then choose File > Close.

Congratulations, you've finished the lesson.

Wrapping up

Sounds are a great way to enhance your movie, and, paired with ActionScript, the applications and ideas are limitless. Always plan carefully when working with sounds, as a certain level of preproduction on your original files will help guarantee the best possible results in Flash. Wherever possible, make sure the user has an option to discontinue or temporarily mute sounds.

Self study

Use the techniques you've learned here to import and place a song from your own MP3 library into one of your own Flash movies. Experiment with different sync and loop options to see which works best for your new soundtrack. Design and add a Mute button that uses the `SoundMixer.stopAll()` action. Make sure to preview your movie to see how the sound will perform for your users.

Review

Questions

1   What three sound formats can Flash import by default (not including additional QuickTime-enabled formats)?

2   What Sync option is best for shorter sounds, such as those that respond to button events?

3   True or False: Several sounds can be added to your movie on a single keyframe.

Answers

1   Windows WAV, Mac OS AIFF, and MP3.

2   Event sounds.

3   False—while your movie can play back several sounds at once, each needs to be placed on its own keyframe and its own layer.

What you'll learn in this lesson:

- Using movie clips
- Creating, editing, and reusing movie clips
- Understanding instance names
- Nesting movie clips
- Viewing movie clip animation

Introducing Movie Clips

As your animations become richer and more elaborate, you may find that they can't be easily managed on a single timeline. Movie clip symbols enable you to break complex animations into smaller pieces that can be manipulated individually.

Starting up

Before starting, make sure that your tools and panels are consistent by resetting your preferences. See "Resetting the Flash workspace" in the Starting up section of this book.

You will work with several files from the fl12lessons folder in this lesson. Make sure that you have loaded the fllessons folder onto your hard drive from the supplied DVD. See "Loading lesson files" in the Starting up section of this book.

See Lesson 12 in action!

Use the accompanying video to gain a better understanding of how to use some of the features shown in this lesson. You can find the video tutorial for this lesson on the included DVD.

The project

In this lesson, you will create an animation of a common, complex machine in motion: an airplane taking off. Using the power of movie clips, you'll break the airplane's various moving parts into individual animations. The graphics for the propellers and landing gear are provided; you'll simply put them all together while learning how to create complex yet manageable animations beyond the main Timeline.

About movie clips

Movie clip symbols have the same advantages as other symbol types: all instances of a movie clip remain attached to their master in the library, and you create new instances by dragging them to the Stage from the Library panel. Each movie clip instance can be modified with transformations and color effects, just like a graphic. The real power that sets movie clips apart is that each movie clip contains its own timeline, independent of the main Timeline. Movie clip animation, therefore, neither depends upon, nor needs to synchronize with, anything happening on the main Timeline. Each movie clip can contain its own animation, which you can place on the main Timeline whenever and wherever you need it.

The lesson's airplane is a good analogy: it's a complex machine made of a lot of separate parts and smaller machines. Although the landing gear, turbines, and wing flaps make up the whole machine, each component has a different motion, rate, and function. Trying to build a plane out of one component would be impossible. Similarly, some complex animations can't be built on one timeline alone; they require the flexibility of separate parts. Each part needs to move at its own pace along its own Timeline. Movie clips allow you to break animations into separate manageable and reusable pieces.

Think about the airplane again: some smaller machines (like the engine) are built from a lot of smaller moving parts, but still need to be treated as one whole piece. Movie clips can contain other movie clips, so you can build a single movie clip from several others. They can also contain any number of graphic or button symbols.

Creating movie clips

As with graphic and button symbols, you create movie clips by choosing Insert > New Symbol, or by converting existing graphics or animations on the Stage by choosing Modify > Convert to Symbol. You'll get plenty of practice with this in the next exercise.

Laying the foundation: Your first movie clip

To begin your airplane animation, you'll build a propeller to power your plane.

1 Choose File > Open and navigate to the fl12lessons folder. Select the fl1201.fla file and press Open.

2 Choose File > Save As. When the Save As dialog box appears, type **fl1201_work.fla** into the Save As text field. Navigate to the fl12lessons folder and press Save.

3   Open the Library panel by choosing Window > Library, if it is not already open. Locate the Propeller graphic symbol. This propeller blade is the foundation for an entire propeller assembly that you'll save as a movie clip symbol.

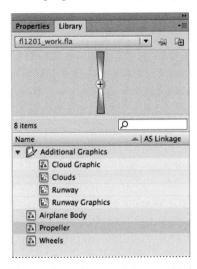

The Propeller graphic in your Library panel is the starting point for your first movie clip.

4   Choose Insert > New Symbol to open the New Symbol dialog box.

5   Name the new symbol **Propeller Animation**, and select Movie Clip for Type. Press OK. The blank Stage and new Timeline that you now see indicate that you're in Edit mode for the new symbol.

Create a new, empty movie clip.

6   Locate the Propeller graphic in the Library panel and drag an instance to the Stage. Choose Window > Align to bring up the Align panel. In the Align panel, make sure the Align to stage checkbox is checked, and then press Align Vertical Center (⊕) and Align Horizontal Center (⊜) to center the Propeller graphic on the Stage.

7   To add a motion tween to the propeller, right-click (Windows) or Ctrl+click (Mac OS) on the propeller instance on the Stage and choose Create Motion Tween from the contextual menu.

8 By default, Flash creates a tween span that is equivalent to one second of play time. The start file was set to 30 fps, so the tween span in this case is 30 frames. Click and drag the end of the tween span to reduce it to 20 frames.

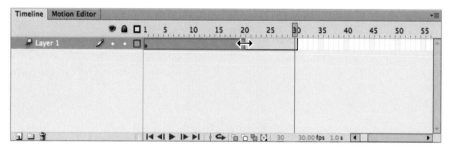

Add a motion tween, then reduce the tween span to 20 frames.

9 Bring the Property Inspector forward by clicking on its tab. If necessary, click on the tween span in the Timeline to make sure it is selected. Choose CW from the Direction drop-down menu in the Rotation section of the Property Inspector. The Rotate drop-down menu enables you to automatically apply rotation to the symbol in your tween. Here, you have applied one clockwise revolution.

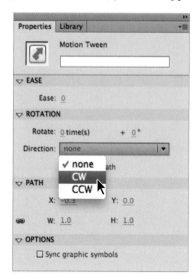

Choose CW from the Direction drop-down menu in the Property Inspector.

10 Press Enter (Windows) or Return (Mac OS) to play your animation. The propeller should now rotate clockwise once.

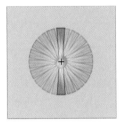

Watch the propeller spin clockwise once.

11 Exit the movie clip by clicking the Scene 1 link above the Stage to return to the main Timeline.

12 Choose File > Save to save the file.

Previewing movie clip animation from the main Timeline

Because movie clips each operate on their own timeline, it's not as easy as pressing the Enter (Windows) or Return (Mac OS) key to see them working on the main Timeline or along with other movie clips. You can view your movie using Publish Preview to see the clips play. Now you'll try placing some instances of your new movie clip on the Stage, and view them all in action.

1 Locate the new Propeller Animation movie clip in the Library panel, and drag an instance to the Stage.

2 Press the Enter (Windows) or Return (Mac OS) key. Nothing happens, but that's OK; nothing is supposed to happen. You must view the movie in Publish Preview to see the movie clip play.

3 Choose File > Publish Preview > Flash, or go to Control > Test Movie > in Flash Professional, to export and launch your movie in the Flash Player. You should see your propeller moving now.

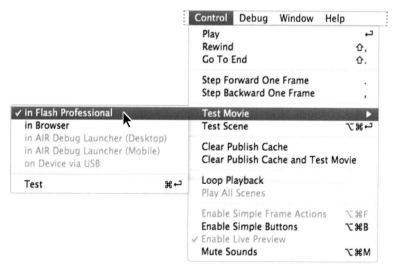

Preview your movie using Control > Test Movie.

4 Close the Preview window and return to the Timeline. Drag another instance of the Propeller Animation movie clip to the Stage.

5 Choose Control > Test Movie > in Flash Professional. Now you should see two propellers spinning at once. With movie clips, reusing animations are as easy as dragging and dropping them.

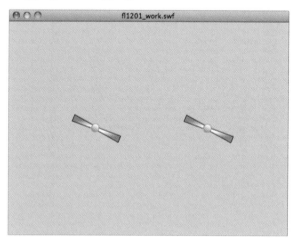

Two instances of the propeller turning simultaneously in Preview mode.

6 Close the preview window.

Creating the landing gear

You've seen two instances of the same movie clip combined. What about multiple instances of different movie clips? Assembling the airplane's retractable landing gear will give you plenty of practice. Before you begin, make sure the Library panel is open, and locate the Wheels graphic symbol.

1 Choose Insert > New Symbol to open the Create New Symbol dialog box.

2 Assign the name **Landing Gear** to your new symbol, and specify Movie Clip for its type. Press OK.

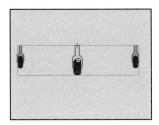

Create a new movie clip symbol.

3 Now you're in Edit mode for the new symbol. Drag a copy of the Wheels graphic from the Library panel onto the Stage, and position it so the top of it lines up with the crosshair in the middle of the Stage.

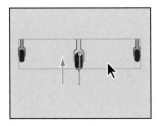

*Position the Wheels graphic underneath
the center of the crosshair.*

4 Right-click (Windows) or Ctrl+click (Mac OS) on the instance of the Wheels graphic on the Stage, and choose Create Motion Tween from the contextual menu. Make sure the playhead is at frame 30, and that the wheels are still selected, and use the up arrow key to move them above the crosshairs as shown in the figure.

Animate your landing gear.

5 To add an ease to the landing gear animation and make it a bit more lifelike, click on the Motion Editor tab and scroll down to the Eases section. Click and drag the number 0 to the right until it reads 100.

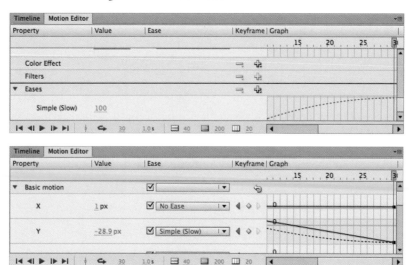

Adjust the Simple ease in the Motion Editor, and then assign it to the animation of the Y position.

6 Scroll up to the Y property in the Basic motion section and choose Simple (Slow) from the Ease drop-down menu. This applies the ease you just adjusted to the animation of the Y position of the wheels.

7 Exit the movie clip by clicking the Scene 1 link above the Stage to return to the main Timeline.

8 Locate and drag a copy of the new Landing Gear movie clip onto the Stage from the Library panel.

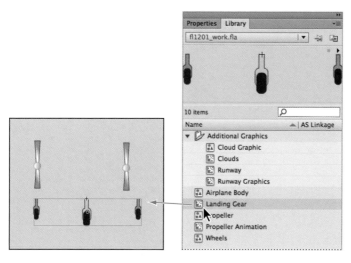

An instance of your Landing Gear movie clip on the Stage.

9 Press Ctrl+Enter (Windows) or Command+Return (Mac OS) to view your movie in the Flash Player and set both propellers and the landing gear in motion.

10 Close the preview window.

Combining movie clips and main Timeline animation

With some key parts in working order, you're ready to match the body of your airplane to these parts. Locate the Airplane Body graphic symbol in the library; you'll be placing this on the Stage in the next steps.

1 Drag an instance of the Airplane Body graphic symbol from the Library panel onto the Stage. Use the Property Inspector to position it at X: **260**, Y: **100**.

Drag and position an instance of the Airplane Body graphic symbol on the Stage.

2 Select the landing gear on Layer 1 and position it at exactly X: **260**, Y: **150**, using the Property Inspector. It should now be in its proper place at the bottom of the airplane body.

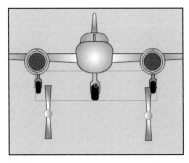

The landing gear is now in place at the bottom of the airplane.

3 Holding down the Shift key, select both instances of the animated propeller movie clip. You need to move these to the front of the stacking order to place them in position on the wings. Choose Modify > Arrange > Bring to Front.

4 Using the Property Inspector, move the left propeller to X:**147**, Y:**132**, and the right propeller to X:**373**, Y:**132**.

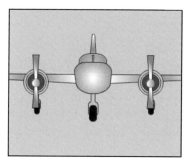

Bring the propellers to the front of the stacking list and position them on the wings.

5 Preview your movie in the Flash Player by selecting File > Publish Preview > Flash, or use the keyboard shortcut Ctrl+Enter (Windows) or Command+Return (Mac OS). The airplane should now be in full force with all parts moving.

6 Close the preview window, and choose File > Save to save your work.

Nesting movie clips

When creating complex animations, you can simplify your main Timeline by leveraging a movie clip's ability to nest, or to include movie clips inside other movie clips. In other words, you can create one single movie clip from several others. (Remember the engine analogy?) This gives you amazing flexibility, and the ability to drag and drop very complex animations to the Timeline as effortlessly as simple graphic or button symbols. Of course, you can modify and maintain movie clips as easily as other symbols by updating multiple instances of a complex movie clip from its master symbol in the library.

In this exercise, you'll convert the airplane and all its moving parts into a single movie clip symbol that you can tween, modify, or duplicate just as easily as any other symbol in your library. Movie clips can be created from existing movie clips, animations, or graphics on the Stage, using Modify > Convert to Symbol.

1 Select the Airplane Body, Propellers, and Landing Gear movie clips by choosing Edit > Select All. Choose Modify > Convert to Symbol to open the Convert to Symbol dialog box.

2   To convert the whole group into a single movie clip symbol, assign the name **Full Airplane** and set the Type as Movie Clip. Use the registration grid to set a perfectly centered registration point. Press OK.

Name the new movie clip **Full Airplane**.

Notice that the group of parts appears on the Stage inside a single bounding box. You can now click and drag the movie clips around the Stage as one unit. Keep in mind, though, that the original movie clips must remain in the library, as the new movie clip depends on them.

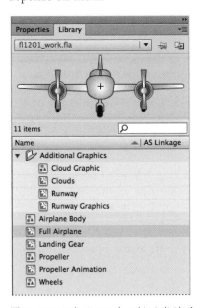

The new movie clip is created, and its individual components remain in the library.

3 Choose File > Publish Preview > Flash to view your movie in the Flash Player. It should play just as it did before.

As the exercise demonstrates, movie clips can contain not only other movie clips, but also graphics (such as the airplane body) and button symbols. This means that you can create entire animations inside movie clips without having to do anything on the Timeline.

4 Close the preview window, and choose File > Save to save your work.

Movie clip facts, myths, and legends

Now that you're pretty deep into movie clips, it's time to review some rules, dispel some myths about how movie clips work, and pass on some important facts you need to know.

Dependencies: When you nest one symbol (movie clip, button, or graphic) inside of another, you create dependencies. In other words, the highest-level symbol (for example, Full Airplane) depends on the symbols it contains (Airplane Body, Propeller Animation, and Landing Gear, in this case) residing separately in the library. Placing other symbols inside a movie clip doesn't copy them, but rather references them. If you remove any lower-level symbol from the library, it will disappear from the larger symbol. If, for instance, you remove Landing Gear from the library, Full Airplane will no longer be able to find it, and the landing gear component will disappear from the grouped movie clip.

Frame Rate: Although movie clip timelines are independent of the main Timeline, they can't use a different frame rate. Frame Rate settings are global to a Flash movie (.swf), and can't be modified from movie clip to movie clip. Changing the frame rate for one affects the entire movie.

Timeline Length: Because a movie clip works from its own timeline, its length is independent from the main Timeline's length or available space. You can place a 200-frame movie clip on the main Timeline, even if there's no more than one frame there. The movie clip will still play as it should. Many movies are built using the main Timeline as nothing more than a container for movie clips, and the main Timeline sometimes contains no more than the first frame of each movie clip.

Timelines: Movie clip timelines work just as the main Timeline does. Anything you can do on the main Timeline, from tweens and layers to ActionScript, you can use on a movie clip timeline. Here's a little-known fact: the main Timeline is a movie clip in itself.

ActionScript: ActionScript on a movie clip timeline has no effect on the main Timeline or Timelines of other movie clips (even included ones), and vice versa. ActionScript on a timeline, such as a stop or play action, affects only that timeline. This means you can use ActionScript across multiple timelines without a problem.

Adding ActionScript to movie clip Timelines

When you preview your movie, you may notice that a few elements need some adjustment. The landing gear, for example, retracts but then shoots back out again (and again, and again) because nothing is directing the landing gear to stop when it has fully retracted. The nature of movie clips is to loop until told otherwise. The default behavior of the Flash Player is to make a movie loop. To override these two behaviors, you'll use a little bit of the ActionScript that you learned in Lesson 9, "Introducing ActionScript."

Controlling movie clip playback

Because movie clip Timelines function just like the main Timeline, placing ActionScript on a movie clip Timeline is exactly the same as placing it on the main Timeline. Prove this to yourself by modifying the Landing Gear symbol so that it doesn't loop.

1 In the Library panel, locate the Landing Gear movie clip symbol and double-click it to edit it. You should be in its Edit mode and see the tween you created earlier in the chapter.

2 Make sure you are viewing the Timeline by choosing Window > Timeline, then press the New Layer button (⬒) to create a new layer, and rename it **actions**.

Although it's not required, separating ActionScript from frames that have content is a good practice.

3 On the actions layer, click on the last frame (frame 30), and press F7 to create a new blank keyframe.

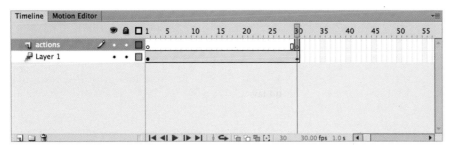

Create a new layer and blank keyframe for the ActionScript.

4 Choose Window > Actions or press F9 (Windows) or Option+F9 (Mac OS) to launch the Actions panel.

5 In the Actions panel, make sure that Script Assist is turned off. Type **stop();** into the Actions panel as shown in the figure below.

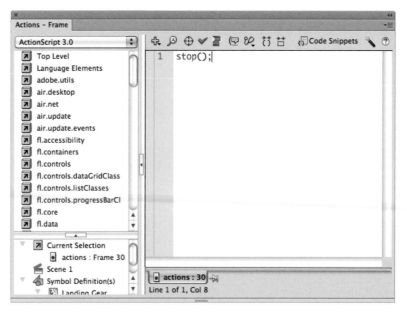

Add a stop() *action to frame 30.*

A lowercase letter *a* on the frame indicates that the frame now contains a script.

6 Close the Actions panel, then exit the movie clip by clicking the Scene 1 link above the Stage to return to the main Timeline.

7 Preview your movie, using File > Publish Preview > Flash. The landing gear should now retract and stay put without looping.

8 Close the preview window, and choose File > Save to save your work.

Adding some variation to the propellers

To make your animation a little more dynamic, you can add two stages of speed to your propeller's rotation. All you need is some additional animation and a little ActionScript. At the moment, the propeller has a single tween that keeps it rotating. Simply add another rotation tween with a higher rate of speed right after the existing one to give the viewer the impression that the propellers pick up speed. To keep them from slowing down and speeding up repeatedly, you'll add ActionScript to animate it over a selected number of frames.

1 Locate the Propeller Animation movie clip in the Library panel, and double-click it to edit it. You should see that the Timeline for this movie clip contains a single tween.

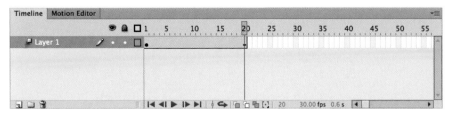

You'll work with tweens to better animate the propeller.

2 Right-click (Windows) or Ctrl+click (Mac OS) on frame 40 and choose Insert Frame.

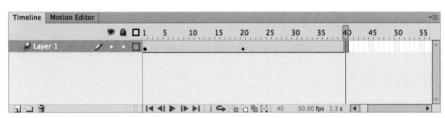

Add a frame on frame 40.

3 Click on the Motion Editor tab and locate Rotation Z in the Basic motion section. Make sure that you have frame 40 selected, and then click the Add or Remove Keyframe button (◆).

4 In the Value field of Rotation Z, type **1800**. This will make the Propeller rotate five times between frames 20 and 40.

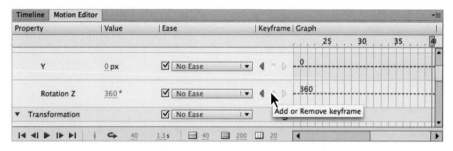

*Add a keyframe on frame 40 and type **1800** in the Value field of the Rotation Z property.*

5 Click on the Timeline tab to bring the Timeline panel forward. With Layer 1 selected in the Timeline, insert a new layer using the New Layer button (⊐), and rename it **actions**. This layer will contain an action that forces the animation to loop.

6 Create a new blank keyframe on the Actions layer at frame 40 by pressing F7. Open the Actions panel (Window > Actions).

7   In the Actions panel, type **gotoAndPlay(21);** as shown in the figure below. This method of the Movie Clip class instructs the playhead to jump to a frame or frame label and play. In this case, when the playhead reaches frame 40, it will jump to frame 21 and play. This will result in frames 1 to 20 playing once, and frames 21 to 40 playing indefinitely.

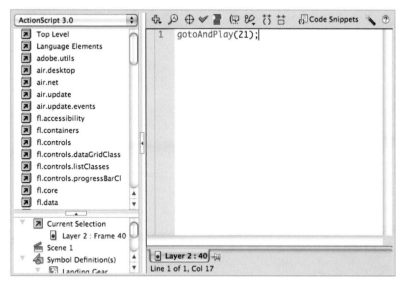

Add `gotoAndPlay(21)` to frame 40 of the Actions layer.

The loop starts later in the Timeline because you want the speed increase to occur only once and then have the propeller maintain a consistent speed as it loops. After the propeller picks up speed through the two tweens, the animation will loop continuously from frame 21, so the speed stays fast as the loop continues.

8   Close the Actions panel and select the Scene 1 link above the Stage. Preview your movie by choosing File > Publish Preview > Flash. The plane's propellers should appear to speed up and then rotate at a continuous rate. Because both propellers were instances of the same symbol, both automatically reflect the changes you made to the master symbol's animation.

9   Close the preview window, and choose File > Save to save your work.

Tweening movie clips

To make your movie clips glide, transform, or change their color tint, you can apply motion tweens to them just as you would to other symbols. Creating a tween with a movie clip is exactly the same as for graphic symbols, and several movie clips can be tweened at the same time on separate layers.

You've already used a few tweens, and, in this exercise, you'll practice using motion tweens to make your airplane take off. Before you start, make sure the Property Inspector is visible.

To tween your airplane and create a take-off sequence:

1   Select the entire airplane on the Stage (instance of Airplane Full). Use the Property Inspector to set its position to X: **280**, Y: **275**. To keep proportions constrained, click the *Lock width and height values together* button and set the width of the airplane to **300**. It should now be slightly smaller and sit on the bottom center of the Stage.

Reposition and shrink the airplane.

2   To animate the airplane taking to the skies, right-click (Windows) or Ctrl+click (Mac OS) on the instance of Full Airplane on the Stage, and choose Create Motion Tween from the contextual menu.

3   With the playhead on frame 30, use the Property Inspector to set the airplane's position to X: **280**, Y: **100**.

Use a motion tween to make the plane rise.

4   To create the impression of gravity pulling down on your plane as it takes off, add an Ease of –100 on frame 1. To do so, select frame 1, then click on the Motion Editor tab and scroll down to the Eases section. Type **–100** in the field to the right of Simple (Slow). Scroll up to the Y property in the Basic motion section and, if necessary, select Simple (Slow) from the Ease drop-down menu.

Add an ease to the airplane's new motion tween.

5   Preview your movie by choosing File > Publish Preview > Flash; your airplane should now lift off and make its way toward the top of the screen with propellers and landing gear in full effect.

6   Choose File > Save to save your work.

Adding a second tween

Now that you have your airplane taking off, you can elaborate further on your animation by making the airplane come toward you as it continues to fly. This will require a second tween after the one you just created.

1   Click on the Timeline tab to bring the Timeline forward. Right-click (Windows) or Ctrl+click (Mac OS) on frame 60 and choose Insert Frame.

2   Click on the airplane and type **400** in the W (width) field in the Property Inspector.

Resize the airplane.

3   Choose Control > Test Movie > in Flash Professional. The airplane takes off and appears to fly toward the camera. This effect may be a bit startling, so hold on to your seat.

As you've seen in these steps, tweening a movie clip instance is very much the same as working with a graphic symbol; so transformations, color effects, and motion can all be applied. Because movie clips can contain entire animations, however, you can fully explore more complex and dynamic animations.

Combining movie clips for complex animation

To make a movie as realistic and dynamic as possible, you can combine as many movie clips on the main Timeline as you need to achieve the full effect. Because each movie clip is an independent animation of its own, multiple movie clips interacting on the Timeline do not interfere with each other. Keep in mind, however, that you may need to carefully orchestrate and sequence animation in different movie clips if one needs to interact with another.

Now that you have your airplane up-and-running, to make the scene more realistic, you'll add two things: a runway and some clouds. Both these graphics will have their own motion, especially as your plane moves off the runway and through the clouds. The movie clips for both of these have already been created for you in the library; all you'll need to do is place them on the main Timeline.

1 Rename Layer 1 **airplane**. Click on the New Layer button to create a new layer above this one and name it **clouds**.

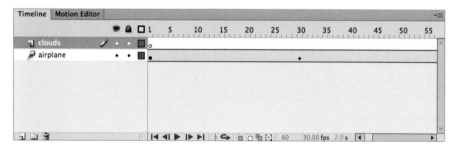

Create a new layer for the Clouds movie clip.

2 Click on the Library tab to bring the Library panel forward. Locate the Clouds movie clip in the Additional Graphics folder and drag an instance to the Stage.

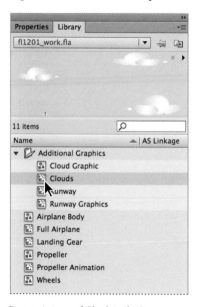

Drag an instance of Clouds to the Stage.

3 Use the Property Inspector to position the new Clouds instance at X: **100**, Y: **220**.

4   While still on the main Timeline, create a new layer and rename it **runway**. Drag this layer to the bottom of the layer stack below the airplane layer.

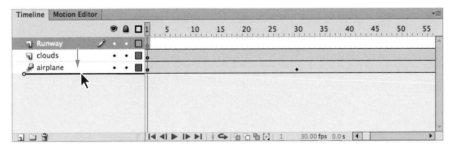

Create a new layer below the airplane tween to make room for your runway.

5   With the runway layer selected, locate the Runway movie clip in the Library panel in the Additional Graphics folder, and drag an instance of it to the Stage. Use the Property Inspector to position it at X: **275**, Y: **260**.

6   Test your movie by choosing Control > Test Movie > in Flash Professional. The newly added clips animate along with the airplane you created; you now have a full animation scene.

7   Close the preview window, and choose File > Save to save your work.

Exercise

To test your new skills, explore both the provided movie clips in Edit mode to see how they were created. Try making modifications to them and see how your overall movie is affected. Because these movie clips were built to work together, major changes in length or animation style may require you to also adjust the other movie clips on the Stage.

Adding filter effects to movie clips

Movie clips have another advantage: they (and buttons) are the only symbol types to which you can apply Flash's built-in, high-quality filter effects, including blurs, drop shadows, and bevels. Because the filter effects are nondestructive, they won't permanently alter the pixel data in a symbol, meaning that you can easily remove or edit filters, as well as apply unique filters to several instances of a movie clip.

Probably one of the coolest features to note is that Flash filters can be tweened, just like any other instance-specific property. For example, you can gradually apply a blur to a symbol to create realistic and artistic effects.

Some CS6 applications (most notably Adobe Photoshop) feature a variety of filter effects. If you're creating graphics in one of these applications, you may choose to apply filters then, or directly in the Flash environment after import. Because Flash natively supports importing Photoshop and Illustrator files, it converts most common filter types to Flash filters. The advantage of applying filters in Flash is that they can be easily edited without the need to switch applications and re-import updated files. In addition, you can manipulate Flash filters with ActionScript, which opens a world of dynamic filtering possibilities.

Using the Filters panel

In this exercise, you'll explore Flash filters by applying effects to the Clouds and Runway movie clips. Then you'll animate these effects with motion tweens to add more realism to the airplane animation.

1   Select the instance of the Clouds movie clip on the Stage.

2   If necessary, bring the Property Inspector forward by clicking on its tab. Click on the Add filter button (⊒) at the bottom of the Property Inspector and choose Blur from the pop-up list of filters.

Add a blur filter to the Clouds movie clip.

The settings that appear to the right enable you to set the desired degree of vertical and horizontal blur.

3   Locate the Blur X and Blur Y text fields, and then type **10** in either field to set the blur amount for both.

4   Select Medium from the Quality drop-down menu. This is a good choice for making sure the effect looks clean without putting too much strain on the Flash Player (as filter effects are resource-intensive).

5   Preview your movie, using the shortcut key combination Ctrl+Enter (Windows) or Command+Return (Mac OS). Your clouds now have an interesting blur effect applied and, as a result, appear more realistic as the animation plays.

6   Close the preview window.

Creating a filter effect

Filtering an entire movie clip instance is a few clicks away using the Filters panel, but you can go a step further by combining tweens and filters to transition into a filter effect. Try this with your Runway movie clip by blurring the runway as the plane takes off, and climbs above the ground.

1   Double-click the Runway movie clip on the Stage to edit it in place. You should see a basic motion tween that moves the runway down. The tween was created between two instances of a movie clip called Runway Graphics. (Graphics symbols cannot be used because you can apply filter effects only to movie clips or buttons.) Move the playhead on the Timeline to Frame 30 and select the instance of the Runway Graphics movie clip on the Stage.

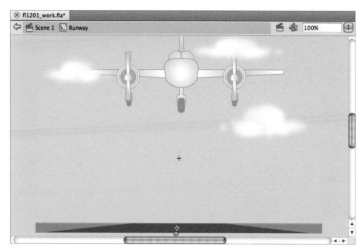

The Runway movie clip at frame 30 in Edit mode.

You can apply filter effects only to movie clips, buttons, and dynamic text fields. If you want to apply a filter to a basic graphic, graphic symbol, or drawing object, you must convert it to a movie clip or button symbol first.

2   Click the Add filter button (⬏) at the bottom-left corner in the Filters section of the Property Inspector, and choose Blur from the resulting contextual menu.

3   Set the Blur X and Y values to **15**, and select Medium from the Quality drop-down menu. Changing the Blur X and Y values to 15 from the default of 5 will automatically create an animation between frames 1 and 30. The effect will be applied for the entire tween span, but it will transition from the default value to the new value.

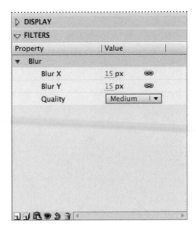

Add a blur to the runway, and then adjust the Blur X and Y values on frame 30 to create an animated filter.

4   To make the transition a bit more pronounced, drag the playhead back to frame 1, select the runway, and change the Blur X and Y values shown in the Property Inspector to **0**.

5   Press Ctrl+Enter (Windows) or Command+Return (Mac OS) to preview your movie.

6 If you like, return to the main Timeline and keep your airplane at cruising altitude by adding a `stop()` action on frame 60. Remember to insert a new layer for the `stop()` action and create a new keyframe at frame 60 before adding the action, to ensure it occurs in the right place. The provided runway and clouds already utilize a `stop()` action.

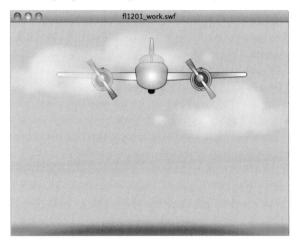

The preview shows the filters you've applied. Now you're flying!

7 Choose File > Save, then choose File > Close.

Congratulations! You've completed the lesson.

Wrapping up

Movie clips open a treasure trove of possibilities, and the best way to master movie clips is to use them—the more you do, the more ways you'll find to create innovative, complex, and eye-catching animations that far exceed what's possible on a single Timeline. To get ideas for your next movie clip, explore ready-made clips, such as the Runway and Clouds movie clips in your library, to understand how they were created. Don't hesitate to modify the movie clips in this exercise by adding keyframes, experimenting with more filter effects, or adding some additional graphics of your own.

Self study

Choose a machine or object with two or more moving parts, and then try to recreate it using movie clips. The subject doesn't have to be complex—get ideas from around the house, in the kitchen, or at the office. Chances are you'll find something worth re-creating that's fun and lets you use your new skills.

Review

Questions

1   True or False: Movie clip Timelines depend on the length and action of animation on the main Timeline.

2   What type of symbols can be contained inside a movie clip?

3   How do you preview movie clip animation along with the main Timeline and other movie clips?

Answers

1   False. Movie clip Timelines are fully independent of the main Timeline.

2   Graphics, buttons, and other movie clips.

3   Use File > Publish Preview.

What you'll learn in this lesson:

- Understanding the principles of working with video in Flash

- Using the Video import wizard to import and convert video files

- Controlling playback of video on the Timeline

- Using the Adobe Media Encoder

Working with Video

Video has become an expected staple of any web or mobile offering, giving viewers a rich and immersive experience beyond graphics and text. Flash Professional CS6 has many tools and capabilities for encoding and delivering video, which has made Flash one of the most utilized platforms for delivering web video content.

Starting up

Before starting, make sure that your tools and panels are consistent by resetting your workspace. See "Resetting the Flash workspace" in the Starting up section of this book.

You will work with several files from the fl13lessons folder in this lesson. Make sure that you have loaded the fllessons folder onto your hard drive from the supplied DVD. See "Loading lesson files" in the Starting up section of this book.

See Lesson 13 in action!

Use the accompanying video to gain a better understanding of how to use some of the features shown in this lesson. You can find the video tutorial for this lesson on the included DVD.

The project

In this lesson, you'll import a video file into Flash and practice various methods of integrating it into your movies. Working through the exercises in this lesson will introduce you to the different ways to work with video in your Flash projects. To view the finished file, choose File > Open and select the fl1302_done.fla, fl1303_done.fla, and fl1306_done.fla files within the fl13lessons folder. Close the files when you are finished, or keep them open as a reference.

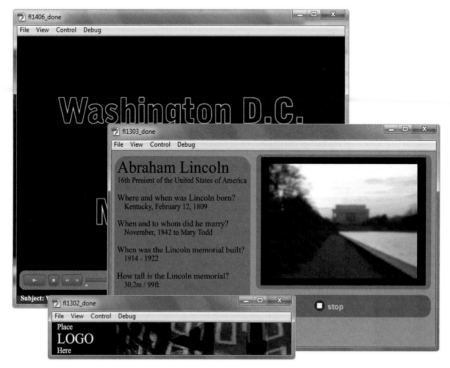

The finished files.

Video in Flash: formats and fundamentals

The first step toward importing video into Flash is to make sure you are equipped and ready. In addition to Flash CS6, you'll need the QuickTime player (at least version 7 for Windows or version 10 for Mac OS) installed on your system. You'll also need a source video file to import and convert (video is provided for the exercises in this lesson).

Understanding video

Like animations on the Timeline, videos are composed of a series of sequential still images played back very rapidly, sometimes with sound, and sometimes without. When played back very quickly, these images seem to form continuous motion. You need to keep two parameters in mind when working with video: frame rate, which is the speed, measured in frames per second (fps) at which the video plays, and frame size, which is the size, measured in pixels, of each frame of video. Both the frame rate and size contribute to the final file size.

Embedded versus linked video

There are two ways to work with video in a Flash (SWF) file: you can embed the video directly onto the Timeline, or have your movie reference an external, linked video file that resides on a server.

External video files can be streamed from a Flash Media Server, a server solution optimized to deliver streaming or real-time media, or downloaded progressively from any standard web server, including the same one on which your Flash movie is hosted. Using external video keeps the SWF file size fairly small, and because the video file exists as a separate object on a server, the SWF container can be repurposed to dynamically display multiple video sources. In addition, because the FLV file exists outside the Flash movie, it can have a different frame rate from the SWF; this avoids messy issues where video and audio end up out of sync, which is common when working with embedded video files. For a comparison of the benefits of streaming versus progressively downloading, see the section, "Working with linked video."

Embedded video is placed directly on the Flash Timeline. This can significantly increase the SWF file size—potentially to unmanageable levels with longer clips. Additionally, because the video file and the Flash document can have two different frame rates, audio and video may end up out of sync when the movie is published. For this reason, embedded video is usually recommended only for short video clips, and even then usually only for short video clips without audio.

Another major difference between embedded and linked video is the way in which they are deployed for distribution. Because embedded video is a part of the SWF Timeline, it is automatically included when you publish the file. Linked video, however, exists independently and must be uploaded to the server in addition to your SWF and any other dependent files. In general, the goal of using linked video files is to create modular content than can be repurposed more easily than embedded video can, and to reduce the initial loading time of your SWF.

Flash Video formats: FLV and F4V

All video in Flash must be converted into the Flash Video format (FLV or F4V) or H.264 formats for playback in the Flash Player. This conversion can be performed as part of the process of importing video into a Flash document using the built-in Video Import wizard, or it can be completed before the import stage by using the Adobe Media Encoder or a video editing application such as Adobe Premiere Pro that can export Flash video.

There are two extensions used for Flash video files. The FLV format is supported by Flash Player version 7 and higher, while the newer F4V format is supported by Flash Player versions 9.2 and higher. The F4V format is intended to provide higher playback quality at lower files sizes than FLV can provide. The Flash Player version that you want to target will determine how you format your video. If you are publishing for the latest version of Flash Player (or even versions 9 or up), it's recommended that you convert video to F4V.

Understanding codecs

Codecs are software routines that compress video files small enough to be e-mailed, or viewed on the Web or mobile devices.

The video creator uses a codec to compress the video file for distribution; the files are then decoded by the viewer's video player using the same codec. Flash video (F4V specifically) supports three codec choices: Sorenson Spark, On2 VP6 (usually called ON2V), and H.264.

The Sorenson Spark codec is supported by files encoded in the FLV format for playback in Flash Player 7 and later. The On2 VP6 codec is the default setting for videos encoded for versions 8 and 9 of the Flash Player because it provides higher video quality than the older Sorenson Spark codec. MainConcept H.264 is supported by Flash Player versions 9.2 and later. The newer codecs provide better video playback quality at lower file sizes than the older ones do. This higher-quality video comes at the price of a slower encoding time and more use of system resources (such as RAM and connection speed) on the viewer's computer at playback time.

Understanding Adobe Media Encoder CS6

The Adobe Media Encoder is a stand-alone application that is installed when you install the Flash application. The encoder exists to convert video and audio media from one format to another. While often thought of as a tool for converting video into the Flash Video format, it can actually convert video into a wide range of formats, such as IPod video and video for sharing sites such as Vimeo and YouTube.

The Adobe Media Encoder can import video and audio in a wide variety of file formats. Some of the more common importable video formats are listed below:

- 3GPP/3GPP2 (.3gp, .3gpp)
- Digital Video (.dv)
- DV stream
- Flash Video (.flv, .f4v)
- QuickTime (.mov)
- MPEG (.mpg, .mpeg, .m2v)
- Windows (.avi)
- Windows Media (.asf, .wmv)

The QuickTime player is available as a free download from apple.com, *and is packaged with all versions of Mac OS X.*

The Adobe Media Encoder is divided into 4 main areas: the Queue, Encoding, Preset Browser and Watch Folders panes. The Queue is a list of the files you are going to convert, and the settings for each. From the Queue, you can choose the type of video you would like to output to, and the specific preset you would like to use for it.

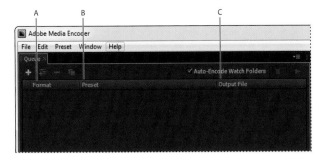

A. Format. B. Presets. C. Output file destination.

When the built-in presets aren't suitable for your project, you can open the encoder's Export Settings dialog box for greater control. The window gives you increased control over things such as output size, video and audio compression, and even the ability to upload directly to a web server. In addition to the output of your video file, the dialog box can be used to set cue points for Flash video and even perform basic editing by trimming the beginning or ending of a video file.

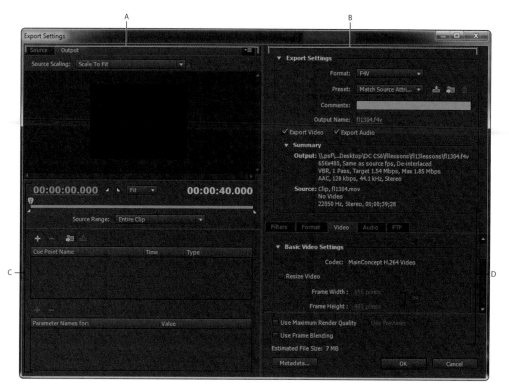

A. The Source and Output Monitor tabs. *B.* Provides a summary of the Export Settings. *C.* Location for setting cue points and trimming video. *D.* Tabs containing the specific settings for Video, Audio, and Format.

Converting video with the Adobe Media Encoder

The first phase is to prepare the video file that you will import into the Flash project using the Adobe Media Encoder. Technically, the Adobe Media Encoder isn't a part of Flash; it is a stand-alone video converter that can take video in one format and convert it to another. In addition to Flash video, the Adobe Media Encoder can also create files for display on mobile devices such as cell phones, iPods, and others. In the following exercise, you will import and convert a video file using the Adobe Media Encoder.

1 Open the Adobe Media Encoder by choosing Adobe Media Encoder CS6 from the Start Menu (Windows) or Applications > Adobe Media Encoder CS6 (Mac OS).

2 In the Adobe Media Encoder, press the Add Source button. In the Open dialog box, navigate to the fl13lessons folder and select the fl1301.mov file. Press Open to load the video file into the Adobe Media Encoder.

You can also drag and drop files into the Adobe Media Encoder window from the Mac OS X Finder and Windows Explorer.

3 There are three editable fields for every file:

- **Format**: Either Flash Video (.flv or .f4v), h.264 or mp3. The h.264 format is used when creating video for mobile devices, and video sharing sites like YouTube.

- **Preset**: Once the format is chosen, AME allows you to select from a wide range of preset options for encoding the video.

- **Output file**: Specifies the location and name of the new file that will be created.

For Format, make sure that the drop-down menu displays FLV or F4V. For Preset, press the triangle button to open the menu and choose Match Source Attributes (Medium Quality). The Output file's location will automatically be set to match the location of the source video file.

As stated previously, if the F4V format is designed to provide better quality video, why are you using FLV-formatted video here? The reason is that for the first part of this exercise you will embed video directly into a Flash file. This procedure can only be done when using an FLV format.

4 Press the Start Queue button and the Encoder will convert your video.

5 Once the video has completed converting, close the Adobe Media Encoder by choosing File > Exit (Windows) or Adobe Media Encoder CS6 > Quit Adobe Media Encoder CS6.

Working with embedded video

Embedding video is the most straightforward method of adding video content to your movies. However, because it can enlarge the size of your SWF file and create issues where your audio and video are out of sync, it is best suited for adding short video clips. On certain projects, embedded video may be the only viable way to work with video in Flash. Often, when creating Flash banners or other advertising material, you have to deliver completely stand-alone SWF files without external links. Embedded video is also a very good way to create interaction or integration between video and Timeline animated assets, or to create a quick closed-captioning effect.

Adding embedded video to the Timeline

Once video has been converted to the Flash Video format, it is ready for use in Flash either as linked video that runs from a location outside your Flash movie (.swf), or embedded video that is placed directly into it. Once you have embedded the video file, the SWF that you create will be ready for deployment just like any other Flash movie. All you need to do is place it in a web page, and it will be ready to be viewed on the Web.

1   Open Flash CS6. Choose File > Open, navigate to the fl13lessons folder, and select the Flash file fl1302.fla. Press Open. This file is a mockup for a banner advertisement.

2   In the Timeline, select the first frame of the Video Here layer, and then choose File > Import > Import Video.

3   In the Import Video dialog box, under the section labeled *Where is your video file?* make sure the radio button labeled On your computer is selected. Press the Browse button and from the fl13lessons folder, select the fl1301.flv file created in the previous exercise and press Open. Select the radio button labeled Embed FLV in SWF and play in timeline.

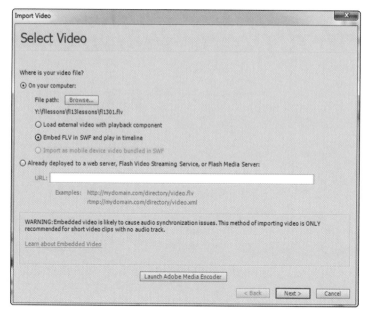

The dialog box displays a warning that embedding video is recommended only for smaller video files and those without audio.

4   Click Next. In the Embedding section of the Import Video dialog box, make sure Embedded video is selected from the Symbol type drop-down menu. Make sure that the Place instance on stage, Expand timeline if needed, and Include audio checkboxes are all selected.

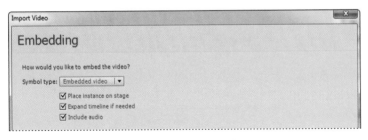

Increase the size of the Timeline to accommodate the new video.

5   Click Next. The Finish Video Import section of the Import Video dialog box provides a summary of the decisions you have made in the Video Import wizard. Press Finish to complete the import process.

6   Use the Selection tool (**k**) to position the video file so its left edge lines up against the second vertical guide to the right of the logo area, and it's vertically centered on the Stage. Lock the Mask and Video layers by clicking them below the padlock column in the Timeline panel. This fully activates the mask layer, and you should see only a portion of the new video revealed.

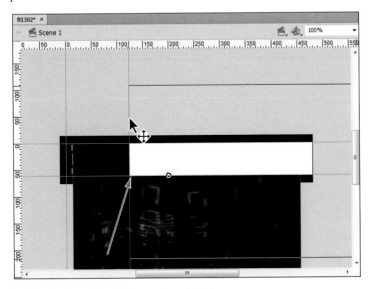

Position the video within guidelines as shown in the figure.

To make positioning the new video as easy as possible, make sure that snapping is enabled by choosing View > Snapping > Snap to Guides.

7 As the Timeline currently stands, the video on the Video Here layer plays for 1171 frames, but the theme, Mask, Logo, and Background layers only exist at Frame 1. You'll correct this in the next few steps by adding frames to the Timeline.

Click the Go to Last Frame button located at the bottom of the Timeline to advance to the end of the timeline at frame 1171. Click on frame 1171 in the Background layer on the Timeline. Hold down the Ctrl (Windows) or Command (Mac OS) key, and click on frame 1171 in the Mask and Logo layers as well, to select them all at once.

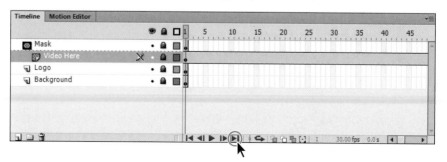

Advance to the last frame of the timeline so you can extend the remaining 3 layers.

8 Press the F5 key on the keyboard to add new frames to all three layers. This ensures that the content of the Logo and Background layers remains on the Timeline until the video finishes playing.

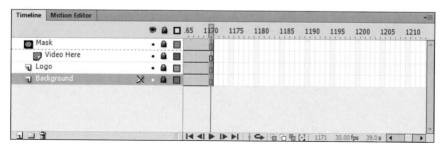

Keyframes act as placeholders, extending the duration of the previous keyframe on the layer.

9 Choose File > Save As. In the Save As dialog box, navigate to the fl13 lessons folder, and then type **fl1302_work.fla** in the Name text field. Press Save.

10 Choose Control > Test Movie to preview your work so far.

11 Close the Flash Player preview window, then choose File > Close to close the FLA document.

Building controls for embedded video

It is the standard behavior of the Flash Player to loop SWF files, but this may not be the effect you want. To prevent this continuous looping, you will use ActionScript 3.0 to control the Timeline and, in turn, the playback of the video. In this exercise, you will import and embed a short video file into a prepared Flash document and use the new Code Snippets panel to create functional Play, Pause, and Stop buttons to control it. The file you will be using for this section is a mock-up of a presentation about Abraham Lincoln and the Lincoln Memorial.

The Timeline of the file lasts for 915 frames. It has an embedded video file, a generic Play and Stop button, and an empty Actions layer where you will place your ActionScript. In order to create a button that will control the Timeline, you will have to define three things:

- Which object on the Stage do you want to control the Timeline playback? For this exercise, you will build two actions, one to play the movie and the other to stop its playback.

- When do you want it to happen? This is called an Event. In this case, you will have the buttons activate when a user clicks and releases the mouse on them.

- What do you want it to do? This is a special type of function called an Event handler. The Code Snippets panel will help you create event handlers that play and stop the movie's Timeline.

1   In Flash CS6, choose File > Open. In the Open dialog box, navigate to the fl13lessons folder and select the fl1303.fla Flash file.

2   Select the first frame of the Actions layer. Locate and expand the Code Snippets panel in your workspace; if the Code Snippets panel is not visible, choose Window > Code Snippets to open it up. To keep the Code Snippets panel open and available, click and drag it by its tab and pull it out of the panel group on the right. Position it somewhere within the left side of your workspace.

3   The first thing you will do is stop the movie's Timeline from playing automatically when the SWF file is loaded. Within the Code Snippets panel, locate and expand the Timeline Navigation folder. Double-click the Stop at This Frame code snippet to place it on the timeline. The Actions panel will appear showing that the code has been added to your project.

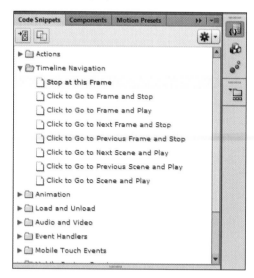

The Code Snippets panel contains pre-created actions for timeline navigation.

4   Select the button labeled Play on the Stage. You will notice when you look at the Property Inspector that the Play button has an instance name of play_btn.

5   With the Play button selected, once again return to the Code Snippets panel. This time expand the Event Handlers folder within this panel. Double-click the Mouse Click Event snippet to add it to the timeline. The Actions panel will appear again, showing you that the necessary code has been added to "wire up" your button for some type of click action.

6   In the Actions panel, locate the line in the new block of code that reads:

```
trace("Mouse clicked");
```

Replace this placeholder line with the following code instead:

```
play();
```

7   If necessary, drag the Actions panel out of the way, or collapse it by double-clicking its tab in the upper-left corner. Select the button labeled Stop on the Stage. Just as you did with the Play button, you'll add some ActionScript to the timeline to make this button do something when clicked.

8   Return to the Code Snippets panel. The Event Handlers folder should still be expanded. Double-click the Mouse Click Event code snippet again to add a new block of code to the timeline. The Actions panel will come forward once again to show you the new code.

9 Just as you did in Step 6, locate the line in the new block of code in the Actions panel that reads:

```
trace("Mouse clicked");
```

This time, replace this line with the following code instead:

```
stop();
```

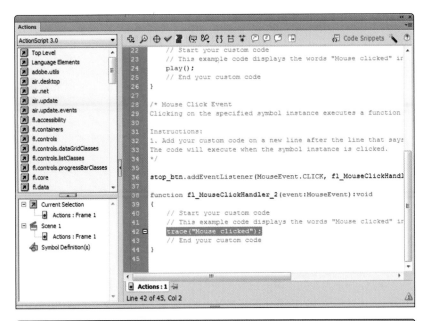

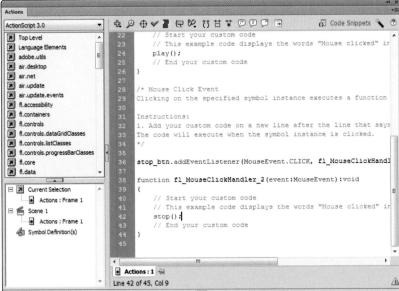

The completed code as it should show in the Actions panel.

10 With the help of the Code Snippets panel, you've added the appropriate code to the timeline that will instruct the Play and Stop buttons to play the current timeline, and stop it, respectively.

11 Close the Actions panel and choose File > Save As. In the Save As dialog box, navigate to the fl13lessons folder and type **fl1303_work.fla** in the Name text field. Press Save.

12 Choose Control > Test Movie to preview your Flash movie and test the buttons. Keep the Flash Player preview window open; you are going to use it in the next exercise.

The Bandwidth Profiler

The Bandwidth Profiler is a useful tool that can help you measure the impact of embedded video on your movie. Even if your movie plays well for you, how does it perform for your target viewers? The Bandwidth Profiler enables you to test your movie's download time under a variety of conditions, and gives you the ability to review the amount of data in each frame of your movie. Check how well your movies from the exercises stack up.

1 In the Flash Player window, choose View > Bandwidth Profiler.

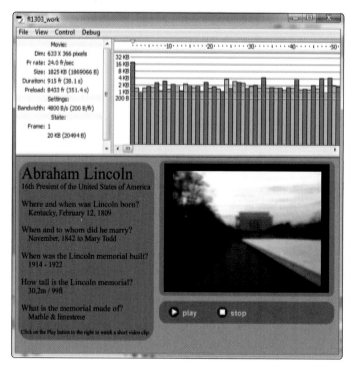

You can access the Bandwidth Profiler through the View menu.

2 Choose View > Frame by Frame Graph to see a breakdown of your movie's parameters on the left, and the size of each frame below that.

3 Choose View > Download Settings > DSL (32.6 KB/s) to see how your movie is treated if viewed over a DSL connection instead of a 56K dial-up connection.

4   Choose View > Simulate Download to preview what viewers experience when they watch your movie at the currently selected download settings.

5   Choose File > Close to close the Flash Player, then choose File > Close from the main Flash menu to close the file.

Working with linked video

If your video file is too large to embed into the SWF file, you should consider importing it as external video. External video remains separate from the SWF file that plays it, keeping the initial loading times for the SWF file fairly small. Linked deployment gives you the choice of three approaches: Web server, Flash Media Server, or Flash Video Streaming Service. Web server deployment enables you to use your current web server or hosting service plan to progressively download video into your Flash movie, using standard Hyper Text Transfer Protocols (HTTP). This allows users to begin watching a portion of your video while the rest of the file continues to load in the background.

Although progressively downloading a video clip from a web server doesn't provide the same real-time performance as using a Streaming Server, this approach requires minimal overhead and works easily with the same server that currently hosts your website.

Video in the fast lane: Flash Media Server

For the fastest video delivery, consider deploying your video content to a Flash Media Server or Flash Video Streaming Service (FVSS).

The stream from a Flash Video Streaming Service for your Deployment option (available from the Deployment Options screen on the Video Import wizard) enables you to upload your video to a Flash Media Server and stream it directly into your Flash movie. Beyond just hosting, these servers also provide many other advanced features for adjusting bandwidth and quality and delivering high performance for large volume usage.

Such providers are often called CDNs (content delivery networks). The Video Import wizard's Deployment Options screen also displays a hyperlink to the Adobe website, *adobe.com*, where you can find a licensed FVSS. Choosing Stream from Flash Media Server on the Deployment Options screen allows you to stream your Flash video from a Flash Media Server that you host, and provides a hyperlink that takes you to the Adobe website to learn more about the Flash Media Server and how to license it.

For both linked approaches, you can use an FLVPlayback component with built-in navigation or ActionScript to control video playback and provide intuitive controls for user interaction.

To explore the linked video approach, you'll build a video player to display a short clip showcasing two presidential monuments in Washington, D.C. Because it is the most easily accessible method, this exercise focuses on progressive downloads from a web server.

Adding cue points in the Adobe Media Encoder

One of the benefits of using linked video is the ability to create navigational cue points and use skins to customize the appearance of the video player. Cue points are added when the Flash file is created in the Adobe Media Encoder, or within the Property Inspector in Flash CS6 (shown in a later exercise).

Cue points can be thought of as bookmarks, or chapter markers within a video. You can navigate through them using the seek buttons on the default Flash Video skins, or using your own mechanism created in ActionScript.

1 Open the Adobe Media Encoder by choosing Adobe > Adobe Media Encoder CS6 from the Start menu (Windows) or Applications > Adobe Media Encoder CS6 (Mac OS). You may see videos that you're previously encoded (if any) appear here. If you want to clear out the display, you can highlight an entry and click Remove. It doesn't remove the files from your hard drive; it merely removes the reference to the file in the encoder.

2 Press the Add Source button on the left side of the workspace. In the Open dialog box, navigate to the fl13lessons folder and select the fl1305.mov file. Press Open to load the file into the encoder.

3 Under Format, make sure that the drop-down menu displays FLV or F4V.

4 In the Edit Export Settings dialog box, choose Web 640×480, Project Frame Rate, 4×3, 800kbps from the Preset drop-down menu.

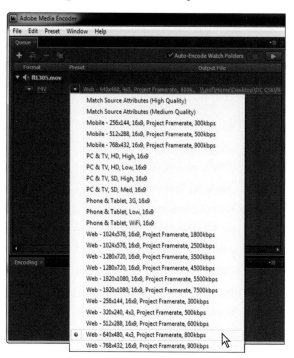

The Preset drop-down menu allows you to select a base group of settings to start with.

5   Click on the title of the newly selected preset in the queue to open the Export Settings dialog box.

6   Cue points are added in the area below the Source/Output monitors. The horizontal orange bar beneath the Source and Output monitors allows you to preview your video and add cue points. Slide the orange handle, called the Current Time Indicator, at the top of the bar until the time above it reads around 5 seconds (00;00;05;00). To get an even 5 seconds, you can click on the timecode and edit it by hand, or use the left/right arrow keys to move one frame at a time. This will move the playhead to 5 seconds, from the beginning of the video.

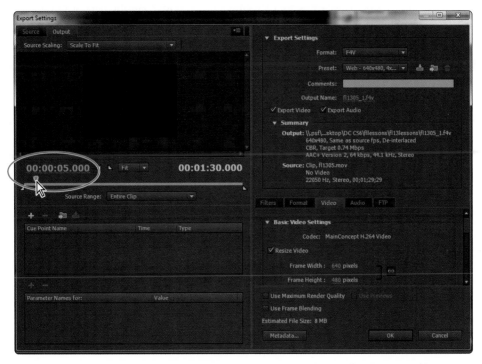

Specific times in a video are located using timecode, shown above. It is denoted by four sets of numbers separated by semicolons. The numbers indicate hours;minutes;seconds;frames.

If you are having trouble moving to a specific time in your video, you can use the left and right arrow keys on the keyboard to move left or right one frame at a time.

7 Press the Add Cue Point button (+) to add a cue point at the current time. In the cue point list, click on the name of the cue point and rename it **washington_monument**. Choose Navigation from the Type drop-down menu.

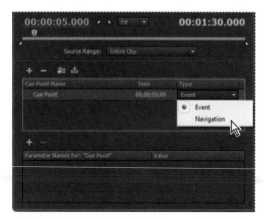

Set a cue point for the navigation.

8 Move the Current Time Indicator to 00:00:35:15. Click the Add Cue Point button. Rename this new cue point **lincoln_memorial** and choose Navigation from the Type drop-down menu.

9 Move the Current Time Indicator to 00:01:15:03. Click the Add Cue Point button. Rename the new cue point **website** and choose Navigation from the Type drop-down menu.

The completed cue points list.

10 Press OK to return to the Adobe Media Encoder. Press the Start Queue button to begin the conversion process. After the file finishes converting, close the Adobe Media Encoder by choosing File > Exit (Windows) or Adobe Media Encoder > Quit Adobe Media Encoder (Mac OS).

Video rendering is a very processor-intensive activity that can take quite a long time. The video included in this lesson could take anywhere from two to five minutes to complete the process. The longer a video file is, the longer the conversion process will take. For your convenience, all the video that you use in this lesson is included as pre-rendered Flash video files in the fl13lessons folder.

Adding linked video to the Timeline

Once the video file is converted by the Adobe Media Encoder, the process for adding the file to the Flash Timeline is remarkably similar to the one used previously for embedding video.

Live Preview

A subtle but useful feature is the ability to preview linked video directly on the Stage within the Flash Professional CS6 environment. Previous versions of Flash required you to Test or Publish a movie first; now you simply use the included controls of the FLVPlayback component to play, rewind, and seek through your movie as you would in a published movie.

1 In Flash CS6, choose File > Open, and open the fl1306.fla file located in the fl13lessons folder. This contains a pre-created layout for your new video preview page.

2 Choose File > Save As. When the Save As dialog box appears, type **fl1306_work.fla** into the Name text field. Navigate to the fl13lessons folder and press Save.

3 Choose File > Import > Import Video to open the Video Import dialog box.

4 In the Select Video section of the Import Video dialog box, press the Browse button, navigate to the fl13lessons folder, and select fl1305.f4v. Press the Open button to return to the wizard. Make sure the radio button labeled Load external video with playback component is selected.

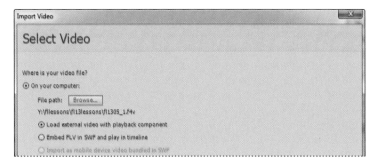

The video import dialog box allows you to embed or load external video.

5 Click Next. In the Skinning section of the Import Video dialog box, choose SkinOverAllNoCaption.swf from the Skin drop-down menu for the movie navigation. Press the Color button, and from the Swatches panel that appears, choose a color and alpha for the skin. In this exercise, the default dark gray was used.

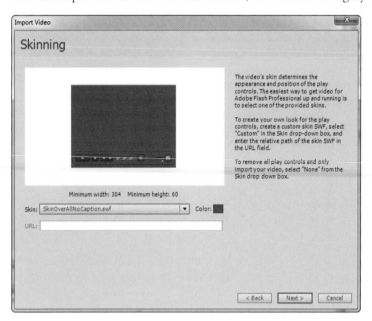

The Skinning section of the Import Video dialog box allows you to control the appearance of the Video player interface.

6 Click Next. The Finish Video Import section of the Import Video dialog box gives you a summary of the decisions you have made in the wizard. Press Finish to complete the video import.

7   Activate the Selection tool (⬥); then click and drag on the FLVPlayback component and move it to the top of the Stage area inside the guidelines.

The positioning of your video should match what you see here.

8   Choose File > Save to save your work.

Adding Cue Points in the Property Inspector

To make working with linked video easier, you can view and modify cue points directly within the Property Inspector in the Flash Professional CS6 environment. This eliminates the need to navigate through a series of complex dialog boxes. All the cue points of a selected video appear in a dedicated panel within the Property Inspector, and you can continue to edit and modify them as needed.

1   Using the Selection tool (⬥), select the FLVPlayback component on the Stage.

2   On the Property Inspector, locate the Cue Points panel, and expand it by clicking the arrow next to Cue Points. You should now be able to see a listing of all cue points that already have been created in this video during the import process.

3   Press the Play button on the FLVPlayback component on the Stage to begin previewing the video. Allow the video to play for about 10 seconds, and the pause it. This is the spot where you'll create a new cue point.

4   On the Cue Points panel on the Property Inspector, click the Add ActionScript Cue Point button (+) above the cue point listing. This adds a new cue point entry in the list.

5   Double-click the default title in the cue point listing to make it editable and change it to read **Chapter 1**.

6   Double-click the Time value for the new cue point to make it editable. Enter 00:00:10:00 to set the cue point at exactly 10 seconds from the beginning.

7 Repeat steps 5 and 6 for a different cue point listed. You can easily add, remove, or edit other cue points as needed directly from this panel.

8 Choose File > Save to save your work.

Working with the FLVPlayback component

The FLVPlayback component is a special Flash object used to control the playback of linked video in a Flash movie, and to provide the user with an intuitive set of controls for interacting with your video. For the most part, you can work with components in the same way you would with movie clips. However, components are far more complex, and you can edit several more parameters from the Property Inspector to control their behavior. In this exercise, you'll use the FLVPlayback component and its included controls for your movie's linked video.

1 Using the Selection tool (⭑), select the FLVPlayback component on the Stage.

2 Locate and expand the Component Parameters area within the Property Inspector to view the properties for this FLVPlayback component.

Components can be edited and fine-tuned using the Component Parameters on the Property Inspector.

3 By default, the autoPlay parameter is set to true, (the box next to it will appear checked), which sets the video to automatically play when loaded. Click on the checkbox to deselect it. This sets the value to false, disabling the autoPlay behavior for this component.

The Property Inspector offers access to most common properties of the FLVPlayback component.

4 Choose Control > Test Movie to test your movie. When the video appears, it should now be paused on the first frame; you will have to click on the Play button for it to play. Close the Flash Player.

You may notice a slight delay between the time that the Flash movie loads and the appearance of the video. This is normal and varies by the speed of a user's Internet connection. Some developers place an image or text on the layer below the FLVPlayback Component to entertain the viewer while the video loads.

5 Choose File > Save.

6 Close your project by choosing File > Close.

Congratulations! You have finished the lesson.

Self study

Use the three Flash video files you created in the last part of the lesson to create your own video player by embedding each of them into a Flash file.

Practice encoding your own video at various settings and compare the results of the different encoding options.

Review

Questions

1 What are the two standard deployment options with Flash video? Briefly describe each.

2 Which linked deployment option can any Flash user with a website immediately use, and why?

3 Which ActionScript command is used in this lesson to completely stop the movement of the Timeline?

Answers

1 **a.** Linked video: This can be a progressive download from a web server allowing you to stream video, using a web server's standard HTTP protocols of streamed video from a Flash Video Streaming Service, or your own Flash Streaming Server.

b. Embed video in SWF and play in Timeline: This places the video directly in the Flash Timeline, which allows you to sync the video with other animation, or add interactive elements to the video area.

2 The progressive download option can be used by any Flash user with a website because it uses a standard Internet protocol (HTTP) to load and display video.

3 The stop() action can stop all movement in a Flash movie by stopping the playhead on the main Timeline or any nested Timelines from advancing.

What you'll learn in this lesson:

- Exploring the Publish Settings dialog box
- Adjust settings for movies on the Web
- Publishing movies as desktop applications with AIR
- Creating Publish presets
- Publishing options for mobile devices with AIR for iOS and Android

What you'll learn in this lesson:

- Exploring the Publish Settings dialog box
- Adjust settings for movies on the Web
- Publishing movies as desktop applications with AIR
- Creating Publish presets
- Publishing options for mobile devices with AIR for iOS and Android

Delivering Your Final Movie

Although Flash is commonly thought of as a web design and development program, it's also a full-featured multimedia authoring tool. With Flash CS6 Professional, you can publish content for distribution to the Web, mobile devices and even as full-featured desktop applications.

Starting up

Before starting, make sure that your tools and panels are consistent by resetting your preferences. See "Resetting the Flash workspace" in the Starting up section of this book.

You will work with several files from the fl14lessons folder in this lesson. Make sure that you have loaded the fllessons folder onto your hard drive from the supplied DVD. See "Loading lesson files" in the Starting up section of this book.

See Lesson 14 in action!

Use the accompanying video to gain a better understanding of how to use some of the features shown in this lesson. You can find the video tutorial for this lesson on the included DVD.

The project

In this lesson, you won't be creating a movie or even a piece of one. Instead, you'll be publishing existing movies so you can put your creations to work. You will also learn how to customize publish settings for a variety of output formats across web, mobile and desktop (AIR).

The publishing process

By now you should be very familiar with the Test Movie command. As you learned in previous lessons, the command generates an SWF file so that you can preview how your animation looks and how well its interactive elements behave.

Although Test Movie works very well for preview purpose, the Publish command gives you a much wider range of options. By default, the Publish command creates an HTML page with your SWF file embedded into it for display in a browser. You can also specify other file types such as web-ready image formats (JPEG/GIF/PNG), stand-alone projector files and more.

Publishing to the Web

For viewing in a web browser (the most common option), a Flash file must be embedded into a web page. Flash's Publish command does all the work for you by creating an SWF file, as well as an HTML wrapper file (web page) that has your SWF file contained within it. Once you have published these files you can easily upload them to your website to display your work to the world.

Publishing a file is simple. With your FLA file open, select File > Publish. Flash then creates HTML, SWF, and any supplemental JavaScript files (for version checking and browser support), and saves them to the directory that contains the FLA file, or another directory that you specify.

Before you publish, you may want to explore, and work with, some of the Publish settings that can tweak the appearance and behavior of your movie, as well as generate any additional file types you may need.

Customizing the Publish settings

The default settings are fine for many situations, but you can customize the Publish settings for better results. Give it a try:

1 From the fl14lessons folder, open the file named fl1401.fla, which is an animated footer for a website.

2 Choose File > Publish Settings to open the Publish Settings dialog box. Make sure you are targeting the latest version of Flash Player by selecting Flash Player 11.2 from the Target drop-down in the upper-right corner (by default, the latest version of Flash player should be selected). The dialog box will display available file formats on the left as shown in the figure below.

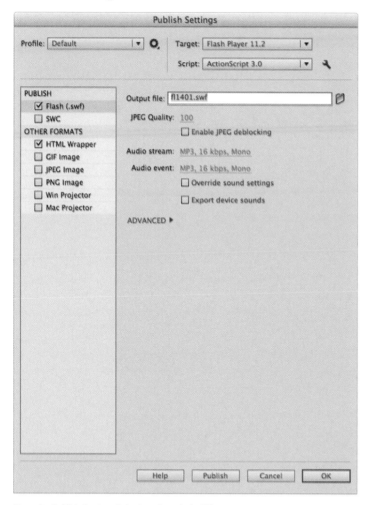

Open the Publish Settings dialog box through the File menu.

3 Under Publish on the left, click and select Flash (.swf) if it's not already selected, so that you display the available publishing options for this format on the right.

4 Here we can tell Flash how much to compress images used in our movie, which helps reduce overall file size. Click and drag to the left over the JPEG Quality value until it reads at about 85. This will increase the amount of compression on the bitmap images in your movie, and lower the file size with minimal sacrifice to image quality.

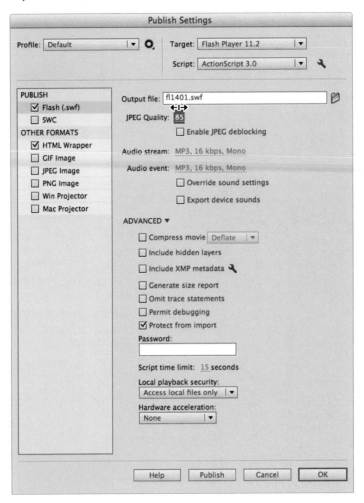

Drag the JPEG quality slider to 85.

5 At the bottom of the Publish Settings panel, click OK to apply the new settings and close the dialog box.

You can set three additional options for the Flash file export under the Advanced options. Omit Trace Action and Permit Debugging are specifically geared toward working with ActionScript, while Generate Size Report creates a text file that breaks down the size of each scene and symbol in your movie.

6 At this point, you can take a quick look at how your selected Publish Settings will affect the final movie. You can do this by using Test Movie and Bandwidth Profiler, both of which you have used previously in this book. Choose Control > Test Movie > In Flash Professional.

7 When the Flash player preview window opens, choose View > Bandwidth Profiler to open up the Bandwidth Profiler at the top of the window. Note: the Size should read about 42 kb. Click the system close button in the upper corner of the window to close it.

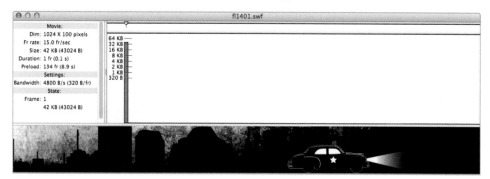

Note the statistics and overall size of your movie as shown in the left side of the window.

Although the example file does not use any audio effects, you can use the Audio Stream and Audio Event options in the Publish Settings panel to control audio quality and how those types of audio objects are compressed. The default MP3 setting is very efficient in most situations.

8 The Publish Settings dialog has some additional options to help compress movies and lower overall file size. Use these options to bring down the overall .swf size a bit more: choose File > Publish Settings once again to open up the Publish Settings dialog box. You should once again see the Flash (.swf) publishing options on the right side of the panel. Locate the Advanced section and click the arrow next to it to reveal advanced publishing options.

9 Locate the Compress movie option and check it. A drop-down list is enabled to let you select one of two efficient and loss-less (no information discarded) compression options: DEFLATE and LZMA. For now, choose LZMA from the drop-down list.

10 Click OK to exit the Publish Settings dialog box and apply the new settings. Repeat steps 6 and 7 once again; you should notice that the file size has decreased slightly to about 38Kb. Every byte counts, so this option can come in handy fairly often.

11 Once more, choose File > Publish Settings. Under the Other Formats category on the left, select the HTML Wrapper option to view the publish options for the HTML file that will contain your .swf file.

12 Locate the Size drop-down list and Width and Height values. By default, the Flash player is instructed to set your movie's dimensions to 100% of the browser window dimensions. This may cause some unwanted side effects, so if you want to keep your movie pixel-perfect, select "Match Movie" from the Size drop-down list. This will set the publish size to match the actual movie dimensions. You'll notice you can't change the Width and Height to arbitrary values any longer. (Those fields are now disabled.)

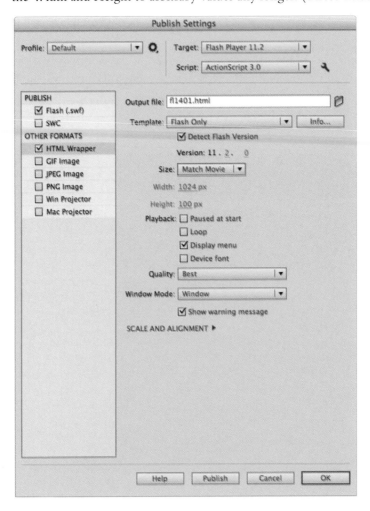

Modify size settings for the HTML Wrapper that will contain your movie.

13 Leave Window Mode, HTML Alignment, and Scale at the default settings. Window Mode controls the appearance of the box in which the SWF file appears; you can use it to create an SWF file with a transparent background. For now, leave this option set as Window.

Note that the example movie uses a nested movie clip symbol, the HTML tab's Paused at Start and Loop Playback options would have no effect; they target the main Timeline only.

14 Click the arrow next to SCALE & ALIGNMENT to reveal these options. Set Flash Horizontal alignment to Center and Flash Vertical alignment to Center, which will place the SWF file in the center of the browser window.

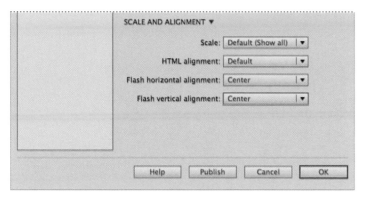

Choose Center from both the Flash Horizontal alignment and Flash Vertical alignment drop-down menus.

15 Click the Publish button to publish your file with the settings you've chosen. Click OK to close the Publish Settings dialog box and File > Close to close the file. You may be asked if you want to save the changes, if so, click OK or Save to save changes.

In the lesson files folder, you should see a newly created fl1401.swf and fl1401.html file sitting in this folder. Double-click the HTML file to view your published movie in a browser.

Creating Publish Profiles

Publish Settings are saved as part of your FLA file, so there's no need to respecify them in between authoring sessions. However, it's possible that you may want to share the same settings across multiple documents. For this purpose, you can create and save Publish profiles from the Publish Settings dialog box.

While in Publish Settings, once you've selected the settings you want, Click the Profile Options button next to the currently selected Publish profile (most likely Default, if you haven't created any before). Choose Create Profile, enter a Profile name and you're good to go! This is saved as part of your application settings, so you can call this profile up at any time within any FLA file.

Publishing for the Desktop with Adobe AIR

With all the capabilities Flash has to offer when it comes to building rich Internet applications, it seems natural that it has evolved to become a great tool for building desktop and mobile applications, as well.

The Adobe AIR runtime makes it possible to deploy your Flash movies as full-blown desktop applications in a few clicks from your Publish Settings dialog box. Your movies will behave exactly as they do in a browser, and with a bit of ActionScript you can extend their capabilities to interact with the user's operating system, work with local files, and connect to outside services to get data.

The Adobe AIR runtime (in version 3.2 at the time of this writing), much like the Flash Player, is available as a free download from the Adobe website, and is a quick install for most users. Best of all, AIR applications are cross-platform, so there's no need to create separate installers for Windows vs. Mac OS platforms. One installer package can handle both.

Before you begin the next exercise, make sure you download and install the Adobe AIR runtime at *http://get.adobe.com/air/*.

> *You can also publish AIR applications from other applications in the Adobe Creative Suite. For example, Dreamweaver CS6 enables you to publish websites, including HTML, CSS and Javascript files, as AIR applications too.*

1   Open the WeatherMate_start.fla file from the fl14lessons folder. This file contains the beginnings of a basic weather application widget. If you do not have the font used in this exercise, you may replace it with any other font on your computer. The exact font you use is not important for this exercise.

2   Choose File > Publish Settings to open the Publish Settings dialog box. Locate and click the Flash tab at the top to see Flash-specific publishing options.

3   From the Player drop-down menu at the top of the dialog box, select AIR 3.2 for Desktop, which will set the necessary publish options to deploy and install your movie as an AIR application on a user's computer.

Set up your Target as AIR 3.2 for Desktop. The Player Settings button sits next to the Target drop-down menu and allows you to open up additional dialog boxes to fine-tune your settings.

4   Click the Player Settings button (✎) next to the Target drop-down menu to open the
AIR Settings dialog box.

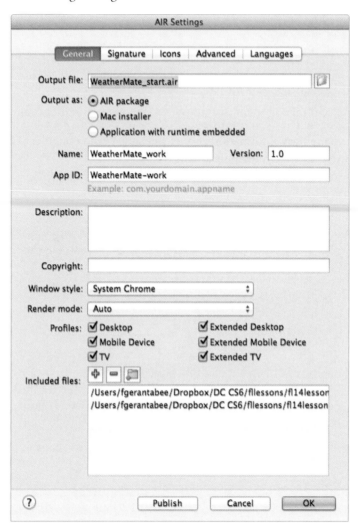

The Air Settings dialog box

Here you can set several options within this dialog box that will affect how your
installer will be packaged, how it appears to the user, and how the application behaves
on the desktop. You'll focus on the most essential ones for this exercise.

5 First, you'll set the general options that determine your file and application name. In the Output file field, change the name of your output file to **WeatherMate.air**; make sure to include the .air extension. This will be the name of the installer file that's created. If you'd like, you can change the save location of the file using the folder icon to the right of the field, but for the sake of this lesson, we'll leave the default save location which is the same folder as your original .fla file.

6 Under the Name and Version, enter **WeatherMate** and **2.0**, respectively. These specify your application's name as your users will see it, and a version number to correspond with the specific release you're offering. If you are not creating an official release, you can enter temporary information and set a default Version number. This is mostly to help your users identify your application.

7 Locate the App ID field; here you can enter a unique ID for your application to distinguish it from other applications the user may have installed on their system. The suggested convention is known as "reverse DNS"—which includes your company domain and application name. If your company is digitalclassroombooks.com and the application is Weather, the ID should read: **com.digitalclassroombooks.weathermate** as stated above. For now, enter this in the field.

8   Next, enter some descriptive text in the Description text field, and relevant copyright info in the Copyright text field. These are optional, so you can leave them blank if nothing comes to mind at the moment.

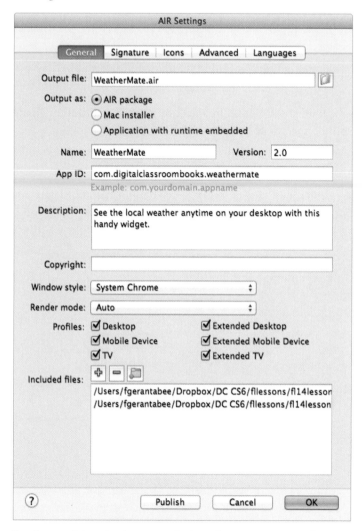

Enter important information about your application such as its name, App ID, description, and any relevant copyright information.

9   Next, you'll set the Window Style, which determines how your application is framed, and how it appears on the desktop. The default option is System Chrome, which places a system window around your application. For this application, however, it would be pretty cool to have it be transparent and reveal the user's desktop below, so select the Custom Chrome (transparent) option instead.

10 Select the Signature tab at the top of the dialog box.

The digital signature of your application verifies its authenticity and provides a level of confidence to your end users/buyers, and is required by most sales and distribution channels. For commercial distribution, it's recommended you purchase a digital certificate (see the section "About Digital Certificates"). For now, you'll continue the steps to create a self-signed certificate for this example.

11 Next to the Certificate drop-down menu, click the New (Mac OS) or Create (Windows) button to begin creating a self-signed certificate.

12 Fill in the text fields for Publisher Name, Organization Unit, Organization Name, and Country (these will be specific to your business).

13 Create a password by entering it in the Password and Confirm Password text fields. You'll be asked for this again later, when signing your application.

AIR Settings	
Publisher name:	Digital Classroom Books
Organization unit:	Application Development
Organization name:	AGI
Country:	US
Password:	••••••
Confirm password:	••••••
Type:	1024-RSA
Save as:	/Users/fgerantabee/Desktop/MyDigitalCerti
	Cancel OK

Creating a self-signed certificate allows you to install and run your application for testing or limited distribution.

14 Next to Save As, click the Folder icon and select a location on your computer to save the certificate in. Enter the file name **MyDigitalCertificate** for your new certificate, and click Save. Press OK to create the certificate and return to the AIR Settings dialog box.

15 The new certificate should be shown in the Certificate field. Enter the password you created for your certificate in the password text field, and for the sake of convenience, check Remember Password for this Session. Press OK to exit the Application & Installer Settings dialog box.

16 In the Publish Settings dialog box, press the Publish button to create your .air installer file. If you are prompted for your password, please re-enter the password for the self-signed certificate you created in step 12. When the process is complete, press OK to exit the Publish Settings dialog box. Note that you may be prompted to enter the password for your new digital certificate again—do so, and then click the Publish button once again, if necessary.

17 Choose File > Save to save your work, then close your document. If you return to the fl14lessons folder, you should see a series of new files created, including a file named WeatherMate.air.

About Digital Certificates

Digital certificates are used to verify the security and authenticity of a software application, and are commonly used for distribution of commercial and non-commercial applications. Depending upon your needs, you can purchase these certificates from vendors such as Thawte (*http://www.thawte.com*) and VeriSign (*http://www.verisign.com*).

While a self-signed certificate will work for testing and limited distribution, if you are considering making your AIR application available for sale, or wide distribution, a certificate can provide an extra level of confidence for your consumers.

Installing Your New AIR Application

Installing your new AIR application is an easy task, especially if you've already taken the time to install the Adobe AIR Runtime. Adobe AIR does the work for you, registering your new application on the system and making it available, just like any other application on your computer.

Make sure you have the Adobe AIR 3.2 runtime installed on your system. If you attempt to install an AIR 3.2 application on a system running an older version of AIR, you may receive an error message.

1 From your Windows Explorer or Mac Finder, locate the WeatherMate.air installer file that you published to the fl14lessons folder.

On Windows, if your extensions are hidden you may need look closely at each weathermate file and choose the Adobe Air application. If you are still unsure, select a file, right-click and choose Properties, then locate the type. You can double-click Adobe Air applications to open them.

2 Double-click the installer file; this will open the Adobe AIR installer dialog box.

3 The dialog box will confirm that you want to install the application. Press OK to begin installation. Note: You may get security warnings if you're using your own self-signed certificate.

The various stages of installing your AIR application.

4 When the installation is complete, locate your new application under the Start menu (Windows) or the Applications folder (Mac OS), and launch it.

You will notice that the WeatherMate application appears with no defined background or window; the desktop below, and only the application artwork itself shows. This is because you chose the Custom Chrome (Transparent) option in your publish settings in the previous exercise. Remember that a Flash movie is actually transparent, so the Stage will not appear in this environment.

Publishing for Mobile Devices

The Adobe AIR runtime has made it possible to take Flash beyond the browser and onto the desktop, and now you can author and publish native iOS and Android applications using the AIR for iOS and AIR for Android document and publish options.

There are many steps to take toward publishing stable and successful mobile applications: you'll need to become familiar with the respective SDKs and developer guidelines, set up developer accounts and testing devices, to name a few. These activities are beyond the scope of this book, but in this section we'll touch on the very basics for setting up your FLA for publishing to the iOS and Android platforms.

Before You Begin

If you would like to get started with mobile application development, we suggest visiting the following resources:

The iOS Developer center on Apple.com Visit *http://developer.apple.com/devcenter/ios/index* to set up a new developer account and get started. You'll also need to make sure you have the SDK and the latest version of Mac OS X and the XCode tools installed.

The Android Developer center at Android OS at *http://developer.android.com/index.html* to get started and download the SDK.

As always, before creating or publishing an application for these mobile platforms, make sure you meet the development guidelines suggested by Apple and Android/Google. You can get started in the right direction by using one of the pre-sized documents from the Start Page or the New Document dialog boxes.

Publishing for iOS

The following steps take you through the basics of publishing an existing Flash document for installation on an iOS device such as an iPhone, iPad, or iPod touch. This assumes you are using the appropriately sized document template and have followed the basic guidelines suggested by Apple.

1   Open the fl14_iphone.fla file from the fl14lessons folder. This file contains a simple movie based on the AIR for iOS document template.

2   Choose File > Publish Settings to open the Publish Settings dialog box. Next to the Target drop-down menu in the upper-right corner, click the Player Settings button (🔧) to open the AIR for iOS settings dialog box.

3   You'll start at the General settings tab. Fill in the appropriate name and output file for your app, as well as the appropriate settings for Aspect Ratio, Render Mode, and Device.

4 Select the Deployment tab, choose the certificate provided to you for iOS development as part of your developer account, and specify your provisioning profile.

These files and settings are available under the Apple Developer Center as part of your profile.

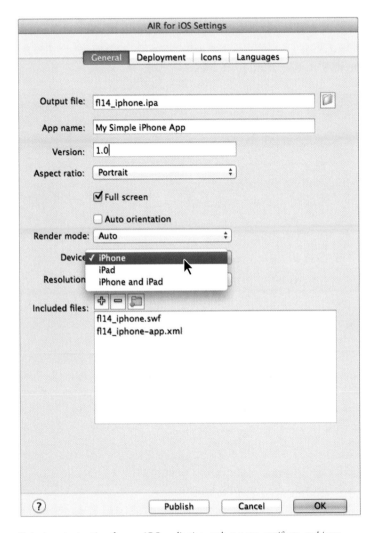

Enter important settings for your iOS application, such as name, certificate, and icons.

A provisioning profile is created as part of your iOS Developer Center account, and connects you and other developers in a group to test devices and to an authorized development group. If you work as part of a larger development team within an organization, it's possible that you can obtain this from your IT or development manager (or the person responsible for your company's developer account with Apple).

5 Choose the Deployment type, which determines how the app is packaged. You can package it for final App Store delivery or specifically for local testing and debugging. If you are still in testing and development, you may want to leave the default setting (Quick publishing for device testing).

6 Select the Icons tab. In each respective field, specify a graphic file for each of the required icon sizes, as shown. For specs and guidelines on preparing icons for an iPhone or iPad application, you can check the iOS developer center or this article at *http://developer.apple.com/library/ios/#documentation/userexperience/conceptual/mobilehig/ IconsImages/IconsImages.html.*

7 Select the Languages tab, and choose the languages you will be targeting for your application. If you are targeting only North American and English speaking users, select English for now. If you are working as part of a team, make sure to consult the project lead or development manager to verify these settings.

8 Click OK to close the AIR for iOS Settings dialog box.

9 Click OK to close the Publish Settings dialog box and save your options, or click Publish to publish your application right away.

To save time, check out the "Creating Publish Profiles" sidebar earlier in the chapter to learn how to save your Publish Settings for reuse across other projects and files.

Publishing for Android OS

Just as with iOS devices, you can target and publish native applications for Android devices, and specify the appropriate settings in the Publish Settings dialog box. With Android devices, however, you have some added abilities to easily install and debug on a connected Android device, a feature added in Flash CS 5.5, to make testing and setup a bit easier. Make sure to consult the Android Developer guidelines for creating an Android application and setting up testing devices.

1 Open the fl14_android.fla file from the fl14lessons folder. This file contains a simple movie based on the AIR for Android document template.

2 Choose File > Publish Settings to open the Publish Settings dialog box, and click the Player Settings icon next to the Target drop-down list in the upper-right corner. (It should read AIR 3.2 for Android.)

3 Under the General settings tab, enter the appropriate name and output file for your app. Make sure that settings for Aspect Ratio, Render Mode, and Device are correct for your specific application.

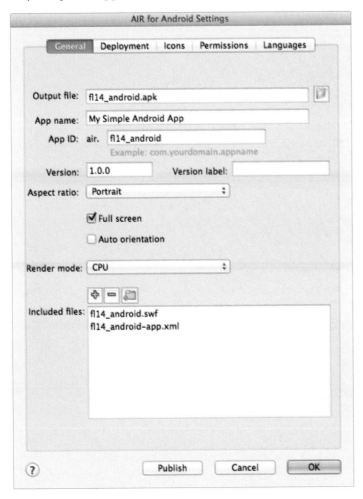

Specify settings for your new Android application.

4 Select the Deployment tab. Choose an .apk certificate provided to you for development, or create a self-signed certificate for temporary use and debugging by clicking the Create button. Certificates are essential for distribution in the Android Marketplace and installation on a test device. For more details and information about app signing, visit *http://developer.android.com/guide/publishing/app-signing.html*.

5 Select your deployment type. This will depend on whether you are creating a final app installer for distribution or a test build for debugging on a connected test device or emulator.

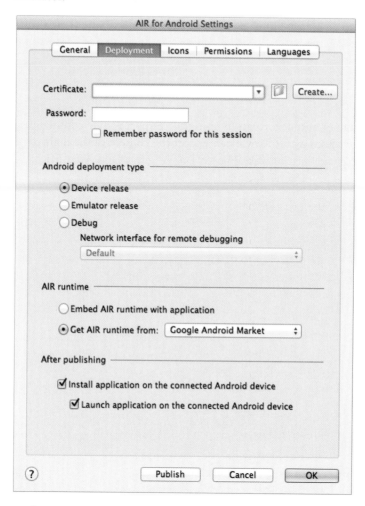

Specify settings for your new Android application.

6 Select the Icons tab, and specify the icon graphic files to use for each required size.

7 Select the Permissions tab, and specify the permissions necessary for your application to function properly. For example, if your application is designed to use the device camera, check 'CAMERA'.

8   Select the Languages tab, select the languages your application is targeting. If you are primarily focused on North American and English-speaking users, select English for now.

9   Click OK to close the AIR for Android Settings dialog box.

10   Click OK to close the Publish Settings dialog box and save your options, or Publish to publish your application right away.

11   Choose File > Close to close the file.

Using Export Movie

You can extend your range of output formats by using the Export Movie command. In addition to creating SWF files, Export Movie can export the content of the main Timeline to still images for editing in applications like Photoshop, Premiere, and After Effects, or FXG format for exchange with other applications that support vector graphics.

1   In the fl14lessons folder, open the file named fl1403.fla, which is a variation of the animated website footer you worked with in the first exercise. The main difference is that here the animation takes place on the main Timeline instead of in a nested movie clip. This is a very important distinction when exporting Flash content to other formats, as the majority of the exportable formats lack interactivity and simply display the content of the main Timeline as it appears in Flash.

2   Choose File > Export > Export Movie.

This exercise covers exporting the entire movie from the Timeline. If you would rather export only a single frame, select that frame, and then choose File > Export > Export Image.

3   In the resulting dialog box, choose the fl14lessons folder in the Save As (Mac OS) or Save In (Windows) drop-down menu, if it is not already listed there.

4   Select QuickTime (.mov) in the Format drop-down menu. This creates a stand-alone QuickTime movie that can be played using the free QuickTime player, converted for display on such mobile devices as PSPs and iPods, or imported into video editing or motions graphics programs, such as Adobe Premiere or After Effects. Press Save. The QuickTime Export Settings dialog box appears.

5   Click the Quicktime Settings button in the lower-left corner; here you can fine-tune options for size, audio settings and other file-specific options. Press OK when you are done, to return to the QuickTime Export Settings dialog box.

6 In the QuickTime Export Settings dialog box, press Export to export your final QuickTime file.

Below the Render height field in the QuickTime Export Settings dialog box, you'll see the Ignore Stage Color checkbox. This generates a QuickTime movie with an alpha channel that you can then import into a video editing or motion graphics program, such as Adobe Premiere or After Effects.

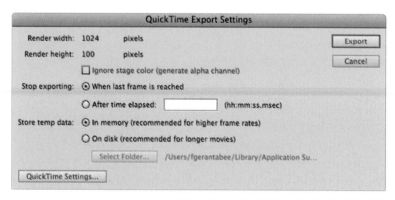

Dial in additional settings in the Quicktime Settings box, or just click Export in the QuickTime Export Settings dialog box to create your new file.

7 Minimize Flash and navigate to the fl14lessons folder. Double-click on your QuickTime movie to play it, and view the animation you have just exported.

8 Choose File > Save, then File > Close.

New: Export PNG Sequence

Sometimes it's handy to be able to export your animations in a way that can be used by other applications. If you need to export graphics for use within a website, mobile application or within a CSS or JavaScript based animation, you can now export a selected symbol as a PNG Sequence.

1 In the fl14lessons folder, open the file named fl1404.fla. You'll see a single movie clip on the Stage.

2 Choose Control > Test Movie > In Flash Professional. You'll see an animation sequence of a small dot expanding into a word balloon. Close the window to return to the document.

3 Right click on the movie clip on the Stage. From the contextual menu that appears, locate the Export PNG Sequence option and select it. You'll be prompted to save the sequence somewhere on your hard drive. Note: It's highly recommended to create a folder for the resulting images, as there may be quite a few! Choose a location to save the resulting images and click OK.

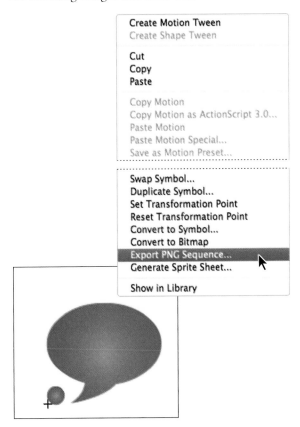

Right-click on any button, graphic, or movie clip symbol to select the Export PNG Sequence command.

4 The Export PNG Sequence dialog box appears. Here you'll see how many frames will be created (based on the length of the animation), and get a chance to adjust width, height and resolution. For now, leave all settings at their defaults and click Export.

5 Navigate to the folder or location where you exported the sequence; you should see a sequence of numbered PNGs, each of which represents a frame in your animation.

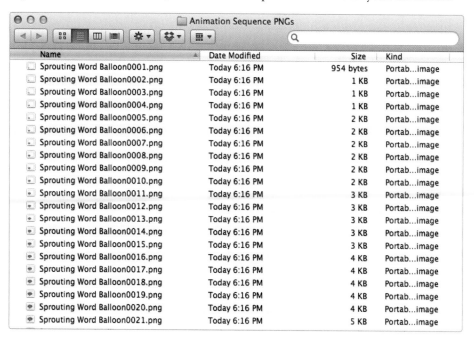

PNG images generated by the Export PNG Sequence command.

An overview of FTP

FTP is an acronym for the phrase File Transfer Protocol. These are the set of rules that allow different computers to connect to each other over the Web. Once you have created and published your Flash movie, you need to upload it to a web server in order to allow people to view it online. Whether this web server is one that you maintain yourself, one set up for you by your company's IT department, or space you rent from a web host, the publishing process is basically the same. While there are stand-alone FTP applications that allow you to connect to a web server, Adobe's industry-leading web design application, Dreamweaver, comes complete with an internal FTP engine that integrates very well with Flash content. The basic steps to follow when uploading Flash content for the Internet are:

1 Create a Flash movie and publish it to your local hard drive.

2 Upload your Flash movie to your web server, along with any secondary content (HTML and JavaScript files) created by the publishing process. Your web hosting service or IT department can provide you with information on where to upload your files, as well as the login and password information you need to connect.

If you published a Flash movie with an accompanying HTML file, chances are that some additional JavaScript files were also created. It is essential that these files are copied with your .swf and .html files up to the web server in order for the Flash movie to appear properly.

3 If you want to make any changes to the movie, edit the file you published to your local hard drive, not the version on the web server.

4 Re-upload the edited version of your Flash movie to the web server, including any secondary content you may have modified.

Self study

Open the masthead.fla file in the fl14lessons folder, and publish it as a Flash movie embedded in an HTML document. Experiment with different JPEG quality settings to see the effects on the resulting SWF file's size.

Review

Questions

1 What is the advantage of using the Publish command instead of the Test Movie command?

2 Why would you want to export a QuickTime Movie or AVI file?

3 What are the advantages of publishing an application as Adobe AIR rather than a stand–alone projector?

Answers

1 The Publish command can create a playable SWF file and automatically embed it into an HTML page. The Publish command also offers a wide range of exportable formats in addition to standard .swf creation.

2 To display your Flash animation on video devices such as iPods and PSPs, as well as to import into a video editing or motion graphics program.

3 Adobe AIR applications are able to interact with the user's operating system and local files. Projectors have security restrictions which prevent this, and don't feature the same ActionScript capabilities necessary to work with the operating system.

Lesson 15

What you'll learn in this lesson:

- Explore new features in Flash CS6

- Publish to iOS and Android devices with AIR

- Leverage 20 new Code Snippets for enhanced interactivity

- Explore new workflow enhancements with the enhanced TLF Text field ruler, PNG Sequence Export and Auto-Save

What's New in Adobe Flash CS6?

Adobe Flash lets you design rich, interactive content for the Web, desktop, and mobile devices, and it's used to create stunning websites, desktop applications, games and video content. Flash Professional CS6 contains new features and small, yet useful, updates that help you build better interactive content more quickly.

Starting up

This lesson does not require any lesson files from the included DVD. You can start Flash Professional CS6 and explore each new feature as it is discussed.

See Lesson 15 in action!

Use the accompanying video to gain a better understanding of how to use some of the features shown in this lesson. You can find the video tutorial for this lesson on the included DVD.

In addition to several new features introduced in Flash CS 5.5, the latest release of Flash Professional includes a number of updates and upgrades to previous features, including publishing options and templates for creating native iOS and Android applications, convenient graphic export features, and workflow and workspace enhancements. In the following pages, you'll get an overview of some of the major and minor (yet useful) features and updates that you will find in Flash CS6. Please note that some features here have been available since the Flash CS5.5 update, and have been highlighted for users upgrading from Flash CS5 or earlier.

Expanded Publishing and Support for iOS and Android Devices

Designers and developers venturing into mobile application development will love the expanded support for iOS and Android devices that's now available, thanks to all new publishing and packaging options built on Adobe AIR. Now, you'll find new device templates in the New Document and Start Page dialog boxes for AIR 3.2 for iOS and AIR 3.2 for Android, sized and ready to go. These feature all new publishing settings and options to package and deploy your applications on iPhone/iPod touch, iPad, and a variety of Android devices on the market.

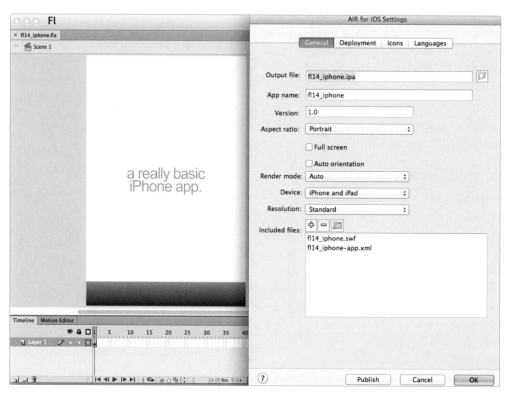

Author, debug, and publish iOS and Android applications from within Flash.

A little ruler goes a long way: Integrated Ruler on TLF text boxes

It's nice to have as many tools and options at your fingertips as possible, and when working with TLF text, it's nice to have a ruler to help you along. The integrated ruler that now appears above all active TLF text boxes on the Stage helps you set margins and other measurements quickly, without having to move to the Property inspector.

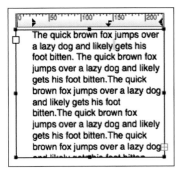

A ruler now appears at the top of TLF text fields to help set margins and other values quickly and easily.

New AIR and Mobile Code Snippets

The introduction of the Code Snippets panel helped new coders hit-the-ground-running, and Flash CS 5.5/CS6 adds 20 new Code Snippets across mobile touch and gesture, AIR for desktop and mobile, to help you maximize the new platforms that Flash can deploy to.

Take advantage of common mobile gesture events, control AIR application windows, or read and write from AIR applications to create extensive functionality.

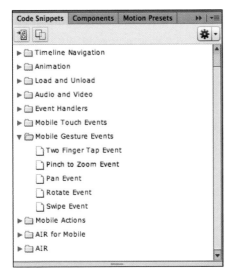

Twenty new Code Snippets across several new categories help you create amazing mobile, desktop, and multi-touch applications.

Convenience Features: Auto-Save and File Recovery plus Scale Content with Stage

Most of us have come to expect Auto-Save as a staple feature of most applications, and the wait is over for Flash Professional users. Now, you can enable Auto-Save for FLA files as part of your Document Settings to make sure important changes are never lost. Set an interval, check the Auto-Save check box, and go.

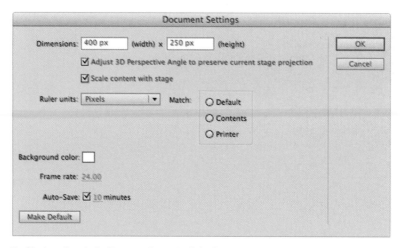

Enable Auto-Save in the Document Properties dialog box.

Another timesaver is the addition of the Scale Content with Stage option, also available under Document Properties. To enable this option, choose one of the Match options on the Document Settings window and select the Scale Content with Stage checkbox:

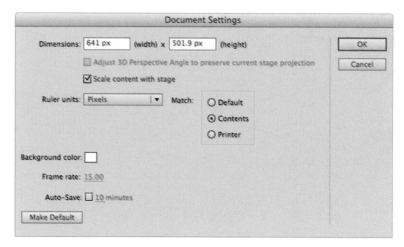

The Scale Content to stage checkbox is found in the Document Properties dialog box.

You have undoubtedly been reluctant to change your document width and height settings after placing content on the Stage, since this usually having to rearrange all of the contents of the Stage. Now, Flash intelligently redistributes most existing content, requiring just minor adjustments to get everything right as shown below.

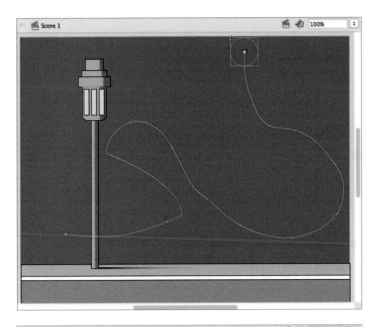

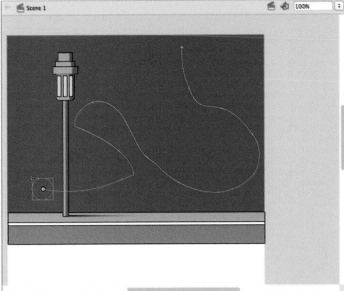

The original document size (top), and resized document (bottom). Symbols and motion paths are resized.

PNG Sequence Export

To share graphics or animation sequences (even individual frames) with other applications, you can select any graphic, button, or movie clip symbol and export its contents as a PNG Sequence. This results in one or more PNG files that you can easily import into other applications or development environments (such as icons for a website).

Bitmap Editing with Adobe Photoshop CS6

For several versions, you've been able to import Photoshop and Illustrator artwork directly into Flash with maximum quality and ease, so it makes perfect sense that you can now do on-the-spot editing with Photoshop CS6 for any bitmap in your movie.

Right-click any bitmap image in the Library panel or on the Stage for direct editing in Adobe Photoshop CS6; changes to the image are automatically reflected in the Flash CS6 application, so there's no need to reimport or update an image from the Library.

And, you're off!

Now that you've had a glimpse of the new and improved Flash CS6 features, use the lessons in this book to prepare yourself for creating interactive files using Flash CS6 Professional. You will find more specific information about each of these capabilities throughout the lessons in this book, which has been fully updated for Flash CS6.

Index

iOS, 426–428, 438
iOS Developer Center, 426–427
iTunes application, 356

J

JavaScript, 43
JPEG compression, 266

K

keyboard shortcuts, 231–234
Keyboard Shortcuts dialog box, 231–232
Keyframe option, 275
keyframes, 31, 152–159, 176, 205

L

Labels layer, 314
Landing Gear movie clip, 366
Landing Gear symbol, 371
Lasso tool, 22, 102
layer folders, 31, 84–85, 205–206
layered Photoshop files, 266–272
layers
  65 Trillion, 204–205
  Actions, 288, 295, 316
  animation, 152
  Armature, 202
  arranging, 83–84
  Background, 153–154, 241, 244, 257, 396
  Background Music, 347, 353
  Classic Tween, 178, 181–186
  Diagram, 153–154, 162–163
  Everything Else, 194, 199
  Guide, 162, 183, 239–244
  hiding, 83–84
  Labels, 314
  locking, 83–84, 175
  Logo, 194–195, 204, 212, 396
  Mask, 199
  Merged Bitmap, 268
  Motion Guide
    for classic tweens, 182–184
    creating, 174
    existing Flash files that use, 174
    troubleshooting, 184
  overview, 81–83
  Screen Mask, 201, 204–205
  Screen Simulation, 204–205
  Shadow, 160, 164, 185–186
  Shape Morph, 175–176, 185–186
  Skip, 194
  Sounds, 340, 343
  Stop Sounds, 355
  Text, 84, 241–242, 307–308
  Timeline, 51
  tween, 156–159
  Video, 394
  Video Here, 396
  Word Balloon, 84–85
layout, 11
Learn More button, 310, 323

lesson files
  fl0101_work.fla, 18, 23
  fl0102_done.fla, 40
  fl0102.fla, 33
  fl0202_done.fla, 46
  fl0202.work.fla, 52
  fl0301_work.fla, 98
  fl0401_done.fla, 132
  fl0501_work.fla, 153
  fl0502_work.fla, 157
  fl0601_start.fla, 190
  fl0701_work.fla, 220
  fl0801.jpg, 261, 265
  fl0801_library.fla, 257
  fl0801_work.fla, 273
  fl0802.jpg, 261
  fl0804.ai, 274
  fl0901_work.fla, 283
  fl1001.fla, 300
  fl1002_work.fla, 302
  fl1101_done.fla, 328
  fl1201.fla, 360
  fl1301.mov, 393
  fl1302_done.fla, 388
  fl1302.fla, 394
  fl1303_done.fla, 388
  fl1305.mov, 402
  fl1306.fla, 405
  fl1401.fla, 413
  fl1403.fla, 431
  loading, 4
  viewing completed, 253
lesson folders
  fl01, 17–18, 23, 33, 40, 44
  fl02, 45–46, 52
  fl03, 98
  fl04, 132
  fl05, 157
  fl06, 190
  fl07, 220
  fl08, 253–254, 274
  fl09, 282–283
  fl10, 302
  fl11, 328
  fl12, 360
  fl13, 388, 393–394, 402, 405
  fl14, 413, 436
  fl0803.psd, 269
Library panel
  controlling views, 129
  deleting items from, 127–128
  features of, 96–97
  Move To command, 126–127
  organizing symbols with folders, 124–125
  overview, 95–97, 124
  review, 130
  self study, 130
  tab for, 175, 379
Library selector, 96
library views, 129
Line tool, 22, 54–56
linear gradient, 76, 91

John Wiley & Sons, Inc.
End-User License Agreement

READ THIS. You should carefully read these terms and conditions before opening the software packet(s) included with this book "Book". This is a license agreement "Agreement" between you and John Wiley & Sons, Inc. "WILEY". By opening the accompanying software packet(s), you acknowledge that you have read and accept the following terms and conditions. If you do not agree and do not want to be bound by such terms and conditions, promptly return the Book and the unopened software packet(s) to the place you obtained them for a full refund.

1. **License Grant**. WILEY grants to you (either an individual or entity) a nonexclusive license to use one copy of the enclosed software program(s) (collectively, the "Software") solely for your own personal or business purposes on a single computer (whether a standard computer or a workstation component of a multi-user network). The Software is in use on a computer when it is loaded into temporary memory (RAM) or installed into permanent memory (hard disk, CD-ROM, or other storage device). WILEY reserves all rights not expressly granted herein.

2. **Ownership**. WILEY is the owner of all right, title, and interest, including copyright, in and to the compilation of the Software recorded on the physical packet included with this Book "Software Media". Copyright to the individual programs recorded on the Software Media is owned by the author or other authorized copyright owner of each program. Ownership of the Software and all proprietary rights relating thereto remain with WILEY and its licensers.

3. **Restrictions on Use and Transfer.**

   (a) You may only (i) make one copy of the Software for backup or archival purposes, or (ii) transfer the Software to a single hard disk, provided that you keep the original for backup or archival purposes. You may not (i) rent or lease the Software, (ii) copy or reproduce the Software through a LAN or other network system or through any computer subscriber system or bulletin-board system, or (iii) modify, adapt, or create derivative works based on the Software.

   (b) You may not reverse engineer, decompile, or disassemble the Software. You may transfer the Software and user documentation on a permanent basis, provided that the transferee agrees to accept the terms and conditions of this Agreement and you retain no copies. If the Software is an update or has been updated, any transfer must include the most recent update and all prior versions.

4. **Restrictions on Use of Individual Programs.** You must follow the individual requirements and restrictions detailed for each individual program in the "About the CD" appendix of this Book or on the Software Media. These limitations are also contained in the individual license agreements recorded on the Software Media. These limitations may include a requirement that after using the program for a specified period of time, the user must pay a registration fee or discontinue use. By opening the Software packet(s), you agree to abide by the licenses and restrictions for these individual programs that are detailed in the "About the CD" appendix and/or on the Software Media. None of the material on this Software Media or listed in this Book may ever be redistributed, in original or modified form, for commercial purposes.

5. Limited Warranty.

(a) WILEY warrants that the Software and Software Media are free from defects in materials and workmanship under normal use for a period of sixty (60) days from the date of purchase of this Book. If WILEY receives notification within the warranty period of defects in materials or workmanship, WILEY will replace the defective Software Media.

(b) WILEY AND THE AUTHOR(S) OF THE BOOK DISCLAIM ALL OTHER WARRANTIES, EXPRESS OR IMPLIED, INCLUDING WITHOUT LIMITATION IMPLIED WARRANTIES OF MERCHANTABILITY AND FITNESS FOR A PARTICULAR PURPOSE, WITH RESPECT TO THE SOFTWARE, THE PROGRAMS, THE SOURCE CODE CONTAINED THEREIN, AND/OR THE TECHNIQUES DESCRIBED IN THIS BOOK. WILEY DOES NOT WARRANT THAT THE FUNCTIONS CONTAINED IN THE SOFTWARE WILL MEET YOUR REQUIREMENTS OR THAT THE OPERATION OF THE SOFTWARE WILL BE ERROR FREE.

(c) This limited warranty gives you specific legal rights, and you may have other rights that vary from jurisdiction to jurisdiction.

6. Remedies.

(a) WILEY's entire liability and your exclusive remedy for defects in materials and workmanship shall be limited to replacement of the Software Media, which may be returned to WILEY with a copy of your receipt at the following address: Software Media Fulfillment Department, Attn.: *Adobe Flash Professional CS6 Digital Classroom*, John Wiley & Sons, Inc., 10475 Crosspoint Blvd., Indianapolis, IN 46256, or call 1-800-762-2974. Please allow four to six weeks for delivery. This Limited Warranty is void if failure of the Software Media has resulted from accident, abuse, or misapplication. Any replacement Software Media will be warranted for the remainder of the original warranty period or thirty (30) days, whichever is longer.

(b) In no event shall WILEY or the author be liable for any damages whatsoever (including without limitation damages for loss of business profits, business interruption, loss of business information, or any other pecuniary loss) arising from the use of or inability to use the Book or the Software, even if WILEY has been advised of the possibility of such damages.

(c) Because some jurisdictions do not allow the exclusion or limitation of liability for consequential or incidental damages, the above limitation or exclusion may not apply to you.

7. U.S. Government Restricted Rights.
Use, duplication, or disclosure of the Software for or on behalf of the United States of America, its agencies and/or instrumentalities "U.S. Government" is subject to restrictions as stated in paragraph (c)(1)(ii) of the Rights in Technical Data and Computer Software clause of DFARS 252.227-7013, or subparagraphs (c) (1) and (2) of the Commercial Computer Software - Restricted Rights clause at FAR 52.227-19, and in similar clauses in the NASA FAR supplement, as applicable.

8. General.
This Agreement constitutes the entire understanding of the parties and revokes and supersedes all prior agreements, oral or written, between them and may not be modified or amended except in a writing signed by both parties hereto that specifically refers to this Agreement. This Agreement shall take precedence over any other documents that may be in conflict herewith. If any one or more provisions contained in this Agreement are held by any court or tribunal to be invalid, illegal, or otherwise unenforceable, each and every other provision shall remain in full force and effect.

Register your Digital Classroom book for exclusive benefits

Registered owners receive access to:

 The most current lesson files

 Technical resources and customer support

 Notifications of updates

 On-line access to video tutorials

 Downloadable lesson files

 Samples from other Digital Classroom books

Register at *DigitalClassroomBooks.com/CS6/Flash*

You have a personal tutor in the Digital Classroom.

978-1-118-12389-8

978-1-118-12407-9

978-1-118-12406-2

978-1-118-12408-6

978-1-118-12409-3

978-1-118-12405-5

978-1-118-01618-3

978-0-470-58360-9

978-0-470-57777-6

DigitalClassroom

A Complete Training Package

**For more information about the Digital Classroom series,
go to www.digitalclassroom.com.**

e **Available in print and e-book formats.**

AGI | WILEY
Now you know.